"I am so excited to have this book available to use with the girls God sends us at Vision of Hope. It is so rich with accurate theological exposition but also so deeply practical. When you combine that with Marie's authenticity and transparency and the book's easy readability, I foresee that this book will become a fast favorite for many biblical counselors working with women. This is an excellently written book, concise yet broad, hitting such a wide variety of topics that it will be beneficial for many addiction issues. What a compassionate and humble way for biblical counselors to be equipped to work with women with addiction issues while, at the same time, completely appropriate to be used for homework and study assignments for our counselees."
—**Jocelyn Wallace, Executive Director, Vision of Hope Ministries, Inc., Lafayette, IN**

"I absolutely LOVED Redeemed from the Pit! You are so consistent with what God's Word says throughout the entire book, and I love that you had constant references for the reader to go discover the truth on her own. I wish I had had something like this to read when I was going through my struggle. But beyond dealing with eating disorders, your book truly deals with where a person's heart is. I love that you lay the Gospel out so clearly throughout the book. Really by the end, the reader has the knowledge; they just have to make the choice. Every chapter I read I was just more and more blown away. I just kept saying, "This is so good…" "Oh, I need to remember that…" "Wow, that's so right on…" It is very convicting and humbling and I absolutely love that it puts God in His proper place—above all and deserving of all glory."
—**Laura Wilkinson, 2000 Olympic Gold Medalist, Platform Diving**

"Having counseled women who have struggled with eating disorders, I highly recommend Mrs. Notcheva's new book, *Redeemed from the Pit*. As a person who has fought the battle with bulimia for many years and overcome it through the power of the Lord and His Word, she has compassion, wisdom and true hope which are carefully and thoroughly delivered through her teaching. This will be a powerful tool for those who suffer and those who desire to help them."
—**Sharon Yaddow, NANC Level I counselor, Raleigh NC**

"I have known women with the same issues who I think would have benefited greatly from this book. There is also much in this book to recommend as a way of dealing with similar sin issues—other destructive habits. It is a very good encouragement to see how someone dealt with her eating disorder in a godly way, and how we can learn from her example."
—**Glenn E. Chatfield, biblical counselor and apologist, founder of The Watchman Ministry, Iowa**

"I've followed Marie's work for quite some time, and have discovered that she cares deeply about important issues. She does not shrink from difficult or delicate subjects, but deals with them with intelligent, courageous faith. And, as far as I can determine, her positions are always solidly based upon Scripture."
—**Don Kimrey, author of God's Comeback Kids: The Road Leads Home**

Redeemed from the Pit

Biblical Repentance and Restoration
from the Bondage of Eating Disorders

Redeemed from the Pit

Biblical Repentance and Restoration
from the Bondage of Eating Disorders

interior PUBLICATIONS

"come inside and learn!"

an imprint of Calvary Press Publishing
interiorpubs.com | calvarypress.com

1-855-2-CALVARY/ 855-222-5827

Published by Interior Publications, an imprint of Calvary Press
Publishing. Visit us at: InteriorPubs.com, CalvaryPress.com

Copyright © 2011, Marie Notcheva
ISBN 978-1-879737-78-5

PRINTED IN THE USA

Dedicated to the staff and residents at Vision of Hope in LaFayette, Indiana. Your testimonies of redemption inspire me. Your joy and love for our Savior, Jesus Christ, is infectious. May you always be blessed.

I love You, O LORD, my strength.

   ²The LORD is my rock and my fortress and my deliverer,
        My God, my rock, in whom I take refuge;
        My shield and the horn of my salvation, my stronghold.
   ³I call upon the LORD, who is worthy to be praised,
        And I am saved from my enemies.
   ⁴The cords of death encompassed me,
        And the torrents of ungodliness terrified me.
   ⁵The cords of Sheol surrounded me;
        The snares of death confronted me.
   ⁶In my distress I called upon the LORD,
        And cried to my God for help;
        He heard my voice out of His temple,
        And my cry for help before Him came into His ears…
He sent from on high, He took me;
        He drew me out of many waters.
   ¹⁷He delivered me from my strong enemy,
        And from those who hated me, for they were too mighty for me.
   ¹⁸They confronted me in the day of my calamity,
        But the LORD was my stay.
   ¹⁹He brought me forth also into a broad place;
        He rescued me, because He delighted in me…
…The LORD lives, and blessed be my rock;
        And exalted be the God of my salvation…
Therefore I will give thanks to You among the nations, O LORD,
        And I will sing praises to Your name.
—Psalm 18:1-6; 16-19; 46; 49 (NASB)

Contents

Foreword
by Martha Peace

Since Mother Eve fell into sin, almost all women, Christians or not, have desired to be beautiful. Different cultures, over time, have defined beautiful in different ways. Remember the bee-hive hairdos of the 1960's? Ancient Roman women thought that beautiful, too! Well, the bee-hive went out and thin came in.

Today, we are greatly influenced by the media to think that the only truly beautiful women are thin; very thin. We want to look like the movie stars, news anchors, and models that are almost always super-slim. I once heard about a movie star who on a very long air flight refused all the meals. On occasion, however, she would become so hungry she would insist on something to eat, eat two bites, and refuse the rest. She was thin and she was beautiful, but I wonder if her almost-starvation diet was worth it in the long run. She struggles with anorexia. Another may not starve herself; in fact, she may often be gluttonous, but maintains her weight by throwing up after the meal. Sometimes her compulsion is repeated several times per day. She struggles with bulimia.

It was forty-plus years ago in nursing school that I learned about eating disorders. As I recall, it was the first time I knew that eating disorders existed. Both were said to be psychiatric diseases and both, especially anorexia, were difficult to treat. What must have been rare back in the 1960's is now, for many, a common practice. The quest for beauty which likely began with Mother Eve has not gone away. It is still labeled a psychiatric disease and anyone struggling with an eating disorder knows what Marie Notcheva means about being in the "pit" and "in bondage."

Redeemed from the Pit: Biblical Repentance and Restoration from the Bondage of Eating Disorders is a gift from God to those struggling and to those helping someone struggling with an eating disorder. This book maintains a high view of God and an accurate view of man. It is written in an engaging style and entwined within it is Notcheva's own personal struggle and how God granted her repentance and real freedom. As a biblical counselor to women, I am looking forward to using this book to help others. Read it prayerfully and thoughtfully. You, too, can, by God's grace, be truly redeemed from the pit!

MarthaPeace
Biblical Counselor and Author of *The Excellent Wife*

Acknowledgments

Last summer, I received the following comment from a young woman:

"You have been able to be that voice and there is no self-righteous tone or condemnation in your words. It's what my heart knew but what my mind did not want to hear…but there is hope and proof that God truly IS bigger than any of our problems and He is the key to our full recovery."

As someone who struggled in the "pit" of an eating disorder for over a decade, it still amazes me that God has salvaged enough of my past to minister to other women. I am humbled and deeply thankful that He used something I wrote to give hope to one of His daughters. I am also grateful to Him for providing so many individuals along the way who helped make this book a reality.

First and foremost, I am extremely indebted to Martha Peace for the countless hours of work she spent reading, correcting and making suggestions in order to ensure this book would be the best it could be. Martha, I will never forget your kindness, and your valuable insights into the writing process. We all need a Titus 2 woman in our life, and you are definitely mine! I cannot thank you enough, and count it an honor to have worked with you.

I am grateful to Dr. Laura Hendrickson, Elyse Fitzpatrick and Drs. Mark Shaw and Rick Thomas for providing the encouragement and "vote of confidence" needed to continue writing, studying, and loving those God brings my way. I have also benefitted greatly from your books and your teaching.

Jocelyn Wallace, who took time out of her busy day on

more than one occasion to talk to me, was instrumental to the chapters about biblical counseling. I stand in awe of the dedication you bring into your ministry to young women, and hope one day to be as compassionate and knowledgeable a counselor as you are.

I am also thankful to Gretchen Smith, whose contributions to Chapter 2 were as insightful as they were articulate. Gretchen, you helped me more than you know back in 2001 when I was still struggling with bulimia myself.

And where would I be without the instruction of Jay Adams and Donn Arms? I have learned so much under your tutelage in the Institute for Nouthetic Studies; never would this book have been worthy of publication without your teaching. Donn, I often hear your voice in my head as I write. And in my head, your voice is asking, "Is this a biblical construct?"

Joseph Bianchi, thank you so much for taking a chance on a first-time writer. I am thrilled and honored to be working with Calvary Press and Interior Publications, and hope that my work will be used by you to lift up the Name of Christ.

Pastor Jason, Joan, Debbie and Marnie—thank you so much for the time you spent reading chapters and making suggestions! The final product is the better for your labor of love, and I appreciate it more than you know

I am so grateful to my children—Valentina, Stanimir, Stefan and Natalia—and my husband Ivaylo for their patience as I worked on this book and watched it come together. You've endured far too many burned meals, blank stares and nights with Mommy holed up in the office. You are the best team I could ask for, and are God's gift to me.

How can I ever express gratitude suficient to my Heavenly Father, Whose mercies are new every morning? Your patience and grace overwhelm me. Thank you for redeeming my life from the pit, and using me to strengthen my sisters. My desire is that you will somehow use my inglorious words to bring glory to Yourself.

Introduction

There is Hope

The loneliness of an addiction is indescribable.

If you have picked up this book, you or someone you love may be suffering from anorexia, bulimia or another seemingly uncontrollable food issue. Perhaps you have tried many times to change this destructive behavior; to quit bingeing, purging or starving, only to fall back into the same pattern again and again. Many anorexics and bulimics describe this compulsion as taking on a life of its own—as if an outside force were controlling them. The cruel irony is that, initially, you had considered your weight the only thing you could control. At one time, you may have found comfort in your admirable "willpower" to refuse fattening food. As the pounds seemed to melt effortlessly away, you experienced a deep sense of personal satisfaction. Self-starvation became a badge of honor you bestowed upon yourself.

Or, perhaps what started as a Spartan discipline one day caused you to cave in. You could no longer endure the metallic taste of hunger constantly in your mouth; the lightheadedness each time you stood up; the gnawing ache in your ravenous belly. That was the day you gave up and began to eat…and eat….and purge. As time went on, you fell back more and more easily into this "escape plan" of getting rid of your food, telling yourself you could stop vomiting any time you chose. No one suspected there was a secret to your slimness. Now, too late, you find yourself enslaved by the behavior you despise, unable to explain the paradox even to yourself. Your days are shrouded in secrecy, shame, and fear. You may be desperate to stop, but deep down you don't truly believe that freedom is possible—you've been this way for so long that it seems to be a part of you. Besides, the fear of how others would react if they knew—especially those closest to you—keeps you from reaching out for help. Inwardly, you may be despairing and feeling very much alone.

If you can relate to this painful scenario, the good news is this: there is hope. You can be completely free of this behavior, as well as of the thought patterns that fuel it. You may, indeed, learn to walk in total freedom. No matter what you may feel, have read or been told, complete recovery from eating disorders is possible. God has promised to restore His children fully from every life-dominating sin when they turn to Him with a changed heart. He Himself supplies this "new spirit"; see Ezekiel 11:19: *"And I will give them one heart, and put a new spirit within them, and I will take the heart of stone out of their flesh and give them a heart of flesh."* While you may realize that the answer lies in the Person of Jesus Christ, applying that truth may be less clear to you. Hopefully, this book will help point you to the One the Bible calls the "Great Physician" and "Wonderful Counselor." While here I discuss eating disorders, and more specifically bulimia, the principles actually apply to repenting of any addiction. You may be thinking, "But I've already tried to 'surrender' my eating disorder! I asked God to take it away, but I still struggle. Now what?"

Be One Who Believes

The Word of God tells us that "All things are possible to him who believes," (Mark 9:23), and this is going to be our thesis as we move forward through the process of leaving this bondage at the foot of the Cross. Let's take a look at this verse in context. Jesus had just come down from the Mount of Transfiguration, where Peter, James and John had seen Him in all of His unveiled glory. A desperate father brings his son to the disciples for healing. We aren't told how old the youth is, but the fact that his father states he had been afflicted with muteness and seizures since childhood indicates he had been tormented for some time. Despite previous success exorcising demons, the disciples were unable to cast out this particular spirit (or spirits). In verse 19, the Lord mildly chastises them for their lack of faith, and then heals the boy.

...He asked his father, "How long has this been happening to him?" And he said, "From childhood. It has often thrown him both into the fire and into the water to destroy him. But if You can do anything, take pity on us and help us!" And Jesus said to him, "'If You can?' All things are possible to him who believes." Immediately the boy's father cried out and said, "I do believe; help my unbelief." (Mark 9:21-24)

Often, we come to God for help, believing only half-heartedly that He can, or will, heal us. While intellectually we will concede that nothing is beyond the power of an omnipotent God, we doubt that He's really interested in our problem (which, usually, we've brought on ourselves). The healing in Mark 9 was a physical one. Sometimes, God may choose to heal physical infirmities to glorify Himself, as Jesus explained in John 9:3 when He gave sight to the man born blind. Other times, He may choose to be glorified through the person's suffering, so that the infirm believer may use his or her life for Christ's glory. Quadriplegic Christian speaker and author Joni Eareckson Tada is a good example of someone who has allowed God to use her suffering for His glory.

When God does not heal a physical condition or disease, we may not understand the reason why He chooses not to. Even so, we must never question His goodness. However, it is always His will for His children to be freed of sinful behaviors and "addictions," which are more precisely life-dominating sins. The Bible is clear on that. Jesus Christ plainly states, *"I came that they may have life, and have it abundantly."* (John

10:10). This "abundant life" comes from walking with God and not being enslaved by sin. The spiritual healing He provides (Isaiah 53:5) is the cleansing forgiveness we so desperately need.

In the first preaching engagement of His ministry, Jesus read Isaiah's prophecy about Himself and candidly told the listeners in the synagogue that He was the Messiah: *The Spirit of the Lord is upon me, because he anointed me to preach the Gospel to the poor. He has sent me to proclaim release to the captives and recovery of sight to the blind, to set free those who are oppressed, to proclaim the favorable year of the Lord.* (Luke 4:18-19)

Inherent in the Gospel message ("good news") Christ came to proclaim is the promise of new life and freedom from the tyranny of sin. If you are bound in the prison of an eating disorder, the new life He offers to His followers is available to you if you will humble yourself before God. Forgiven, cleansed, and given a new start, He expects you to get up off your knees and get started—walking in repentance. Even as Christians, it is challenging to grasp the fact that He has already freed us, and then to find the courage to walk out of our prison cells of sin. As you seek Him and learn to repent of the idolatrous place you have given to food and weight, He will open your eyes to behold His beauty.

"Recovery" versus Repentance

Anorexia and bulimia, like other addictions, are "spiritual diseases" (sin) masquerading as physical ones. In fact, for this reason, I believe the term "recovery" is slightly inaccurate and therefore I try to avoid using it. Recover connotes the convalescence and passive improvement typical of physical diseases. What I hope to show you is how to repent, so that God will restore you. Since the Bible speaks of overcoming sin, we may also use that term here. To all who are in Him, Christ promises victory, and that is our ultimate goal.

Did you notice anything about the verbs I used to describe our game plan? They are all active. "Recovery" is something that happens on its own as a natural course. When you break your leg, the doctor sets it in a cast and eventually you will recover. You cannot force the osteoblasts to knit themselves together any more quickly or coerce your femur into re-calcifying. All you can do is sit back and wait. The same is (generally) true of treatable diseases—if you take your medicine, you may anticipate recovery. In the spiritual realm, however, God expects us to take a more pro-active role.

Regardless of what contemporary philosophies or prevailing theories you may have heard, you are not a victim. If you are a Christian, you are not helpless. You have the strongest Person in the universe standing right by your side, interceding for you, and indwelling you through His Spirit. For your part, you need to agree with God that your thoughts, desires and actions run contrary to His (confession); determine in His power to turn away from your self-centered way of living (repentance); and do what He commands (obedience). Biblical change involves a commitment and work on our part. We can commit ourselves to this wholeheartedly, fully trusting that Our Savior's thoughts and ways are infinitely better than ours. Often, after our conversion, we tend to forget that our lives do not belong to us. Our true purpose in this life, to glorify God, can only be realized as we give up what we think are our "rights" to do things our own way. True joy and lasting freedom is only found in the obedience that demonstrates our love for the One Who gave His life so that His children might live (John 14:15, 21).

"Dependent Responsibility"

While overcoming sin is not done in our own strength, we cannot remain passive and expect God to spontaneously change us, either. In his books on rooting out personal sin, author Jerry Bridges talks about what he calls the principle of dependent responsibility. Bridges explains,

> We are 100 percent responsible for the pursuit of holiness, but at the same time we are 100 percent dependent upon the Holy Spirit to enable us in that pursuit. The pursuit of holiness is not a pull-yourself-up-by-your-own-bootstraps approach to the Christian life. It's not just trying harder. But it's going through the Bible and seeing what God requires of us in the way of obedience to him and likeness to his character, and then setting ourselves to doing that. But at the same time recognizing that we are absolutely dependent upon the Holy Spirit to enable us.[1]

There are no quick fixes or "magic bullets." Overcoming an eating disorder requires our constant, active commitment to inward change. We effect this change by renewing our minds with God's Word. When there is a deep-seated area of sin in our life, even as His children, we need to fall on our faces before the Throne. We simply cannot "do better" under our own steam. Fortunately, God has promised us all the help we need through His Word and the indwelling Holy Spirit. Learning to lean on His strength even as we obey His clear instruction is crucial to resisting the seductive bondage of an eating disorder.

There is no pit so deep that Christ can't pull you up out of it. (I use the term "pit" because that is truly how being trapped in an eating disorder feels—as if you are a prisoner all alone in the pit.) The Bible says, "God is our refuge and strength, a very present help in trouble" (Psalm 46:1). In a metaphorical sense, He has His strong arms wrapped around you right now, holding you up. Innumerable times, the shame I felt after purging would cause me to run away from God, further increasing my isolation and defeat. When I began to make faltering steps back in His direction, His call to me from Scripture became clear: "Why didn't you just come to Me? Don't run. Let Me in."

If you are willing to follow Him, Christ will renew your mind and break the chains of this isolating sin once and for all—no matter how many times you may have tried, and failed, in the past. He has already made a way out, and is patiently waiting. As much as you want to be free, God wills your freedom even more. After all, He sent His Son to die so that sinners would no longer be slaves to sin (Romans 6:6). Freedom starts with realizing that you have a choice not to give in to destructive eating habits.

"Will bulimia send me to hell?"

I remember early on in my struggle finding a crushing statement by a pastor on the Internet. On an "Ask the Pastor" website forum, someone had submitted the question, "If someone is bulimic and dies from it, will she go to hell?" The question was clearly inquiring whether the bulimic could lose her salvation, as the context assumed salvation by grace through faith in Christ (Ephesians 2:8-9). I was disheartened by the pastor's response, which circumvented the doctrine of eternal security. The gist of his answer was, "I do not believe a true child of God would fall into such behavior." Essentially, he was denying that a bulimic could be a Christian. He assumed that she must be unsaved to have such an addiction. This is as dangerous as the position at the other end of the spectrum—well-meaning Christian counselors who tell clients that bulimia is not a sin.

Over the past few years, I have received this same question many times from women who e-mail me for counsel. Typically, they are young Christian women who know and love the Lord, but cannot seem to overcome this one area of sin in their lives. I used to be just like them. Even though Christ has redeemed and justified these women, they are terrified that if they die of complications arising from bulimia, He will banish them to hell. Let me say upfront: if you have heeded

Christ's call to believe on Him and repented of your sin, and have received Him as Lord and Savior, you are a child of God and cannot lose your salvation. This is very often one of the doubts plaguing a bulimic or anorexic woman. Instinctively, she knows her behavior is sin and not a "disease" or simply an "issue," but since she feels powerless to stop, she wonders if she was ever really saved in the first place.

Actually, the Bible is clear that a born-again believer is permanently in Christ, and as such will always be a part of the family of God. Salvation is a gift of grace—you cannot "lose" it; you did nothing to "gain" it in the first place. This doctrine is known as "the eternal security of the believer," or more commonly, "once saved always saved." We are justified before God when we respond to His call. We come to Him in repentance, believing on His Son Jesus Christ for salvation. Ephesians 2:8-9 sums up this concept: "For by grace you have been saved, through faith; and that not of yourselves, it is the gift of God; not as a result of works, so that no one may boast." At the moment of conversion, the Holy Spirit indwells the regenerate child of God. He or she is declared righteous in God's sight because of Christ's finished work on the cross. This is what it means to be "born again"—we pass from death into life and are a new creation. We have become a Christian, a disciple of Christ. (If you have never turned to Jesus Christ in faith and received this new birth, please see the Appendix for a more detailed explanation on how to know for certain you are a Christian).

Grace is Free, but is Not Cheap

While Scripture is unequivocally clear that redeemed believers cannot lose their salvation, we are also warned to "test yourselves to see whether you are in the faith; examine yourselves!" (2 Corinthians 13:5). Repeatedly, we are told that a true Christian will have evidence of a changed life by the way he or she thinks, acts, and behaves. This transformation occurs as we surrender to Christ's authority and strive to obey Him out of love and gratitude. The Apostle Paul lists nine fruit of the Holy Spirit which will manifest in a believer's life: "But the fruit of the Spirit is love, joy, peace, patience, kindness, goodness, faithfulness, gentleness and self-control." (Galatians 5:22-23). When the Lord calls us, He changes us from the inside out. Certainly this "fruit" does not show up overnight, but a gradual growth and increasing measure of these qualities should be apparent in a true child of God.

Unfortunately, our current era of permissiveness has given rise to the popularity of a repentance-free "gospel." Sometimes termed "cheap grace" or "easy believism," this misguided version of Christianity assumes a salvation based on emotional or intellectual acceptance of Jesus Christ as Savior, with no real recognition of one's sinful state, remorse over personal sin, or true desire to change. This distortion lets us "have our cake and eat it too"– it presents salvation as something God wants to do for us (which He does); but with no subsequent expectation from us (He requires us to put the old, self-seeking nature to death).

Emphasizing God's love while ignoring what the Bible says about His holiness is a fatal mistake—He is both perfect love and perfect holiness. He expects His children to pursue holiness as well. We will never realize perfection this side of eternity, but to knowingly continue on in our sin is not the mark of a true Christian. God's ultimate goal is to transform us into the likeness of Christ. That means we are progressing in greater holiness. The Bible calls this ongoing process "sanctification," becoming in practice what we already are in standing—saints.

Tragically, many in the Church today have made a profession of faith, but with no inward heart-change toward sin. This is why it is so important to examine our heart for hidden motives and unconfessed rebellion. The assurance that we are truly God's redeemed children comes from the Holy

Spirit within us, guiding our consciences (1 John 3:21-24; Hebrews 10:22). Are you in the Truth? If not, it is never too late to trust in Christ for salvation. If you are a Christian, yet feel overwhelmed by the nightmare of an eating disorder, there is still great hope for you. Are you trusting Christ today? Have you repented of sin and turned to him in submission as well as belief? Have you had His assistance in overcoming sin? What fruit of the Spirit have you seen in your life thus far? Those are the questions that matter—not being able to pinpoint a specific date when you "prayed a prayer."

Although I have been a Christian since age nineteen, I struggled for many years to grasp what my role was to play in sanctification. I didn't understand what it meant to be changed by the Gospel, or that God does not work with a half-hearted commitment to change. Bulimia consumed me for seventeen years, but ultimately God broke those chains and restored my physical and spiritual health. It is my hope that the lessons God taught me will help others struggling with this bondage. I thank God for the freedom He has given me, and the strength He supplied along the journey to wholeness. Tenacity—a stubborn refusal to give up, no matter how many times you fall and have to get back up—is essential to victory. We cannot win the battle over an addiction effortlessly or independently. We desperately need the supernatural help and strength that God has made available to us, and we need to actively draw on it regardless of what we feel like doing. It is God's will that you to turn to Him with each and every burden and even the darkest of secrets. A book, program or hypnotist will not heal you, but all things are possible with the God Who is on your side. Are you ready to turn away from this self-destructive lifestyle, and embrace true freedom in Christ? Let's start this journey today. All you need is a Bible, a place to spend uninterrupted time with God, and a contrite heart. He will supply everything else you need.

Chapter 1
My Story

One of my earliest childhood memories is of rushing downstairs into the kitchen, half-naked, as a four-year-old. A plumbing mishap in the upstairs bathroom sent me bolting to report the problem immediately to an adult. Clad only in my pajama bottoms, my mother surveyed my "pot belly" with a raised eyebrow. As my six-year-old brother Jay cackled in the background, she categorically informed me that I was going on a diet. Too young to really understand what the big deal was, I became aware that something about me was wrong: Flawed. I asked my mother what a "diet" was, and she replied, "It's when you cut out all the fattening foods." Now I was really scared! My literal-thinking, preschooler's mind conjured up terrifying images of my mother slicing me open with a knife, and "cutting out" all the sweets I had eaten, right there on the kitchen counter. No wonder it had the word "die" in it!

Each morning I would fearfully ask, "Are we going to do the 'diet' today?" Confused by my mother's answer that it was "already going on," I was extremely relieved when she clarified what a 'diet' actually meant. Since this was 1975, it meant almost no carbohydrates. I didn't understand why I couldn't have mashed potatoes anymore, or why my mother never rebuked Jay for calling me "fatso." I had not yet begun kindergarten, but I was already being conditioned to hate my own body.

I grew up in a turbulent, unsaved family as the middle of

three children. Although we attended church as a weekly matter of obligation, no one in my family had heard the Gospel and our denomination did not tell us about the new life in Christ available to us. Empty ritual and familial discord, combined with attempts to present a "normal" façade to the outside world, shaped our upbringing. My mother, outwardly an extremely "religious" woman, was very image-conscious and preoccupied with appearances. Both family and culture at large play a role in influencing the way an individual thinks and relates to others, so I can only assume these two factors played a part in making her this way.

The culture of the 1950's and early sixties, when my mother was a young adult, was aesthetically much more exacting than it is now. The expectations on women to have a "perfect" appearance seem almost comical by today's standards, as satirized by the recent hit movie Hairspray. Beauty "how-to" books of this era demanded perfectly tweezed eyebrows, manicured nails and unnaturally high, teased beehive hairdos. Women were indoctrinated into an almost unattainable standard of thinness, with very low-carbohydrate diets coming into fashion. One cigarette company's advertising slogan at the time was "reach for a [cigarette] instead of a sweet." Smoking was cool among the female baby-boomer generation. Eating, most definitely, was not. A diet book of my mother's, published in the sixties, encouraged women to subsist on lean turkey and cottage cheese. Presumably, those of my mother's generation would have considered these types of diet tips healthy.

While she was in graduate school, my mother began eating dessert regularly, and at one point her weight reached 130 lbs. Although she was 5'5" tall, she considered this grossly overweight and managed to take the extra pounds off. "I had to diet just to maintain my weight," she later recalled of this period. Although my mother never had a full-blown eating disorder, she did seem to harbor many hang-ups about food.

Throughout the 1970's and '80's, she subsisted mainly on black coffee and cigarettes and was very proud of being able to keep her weight at 111 lbs.

"Thin is In"

My mesomorphic form was a source of embarrassment to her. In her eyes, my being a chubby youngster was a sign of weakness. As an adolescent, I'd often hear her bemoaning to other women, "Oh, if my daughter could only lose fifteen pounds!" She, my father and my grandparents, consistently made an issue of my weight—especially at holidays, which were observed with calorie-laden food. To make matters worse, Type II diabetes ran in both sides of my family, and my mother was driven to distraction by the fear that my being slightly overweight would lead to a lifetime of insulin shots. In the 1970's, when I was a child, sugar was seen as a near-toxic culprit. Artificial sweeteners were fairly new on the market, and their popularity boosted the notion that sugar and starches must be avoided at all costs. Low carbohydrate diets were actually considered healthy (a fad that came full-circle in the nineties, with the popularity of the Atkins diet and the Zone). Nutrition science was a relatively unknown field at the time. It was against this cultural mindset that I rolled onto the scene in 1971.

From the time I was a toddler, I was slightly heavy with a full face. Since my growing body didn't magically become sylphlike just by taking away starches, my mother then enrolled me in weekly tap-dancing lessons when I was four. Like all little girls, I loved to put music on the record player and spontaneously twirl around the living room, improvising just for fun; now I disliked the repetitive drills and combinations I was expected to practice at home. Besides, my pink tights were always falling down! By the time I quit in third grade, I still wasn't skinny.

Looking back now at pictures of me from that time period,

my husband and others ask, "Where's the fat girl? You were adorable!" Certainly, I was carrying a few extra pounds; but I was barely overweight and nowhere near obese. Very early on, however, I internalized the lie that physical beauty is a measure of worth. Thinness, I was taught, was a high virtue to be pursued at all costs; corpulence was a moral failing to be disdained. Without being taught to view people as God does, I was simply unable to discern that this attitude was a demonic trap with eternal consequences.

The Soul-Killing Poison of Shame

As early as age seven, I remember praying fervently to God that He would make me thinner and therefore acceptable to my mother. Sometime in middle school, I began to walk in shame. Generally, I avoided eye contact and walked with my head down. Shame can either be the result of guilty feelings (remorse over our own sin) or of others' sin against us. In the first scenario, it can be the motivating factor God allows to lead a sinner to Himself. When we feel guilty, we can usually pinpoint some failing or sin which we have committed. Guilt is the conscience's natural response to wrongdoing, and ideally should drive us to make amends. While shame may be caused by a guilty conscience, it may alternately be an ill-defined or irrational indictment of who we are, coupled with a fear that others will see us in the ugly light we view ourselves. It began in the Garden when Adam and Eve, suddenly aware of their sin, hid themselves from their all-holy Creator.

In a sense, shame is biblical in that we do realize naturally that we are morally flawed and lacking in holiness (Romans 2:14-15). We know instinctively that we do not measure up to the standard God originally intended. However, He Himself provided the solution to legitimate, sin-induced shame at Calvary. God never intended for us to carry a destructive burden of shame based on worldly values ("I'm too fat/ugly/etc. to be accepted."). We develop this toxic sense by believing the lies and negative messages we receive about ourselves, rather than what God's Word says about what He values. What is desirable, important, or highly esteemed by parents or society is not necessarily what matters to God. Without a biblical worldview, deception sneaks into our minds and shame takes root in our souls. At twelve, I had no grasp of what mattered to God and began thinking God was also disappointed in me because I weighed too much. Being thin became inextricably linked to being holy in my mind, because of the near-sacredness my mother placed on it. One Sunday morning, I was enamored by a troupe of performing liturgical dancers. "Yes," my mother noted, agreeing with me. "See how nice and thin they all are?"

Gradually, shame became a part of who I was, and I slowly began to internalize that I was inferior and unloved. Many things that were said to me during my childhood and adolescence affected me deeply, but God has shown me that His grace truly is sufficient (2 Corinthians 12:9) and healing has come through forgiveness. Looking back with the perspective of an adult, I can see how careless words cut deep into my soul and caused wounds; but I can also understand that parents often say things casually without considering the destructive effect their comments will have. Most importantly, I have chosen to forgive and not blame others for my equally sinful responses—just as God has graciously forgiven me. My purpose in sharing specific, traumatic incidents in my testimony is to illustrate how a dangerous pattern can emerge from such experiences. Emotional abuse, intentional or not, can be far more destructive than physical, and the wounds take much longer to heal. Parents of girls who have developed eating disorders may be able to learn the power of words from my parents' mistakes, while their daughters may take counsel from my own error and be warned from going down the same path.

The Nightmare Begins

When I was eleven years old, I read an article in Young Miss magazine about bulimia, which in 1982 was not yet a household word. Undaunted by the author's deterioration and suicide attempt, I decided to try it. The next time I ate ice cream, I attempted this new strategy—only to discover how easy it was to throw up. Shaken, I realized the enormity of what I had done and resolved never to do it again. It would be another four years before I again considered purging.

Things heated up in junior high school. Between sixth and seventh grade, I hit puberty and went through a growth spurt. Within a year, I grew four inches and gained about thirty pounds. In seventh grade, I truly was overweight and began to discipline myself to eat carefully. I also began doing gymnastics, which greatly increased my coordination, endurance, and overall fitness. Although I never became a formidable gymnast, participation in the sport itself helped me get into shape and develop good muscle tone. Over the course of a full year, I lost twenty pounds. That summer, after my fourteenth birthday, I had a routine check-up at our family doctor. I was excited about starting high school, but still a little insecure about my body—my mother had been certain all the girls at the prestigious prep school I was to attend would be "rail thin." Had I lost enough weight to fit in? I tried to push that thought from my mind, and concentrate on the progress I had made.

On the way into the office, my mother instructed, "Now, be sure and ask Dr. Maloney about putting you on a diet." My heart sank. Following me into the exam room, she parked herself across from our family doctor and answered all of the questions he asked me. At the conclusion of the check-up, with lowered eyes, I mumbled, "Um, my mother told me to ask you about some sort of diet." Before he could respond, my mother leaned forward and interjected in an unnaturally loud tone, "She knows she's overweight!" Dr. Maloney turned to face her. "According to my chart, she's perfectly normal," he countered. By my mother's standards, I was still overweight at 5'5" and 131 lbs. All of that hard work and discipline had been for nothing. My face burned with frustration and shame. Dr. Maloney, however, attempted to inject some sanity into the situation. He refused to prescribe a restricted-calorie diet, calmed my mother's fears about my "athletic" physique, and wished me luck in high school. As we exited the office, my mother suggested we stop at the Armenian café next door, where she proceeded to inhale a large wedge of baklava in front of me. I sipped a diet soda and wondered silently whether or not to count the morning as a victory.

As high school began, I resolved to be thinner, like a "real" dancer or gymnast. My love of gymnastics evolved into an obsession, as I sought to prove that there was something at which I excelled. Inspired by a movie about Nadia Comaneci, my diet became increasingly Spartan and my workouts more intense. I idolized Nadia; thinking she was the epitome of discipline and perfection. (Years later, I read that she had battled both anorexia and bulimia during her competitive days, as well). As the pounds and my dress size dropped, my mother could barely conceal her delight—at last, a daughter in whom she could be proud! In tenth grade, I went on a lettuce and Fresca™ regimen for a while, and then became bulimic.

Starving for Acceptance

I don't remember exactly what caused me to snap. It wasn't the gymnastics coach who suggested that a classmate and I compete to see who could lose the most weight—that comment was simply another nail in my coffin. (The other girl laughed it off—she had been conditioned to accept her athletic body). I dealt with more pointed criticisms than that at home on a daily basis. I never got used to constant hunger. Unlike quitting smoking or drinking, in which the cravings decrease in intensity and gradually subside entirely, the longer one restricts food intake, the stronger the urge to eat becomes. This is why the stricter a diet, the more likely the dieter is to fail at her long-term weight loss goals. An anorexic may quell her physical hunger pains with appetite suppressants and water loading, but she is constantly thinking about food. She daydreams about cooking, pores over recipes, and obsessively reads nutritional labels. Even in the refuge of sleep, her senses are still tormented by dreams of food. Most bulimics were, at one point, anorexic. A BMI^2 -obsessed young woman considers resisting the "enemy" of food noble and stoic in the midst of a hedonistic, over-indulged society.

Once the anorexic gives in to her hunger, she has crossed the line. It is impossible to go back to "virtuous" self-denial (starvation) when indulgence is there for the taking. The "safety latch" is the purge. Once vomiting has become a viable option, it is increasingly difficult to resist its lure. The out-of-control, compulsive attempt to satiate that unquenchable hunger began when I was fifteen and in the tenth grade. After so many years of constant exercise, hunger, self-denial and maddeningly slow progress, I gave in. I couldn't live on Slim-Fast and vegetables anymore. My weight dropped with barely a hunger pang. In the dance studio where I sweated on Wednesday nights, a medical scale stood in the bathroom, silently mocking the wiry dancers who vomited nightly.

My menstrual period disappeared that same year. Soon, the dentist began noticing symmetrical cavities on each of my previously perfect molars. My mother's suspicion grew. By the time my mother and grandparents figured out I had bulimia, I desperately wanted to be free of this addiction but couldn't stop purging. During the summer of 1987, before beginning eleventh grade, I wrote my mother a detailed letter confessing that I was bulimic and how out of control my life had become. I left it on her nightstand and spent a sleepless night worrying about the fallout. Much to my relief, she did not get angry and informed me that she had, in fact, known about my "secret" for some time. We decided I could stop on my own, and did not pursue professional help.

I did not stop on my own. I couldn't. With no spiritual grounding, being thin was my ultimate goal and what I essentially "worshiped." The thought of gaining a pound terrified me, and I was by this time completely in the grips of the addiction. While I was ashamed and disgusted by my own behavior, paradoxically the bulimia was the most valuable thing I could hold onto.

As my fear of gaining weight grew, so did my obsession with food, to where I was bingeing and purging every day. I began eleventh grade with a lean 110 lbs. on my 5'5" frame. The gymnastics coach and dance teacher adored my new physique, and I received many compliments from classmates and teachers alike. Soon, however, the praise and admiring looks turned into worried glances and confrontational questions in the hallways. Not long thereafter, several students and teachers realized I was vomiting in the school bathroom. I was no longer in control—the bulimia was controlling me and I was on a roller coaster rapidly gaining momentum. The more I tried to restrict myself to "safe" foods in order not to gain weight, the more intense my cravings became and the frequency of binge/purge episodes increased. I was killing myself, yet I was unable to stop.

About the same time, my fourteen-year old brother started drinking and using drugs. He despised school, and escaped from the unhappy atmosphere of our family life by hanging out with his friends, many of whom had been in trouble with the law. Several nights, I would come home from work to hear him drunkenly vomiting into the basement garbage can—the aftermath of an evening swilling vodka. He was expelled from the parochial high school he attended, and was later in court on assault and battery charges. Unlike Jay, who had been put on Ritalin for hyperactivity and "anger management issues" as a preschooler, Philip was never treated with prescription medications. He preferred to self-medicate, and was attending Alcoholics Anonymous meetings before he was legally allowed to drink. During the late eighties, my brothers' more blatant problems served to camouflage mine for a while. I was the stereotypical "good girl" who studied hard, never drank, and kept a low profile.

Hardened Inside and Out

By my senior year of high school, my weight dropped to just below 90 lbs. When I saw pictures of myself during this period, I was shocked and embarrassed by my emaciated appearance, but I didn't see the same thing in the mirror. I could not bring myself to keep food down, and the feeling of anything in my stomach was abhorrent. At the same time, physical hunger and powerful cravings (survival instinct kicking in) would not allow me to "control" myself when confronted with the smell and sight of food. It became a daily battle to enter and leave the school cafeteria without bingeing on everything in sight. One solution I developed was to bring a diet shake to school and drink it in the student lounge at lunchtime in the guise of studying. Sometimes, I would take appetite suppressants to "help keep it in check," but these pills had the unfortunate side effect of making me fall asleep in class. My exhaustion, even without diet pills, was painfully apparent to my teachers, who took turns confronting me and calling the school headmaster. I was assigned to weekly sessions with the school guidance counselor, to whom I expertly lied, and was given a referral to see a psychiatrist.

As senior year of high school dragged on, my bulimia became so entrenched that it came to seem almost normal to me. My parents alternated between pretending it didn't exist to acting shocked and concerned when the school nurse and headmaster called in alarm. My mother waited until the weekend after I had taken the SAT examination to tell me that she had received yet another call from the school; she did not want to "upset" me beforehand, lest my test scores suffer. My classmates were aware of what was going on and grew uncomfortable around me. Some of the girls tried to help by talking to me, but I was convinced that everyone in the class hated me and I withdrew even further. During the mid-morning break in our Advanced Placement biology class, my eyes fell on a note one student had scribbled to another on the textbook page: "That skeleton has more fat on it than Marie." The girl's lab partner had replied, "My God you're right." I didn't make eye contact with either girl again until we graduated. My shame and alienation grew to the point I would have nightmares about going to school. I learned to "turn off" all feeling and grew completely numb. Hundreds of sit-ups each day transformed my concave abdomen into sheetrock. Rejection of all emotion did the same thing to my heart.

A year after the school had initially intervened and I was seeing a psychologist weekly, my father overheard a telephone conversation between my mother and a concerned party from the school. I don't recall if it was a teacher or the headmaster, but my mother was discussing details of my eating disorder with the individual while my father eavesdropped from the foot of the stairs. He demanded to know why no one had told him about my bulimia, exclaiming: "This is something serious, which needs professional counseling!" My mother countered, "Everyone else has known for over a year. Where have you been?" Devoid of the presence and peace that only the Holy Spirit can give, there was simply no unity or mutual concern in our family. Each of us developed our own means of self-preservation and a mentality of "every man (or woman) for himself."

I took refuge in gymnastics. My performance in the gym suffered greatly, although all I could see was that my weight rivaled that of Olympic gymnasts (many of whom are less than five feet tall). As my strength and coordination deteriorated, my purpose became singular: if I could not be the best gymnast, I would be the thinnest one alive. Practicing on the uneven bars was excruciating—huge bruises covered my hips and legs. The bars were much closer together in those days than they are now, and with no fat left to cushion the impact, my bones took the full brunt of each hit. My chest was every bit as flat as those of the tiny Soviet gymnasts I idolized. One morning, I became light-headed in the shower and had to sit down under the frigid spray to revive myself. Toweling off, I stepped on the scale and watched it register 86 lbs. I remember feeling a very real sense of personal achievement at being the exact same weight that Nadia had been at the Montreal Olympics. I was seventeen years old.

Playing the Game and Killing Time

Although I managed to avoid inpatient treatment, my school mandated outpatient counseling for most of my senior year. A psychiatrist who specialized in eating disorders in adolescents, "Terry" was a low-key, non-judgmental therapist who practiced in an upscale suburb of Boston. During the first couple of sessions, I mentally checked out while my mother bemoaned the messages of the media, the pressures of high school, the unrealistic expectations of dance studios, and the offhand comments of my gymnastics coach. All these factors combined, she felt, to cause my eating disorder. The most assertive thing I remember Terry ever saying came on week three, when my mother again tried to step into the counseling office. Placing herself squarely between my mother and the door, she said firmly, "I think I'd like to talk to Marie alone this week." I don't recall talking about anything of substance, certainly not my compulsion to binge and purge. I spent most of these counseling sessions staring out the window and listening to Terry's clock tick.

Once alone in the room, the psychiatrist tried to prompt me to pin-point specific moments, which she called "markers," that might have led to my becoming bulimic. I didn't think any one particular incident had catalyzed my behavior, but rather saw the eating disorder as a natural progression of events that had been a long time in the making. In a roundabout way, Terry probed my fears about how I thought the opposite sex perceived me. I duly recited the refrain of my early adolescence: "'You're never going to have a boyfriend if you don't 'slim down', because boys don't date fat girls.'" I looked up, and returned Terry's gaze. "That's what my mother said, and my grandmother backed her up." Terry winced. "The funny thing is," I continued, "now the boys don't ask me out, anyway. Apparently they don't go for the 'inmate at Auschwitz look', either." As soon as the words were out of my mouth, I regretted my tactlessness: I had forgotten that Terry was Jewish.

Terry, however, had regained her composure and calmly asked, "How did that make you feel?" "How was it supposed to make me feel?" I thought. "Well, at the time I first heard it, I was so young I wasn't even interested in boys yet," I admitted. "When I was ten, she was driving me home from a piano lesson and I made the comment—I don't even know where this came from—that modeling seems like a fun career. She says, 'What would you model; maternity clothes?'" Terry cringed, then asked about my mother's eating habits. "Well, she basically just eats dinner, and lives on black coffee and smokes Old Golds the rest of the time," I reflected. I saw no direct connection, but I welcomed the chance to throw the attention off of myself. "Maybe she's the one who needs therapy," I added. Terry could see where this was going. "Maybe, but right now we need to work on you learning some healthier coping mechanisms." "I already have a coping mechanism", I thought. "I eat mechanically and then throw up. Works for me."

"Yup," I responded, trying to infuse conviction into my tone.

After a brief pause, Terry asked, "Do you want to make changes?"

"Sure," I said.

We both knew I was lying.

College-Bound and Still in Bondage

Crossing off the days on my calendar in red ink, I convinced myself that as soon as I went to college, the bondage I was in would go away. I left for college at Syracuse University in late August of 1989. My last night at home was marked by a violent outburst that seemed to symbolize the previous eighteen years I'd spent there. A petty squabble between my older brother and father escalated into a shouting match. When I tried to intervene, Jay turned on me, screaming that I was an "(expletive) bulimic." My calm demeanor enraged him further, which he vented by picking up a piece of chicken cordon bleu and hurling it at my head. I ducked, and it splattered all over the kitchen wallpaper behind me. I left the house and walked the mile or so up to the community college's athletic track. As I sat on the embankment reflecting on life, I was uncharacteristically serene. The events that had transpired earlier in the evening somehow seemed a fitting end to a chaotic and unhappy chapter in my life.

As I began college, my weight still hovered in the low nineties. I rarely kept down a meal of any size, although I still did not see the bulimia as a sin that was controlling me. I truly believed that I was the one in control, but simply chose not to give it up. After only two weeks at college, the dormitory resident advisor confronted me and I was placed back in counseling. I was required to attend off-campus group therapy for eating disordered women once a week, and to check in with the student health center twice a week to have my blood drawn. A nurse practitioner was keeping a close eye on my electrolyte levels, as each time vomiting is induced the potassium level drops. At one point, my potassium level was as low as 2.0, and there was a possibility I could go into shock or cardiac arrest (Anorexics and bulimics are considered liabilities by universities, because while they may appear healthy, they are at risk for sudden death). I have read about incidents since I was in college where anorexic women are asked to move off-campus in order not to risk the school's reputation.

During one of my semi-weekly checkups, my electrolytes so alarmed the nurse practitioner that she brought in an attending physician to review the blood profile. Horrified, he demanded to know why I wasn't in inpatient treatment, and asked me if I knew what an electrolyte imbalance meant. "Yes," I replied calmly. "The sodium-potassium pump transmits ions across the plasma membrane." I had aced AP biology in high school, and was glad for the opportunity to show off. "That's exactly right," the doctor replied. "And what happens when the concentration of potassium ions is too low?" Now I was out of my depth. "Umm…the signals don't get transmitted?" I was guessing, but it was irrelevant to the doctor's point. "And what happens then?" he pressed. Backed into a corner, I conceded, "You die?" "That's right," he said sternly. He lectured me for a few more minutes, and I began to wonder if I was expected to show some sort of remorse or fear. I have never been a particularly emotional person, and although I may feel a certain way in private, I cannot simply produce emotion on demand the way one would squeeze the last bit of toothpaste out of a tube. Although I was somewhat shaken inwardly, I couldn't have cried if he had wanted me to. At all costs, I had to maintain an imperturbable façade.

Somehow, the doctor's initial sentence of inpatient treatment was reduced to a weekly appointment with a psychiatrist. Referrals were needed and insurance claims filed before I met Syracuse's renowned specialist in eating disorders, Dr.

Pradahn. A diminutive woman of Indian origin, she was even quieter and more non-committal than Terry had been. Once I was seated on her office couch, she peered at me quizzically from behind her desk and asked profoundly, "What would you like to change?" Lord, have mercy, I inwardly groaned. Here we go again.

My Heart's Cry

C.S. Lewis is usually credited with penning the famous line, "There is a God-shaped vacuum in the heart of every man." Truer words have never been written. It is also true that most people go through life not recognizing the one true God as the object of their desire. Without knowing God, as opposed to merely knowing about Him, we seek to fill this intangible "hole" in our souls with the things of this world, only to find that no such idol will truly satisfy.

Things like acceptance, affirmation, and popularity are what we often think we are lacking. Of course, we don't see these "felt needs" as idols; we label them as "values" and "priorities." Until we realize the depths of our own depravity, we don't see our real needs—forgiveness, salvation, and fellowship with our Creator. Others go through life pretending this vacuum doesn't exist. Either way, we wind up pretty miserable. Like everyone else, bulimics and anorexics desire close relationships, but we always feel the need to keep people at a distance in order to guard our secret. Thus, any kind of intimacy eludes us and we often come across as standoffish.

I had virtually no friends at this point in my life. I was either ignored or outright rejected by everyone, as my condition was painfully obvious. I was frightened but powerless to change—even in moments when I saw my situation with clarity. I dutifully took the Prozac Dr. Pradahn prescribed. It wasn't helping. My compulsion to use food to comfort, stifle, or soothe (or sometimes just for no reason at all) was just as intense as ever, and only increased my alienation.

Since the Greek system was popular at S.U., I decided to participate in Rush Week as a freshman, hoping to find my niche. Perhaps not surprisingly, no sorority wanted me and, once again, I had to face being a "reject." I remember crying out to God one night from the floor of my dorm room, asking why He had created me. I just wanted to die so badly; but could not bring myself to consider suicide, which I had been brought up to believe was a one-way ticket to hell. I was convinced I was on my way there anyway, knowing how stuck I was in sin, but I had no idea how to turn around. I truly believe that it was at this point that my heart began to yearn for God. I simply could not fully recognize my deepest need and longing—to be loved, fully forgiven, and wholly accepted by Him. Even if I had, I would not have known how to let Him rescue me, since I knew nothing of grace.

When I thought about God at all back then, I figured He was angry or disgusted with me for my shameful secret. I had loved Jesus since childhood; that had never changed. At the same time, though, I was a little afraid of God the Father. Growing up, I instinctively knew that the works-based religious system I was reared in was wrong. If God existed, I knew that He was not pleased with man-made rituals and an elaborate merit/demerit system. An all-loving God could not be interested in contrived piety and empty ritual. Unlike my brothers, I never denied His existence. The hypocrisy of those who claimed to represent Christ never caused me to grow hostile or apathetic towards Him. However, I was as yet unaware that biblical Christianity offered a relationship with God only through faith in Christ and His righteousness. If anything, the hollowness of empty religion pushed me instinctively towards the One the Bible calls the God of all Comfort (2 Corinthians 1:3). I just didn't recognize it at the time.

Although I had not yet read the Bible, I knew enough about Jesus from the Gospel readings I'd heard in church to know He was gentle, tender-hearted, and compassionate. I knew He forgave sin. When I let my mind linger there long enough, I hoped that someday there would be hope for me. I was so ashamed of my bulimia that I could not bear the thought of God seeing it. Surely He had given up on me. The stories of the sinful women being forgiven by Jesus (Luke 7 and John 8) were touching and inspirational…but they were not bulimics.

After a semester of meeting with the university's nutritionist, dutifully attending group therapy, and meeting weekly with the psychiatrist, my weight was up to about 110-112 lbs. Clearly, I was keeping some food down, but mostly the weight gain just made the purging easier to hide. I knew exactly how to keep myself out of the hospital, and had long since figured out how to give psychiatrists the answers they wanted to hear. By external appearances, I was "recovered." In reality, I was just gaining skill at concealing my secret.

Jesus and Ice Cream Parties

In September of my sophomore year, intrigued by the name, I joined a group called Campus Crusade for Christ. A group of students was distributing informational leaflets outside the dining hall, and I lingered self-consciously. The flyer promoting Campus Crusade's kick-off meeting promised fun, music and free ice cream to all in attendance. The outgoing sophomore behind the table chatted with every student who stopped by, answering their questions and making them feel welcome. "Um…can, like, just anyone go?" I asked timidly, without making eye contact. "Sure! Everyone's welcome," he replied, pulling an announcement out of his guitar case. I decided to attend….and not for the ice cream, either. The students at the Campus Crusade meetings were friendly and seemed filled with joy. At each gathering, an upperclassman or staff member would get up and share his or her personal story of how they had come to know the Lord—which I later learned was called a "testimony." These students sang Christian songs, talked freely about Jesus, and seemed to have little interest in the more banal aspects of campus life. A few of them invited me to attend the New York State Fair, and for a little while, I began to forget my isolating badge of shame. I was able to relax a little bit, and realized I wasn't the only one in the world who sincerely desired to follow Jesus. I was just completely clueless as to where to start.

When a young staff woman shared the Gospel with me and meticulously pointed to what the Bible says about salvation, I decided to trust that God would actually forgive all my sins. For the first time in my life, I heard the term "unconditional love." I knew Christ was calling me out of my spiritual darkness, and I put my faith in Him, but at the time it was more an intellectual acceptance of His grace than a sincere repentance. Deep down, I was frightened that I would never be able to completely submit this ugly, dominating secret to Christ's authority. I could not imagine a life not controlled by food. My days were ordered around the next binge and how and where I could purge undetected.

I did not tell anyone, including the woman discipling[3] me, about the bulimia. I was still too ashamed, even to talk about it privately or seek help from God. I still wrestled with doubts over where I stood with God, and wondered whether He actually wanted someone like me around. The memory of last fall's sorority humiliation still fresh in my mind, I tried to comfort myself with the knowledge that I was now in the only "sorority" that mattered—the family of God. Rather than assuring me that I was loved, this realization made me think that Jesus simply had no standards whatsoever. The "Jesus" with whom I'd grown up had had very demanding criteria to stay on His good side, and I'd never come close to measuring up. Still, I suppressed whatever doubts I may have had about God's personal love. I was gifted at memorizing Scripture, learned systematic theology in no time, and was leading a small group Bible study by the following year. All the while, the purging continued in secret.

Rejoice and Be Glad?

Often, I have thought that if I had pursued biblical counseling while in college, my long road to freedom would have been shorter. The pain, anger, pride and self-absorption, which the bulimia masked, needed to be countered by a proper concept of God. At the time, however, I kept promising that eventually I would make it go away on my own. What I still did not realize was that being thin had become my idol. While I realized full well that bulimia was a sin, I did not see the root problem as an idol of the heart that could only be torn down in Christ's power.

Ironically, once I became a Christian, I had a new excuse to seek solace in food: I became further alienated from my family. My mother and maternal grandfather, in particular, were horrified that I had been "born again," a taboo word in their lexicon. As the only Christian in my family, (and a vulnerable one at that), the constant criticism and passive-aggressive barbs further eroded any joy I might have experienced in my new life in Christ. I longed for my family to know Christ and prayed daily for their salvation, all the while contemplating serving Him overseas on a short-term summer project with Campus Crusade. I had a strong desire to reach the lost and, as a print journalism major, anticipated an eventual career based in Eastern Europe. The Berlin Wall had just come down three years earlier, and the former Soviet Bloc was the new frontier of limitless possibilities, both for evangelists and foreign investors. Although I had no delusions about going into full-time ministry, as an aspiring journalist I greatly desired to be close to this exciting, exotic new world. I vacillated between Romania and Yugoslavia (the latter being the war-torn topic of my senior thesis), but ultimately was sent to Bulgaria.

As I began raising financial support for the mission, my family provided anything but moral support; my mother even informed me of how "scandalized" she and my grandfather were by my activities. Her parish priest told her that Campus Crusade was a cult, and she believed him. During semester breaks when I stayed at my parents' house in Massachusetts, I would walk the mile each Sunday to the nearest Baptist church—although my mother was paranoid "one of the neighbors would see an O'Toole child (sic) walking into a Protestant church on Sunday." (My father, an agnostic, really didn't have "a dog in the fight" and limited his remarks to mockery of Christ's teachings). As graduation approached, the hostility intensified. Initially I turned to God, pleading with Him to open their eyes. I found solace in Psalms 25 and 27, which I memorized: "For my father and my mother have forsaken me, but the LORD will take me up. Teach me Your way, O LORD, And lead me in a level path because of my foes. Do not deliver me over to the desire of my adversaries, For false witnesses have risen against me, and such as breathe out violence" (Psalm 27:10-12).

As a new and immature Christian, however, I found it impossible to comply with Jesus' command to "rejoice and be glad" when my family slandered me. Forgiveness seemed elusive and unnatural. Resentment at their insults was compounded by the pain of old wounds. Predictably, I turned back to my familiar security blanket—food. As bitterness grew in my heart, the bulimia intensified with a vengeance. Praying and reminding myself that God understood rejection all too well didn't seem to help—I expected Him to change my circumstances. When He didn't intervene, I reverted to my carnal "coping mechanism" and inwardly grew cynical. I filled out my project application with high hopes, and after graduation arrived in Sofia with the best of intentions. During the mission trip, I landed a job as an administrative assistant for a newly-established international business association. I agreed to an employment-at-will contract, and immediately rented a studio apartment. Starting a new life, I determined to forget my painful past and put as much distance between my parents and myself as possible.

For the first several months in Bulgaria, I attended a home church in Sofia run by a middle-aged Southern Baptist missionary couple from the United States. When they were transferred to another city, I started going to a Bulgarian Reformed evangelical church in the city center with friends. As I met other young professional people in other circles, I slowly began to disassociate myself from the insulated, Christian micro-culture. Inebriated with the freedom of being young, independent, and alone in Europe, I began partying with my newfound friends and wealthy business associates. My skirts got shorter and I began smoking, as night after night we explored the exotic new world of discothèques and mafia-run nightclubs.

C.S. Lewis, whom I have already quoted, once said that if he wanted something easy and pain-free, he would have chosen a bottle of wine over Jesus. Unlike the very proper British author, I opted for the bottle of wine.

Within a year of moving to Bulgaria, I had developed a serious drinking habit. I convinced myself that this was a more "socially-acceptable" vice than bulimia. Both addictions intensified quickly, all the easier since I lived alone. The few times I had tried drinking in college, I had found the feeling exhilarating. When I was drunk, I felt like a different person—a smarter, wittier, more confident woman with the world at her feet. The alcohol served as anesthesia to ease the pain and shame of purging for a few hours at a time, but no number of bottles was ever enough to fill the aching emptiness inside.

At age 24 I got married to a wonderful man, who knew nothing about eating disorders or the fact that his American wife had had one for nearly a decade at that point. After so many years of practice, I had become really good at hiding it. My husband, Ivaylo, was concerned about my inability to moderate my drinking, so I no longer had that as a "crutch." I hated myself sober and naturally drifted further away from God. I had stopped going to church because I felt like a hypocrite. How could I have that close, intimate relationship with God they always talked about, with such a filthy secret? Each time I heard a Christian give his or her glowing, "happily ever after" testimony about how Jesus changed their life from the inside out, I would feel depressed and frustrated. I even began to doubt my salvation.

Back to Square One

Soon after our wedding, we moved back to the States. For a while, in the early months of our marriage, I had managed to reduce the frequency of purging episodes by sheer discipline. Things were going well, and I had a false sense of confidence that the bulimia would gradually disappear on its own. Within a matter of days after arriving in Massachusetts, the strain of my family's dysfunction began to take a toll on both my husband and myself. My mother had long since established idolatrous emotional ties to me, which she was unable to see, much less break. Since childhood, I had been able to see through her "guilt trips" and manipulation tactics and resented being used as a "sounding board" for adult problems that were not for me to carry. Now, gossip and inappropriate interference in our personal lives led Ivo and myself to establish boundaries, which were ignored, and ultimately forced us to implement a no-contact policy for a while. My mother retaliated by referring to me as "the nut," a title my sisters-in-law felt more accurately described her bizarre and intrusive behavior. Ivo and I had done nothing to provoke anyone's hostility, yet we were forced to deal with manipulation, fabricated stories about us, and even obscene phone calls my grandfather made to us in a drunken rage.

Stress is a predictable trigger and convenient excuse to slide deeper into addiction. I lost ten pounds the first six months.

I could not even stop purging during my first three pregnancies, although thankfully the babies were all healthy with high birth weights. I maintained a low-normal weight and no one knew the dark, terrifying secret that ruled my waking moments. During this time, I was so hungry spiritually; I desperately wanted to come back to God, but I knew that He could not tolerate or even look upon gross sin (Habakkuk 1:13). I wanted to repent and be in fellowship with Him so badly.

It was nearly impossible, seeing myself as a literal slave to sin, to believe that in spite of my addiction God still loved me and offered repentance. Obedience may be the key to freedom, but what do you do when you feel hopeless to obey? We attended church and many times I tried desperately to turn away from this sin, only to find myself inexplicably drawn back in. One Christmas Eve years ago, I remember sitting in the evening service—surrounded by subdued holy music and flickering candles– and felt like such a failure. I had resolved that year to quit drinking and bulimia as my "birthday present" to Jesus. Needless to say, Advent had barely begun before I had given up.

One subject you will rarely hear addressed in church is that Christians can, and often do, suffer from addictions. I had insight into the fact I was sinning, but it didn't stop me from bingeing when the uncontrollable urge kicked in. One day, as I passed a new church built next to a chain store I often frequent, I noticed a "Healing Room" sign for Saturday mornings. A small ad in the newspaper for the same prayer room had also caught my eye. The ministry promised "confidential prayer for physical, emotional and spiritual healing." I was so desperate; I thought what could it hurt?

The following Saturday morning, I walked in timidly, al-

most in tears, not knowing what to expect. Three very compassionate, mature Christian women put their hands on me
and prayed earnestly that God would break this curse in my
life. They implored God to let me know His forgiveness and
healing; even that He would "re-wire" the endorphins in my
brain. One of them told me that God was calling me to know
Him better; that I knew a lot about Him, but didn't really
know Him. They prayed earnestly for a while longer, and I
really felt better; cleaner than I had in a long time. Nothing
mystical or esoteric happened, but something greater did: I
knew I was forgiven. I had such a strong faith that God had
heard their prayer that I resolved to try to again, with Jesus
on board this time. I went back for intercession several more
times over the next few months.

Turning Darkness into Light

After my first visit, I stopped drinking completely. All desire
for alcohol simply left me. Even when the fleeting thought to
join my husband in a Friday night whiskey passed through
my mind, it was easy to dismiss. One of the women on the
prayer team had told me that Jesus had been watching me for
a long time, as if He had had His arm around my shoulder
while I was unaware of His presence. I kept that image in
my mind whenever I was briefly tempted to seek solace in
alcohol, and it worked. The warmth of that loving assurance,
unconditional and unchanging, was far more satisfying than
any "buzz" I'd ever gotten from drinking.

I wish I could say that the bulimia disappeared just as
quickly, but I'd be fibbing. While I do believe that God forgave and enabled me to change the first time I confessed
this sin, it took me a while (about five months) to fully walk
in that freedom. In other words, on the "high" of that first
prayer session, I went several days without bingeing and
purging. Over the course of the next few months, I would
regularly go about six days on average without an episode.

For years prior to this, I had been purging once or twice on average each day.

It is important to understand that we have to co-operate with God in overcoming sin in our own lives. My desire for Him grew; for reading the Bible, and for fellowship with Him through prayer. I had to deliberately choose, over and over, to lay my wrong thinking (preoccupation with food and weight) down on the altar and reprogram my mind with the truth of God's Word. I learned to "put off" my selfish desires and "put on" the mind of Christ (a discipline we will discuss more fully in later chapters). Little by little, my idol of thinness crumbled and was replaced by the joy of knowing I was a daughter of the King. With each subsequent victory over temptation, I grew stronger and my faith deepened. This was the clearest evidence of the Holy Spirit working in my life that I had ever experienced.

Sometimes, out of habit, I'd still be tempted to binge while mid-meal. I had been using food as a narcotic for half my life, and I still had to struggle against this deeply ingrained pattern. At those moments, I would yield to the Spirit's promptings to pray for strength. I would silently say, "No; Lord, you know how I feel right now. You know this unhealthy temptation that threatens to overcome me. I turn to You; I am spiritually hungry. I crave fellowship with You; this food will never satisfy. Help me not to give in to this self-destructive habit," or something along those lines. Then, if I were alone, I would leave the kitchen and open my Bible. Removing one's self physically from temptation is crucial, especially in the beginning stages of overcoming deep-seated sin. Typically, I would then spend an hour or so in a favorite Bible study (at the time I was doing Max Lucado's "Experiencing the Heart of Jesus"). By the end of this time with God, I would feel refreshed and peaceful with a renewed sense of joy.

This is not a distraction tactic, it is allowing God to help and strengthen you. Repentance and self-control (which is a fruit of the Spirit) were the ultimate keys in my finally forsaking this sin once and for all. Yes, there were some failures, and yes; I got discouraged sometimes. Nevertheless, I never gave up (which is what Satan would have wanted) and in the end I was truly victorious through Christ who strengthens me (Philippians 4:13). Psalm 40 became my lifeline—I saw bulimia as the "miry pit" from which He saved me. Finally, after so many fruitless years, I was beginning to stand on solid Rock!

Mourning into Dancing

Over the course of those months, I did initially gain a few pounds, but it leveled off quickly and I neither restricted, worked out, nor got fat. Later, after my fourth child was born, the additional pounds melted away on their own without any extra effort. When I decided I wanted freedom from bulimia no matter what it took, I accepted that I would inevitably gain some weight, but it was not as much as I feared. A person will not get fat simply from eating as her body needs. God helped me to overcome that irrational mindset as well, which is where changing my heart attitude came in. As you repent from an eating disorder, one of the first steps is to give up your preconceived notions about weight and beauty. God created our bodies and knows exactly how they work. Just as we can trust His plan for every aspect of our lives, I came to realize I could trust Him with His plan for my weight. God even healed my metabolism in addition to renewing my mind. Once my mind became set on things above, (Colossians 3:2), I no longer craved constant compliments on my figure.

In September 2004, fourteen years after trusting Christ, I made the decision to be baptized. More than a public declaration of faith, this event represented a covenant between God and me that there was no turning back. Finally, by God's grace, I was beginning to walk with the Lord in trust and obedience. Being baptized was a joyful yet intensely personal celebration of the depth of victory over sin known only to my Savior.

Another area in which I needed to allow God to heal me was in forgiving my mother. Once I was able to come to terms with what true forgiveness is, I realized that I would have to "let her go" in my heart for her part in the development of my eating disorder. While certainly things in our past can greatly affect us, especially parental influences, blaming another person for our sin is not biblical and will hamper spiritual growth. I needed to learn to accept personal responsibility for my actions and the years of choosing a lie over the truth. Also, God has taught me that true forgiveness is rarely a one-time deal. It means continually making the decision to keep on forgiving her, regardless of old memories, new circumstances, and whether or not she ever repents. To truly extend grace, I need His supernatural strength. Over the years I have learned that I am powerless, in my own strength, to overcome my natural bitterness and resentment. (For a more thorough look at forgiveness and why it is such an important part of overcoming an eating disorder, see Chapter 12).

As this book goes to press, it has been over seven years since God completely restored me from the chains of bulimia. I have never relapsed, been severely tempted, or looked back at the life I used to live in the pit of food and alcohol addiction. My thinking has been totally transformed, and I am more productive and able to serve God and others than I ever was when encumbered by bulimia. Until writing this manuscript, I hardly ever think about it anymore. Still, the memories are fresh enough that I can readily testify to God's great faithfulness. When I feel discouraged or defeated in another area of my life, I go back and remember the valleys He has lead me through, and realize there is nothing insurmountable to God. If His grace alone could free me from a seventeen-year addiction, He can truly move mountains!

Chapter 2

What Really Causes Eating Disorders?

In her 1991 bestseller "The Beauty Myth," feminist author Naomi Wolf writes:

> The youngest victims, from earliest childhood, learn to starve and vomit from the overwhelmingly powerful message of our culture….[my parents'] love contradicted the message of the larger world, which wanted me to starve in order to love me. It is the larger world's messages, young women know, to which they will have to listen…I kept a wetted finger up to the winds of that larger world: Too thin yet? I was asking it. What about now? No? Now? The larger world never gives girls the message that their bodies are valuable simply because they are inside them. Until our culture tells young girls that they are welcome in any shape…. girls will continue to starve.[4]

With all due respect to Ms. Wolf, an extremely intelligent and articulate woman, I disagree with this statement on the grounds that it is completely unbiblical. There is no Scriptural precedent that allows us to indict society at large for our own imprudent, dangerous, or self-destructive behavior. While it is true that we live in a fallen, sinful world, and girls internalize unrealistic messages of beauty and vanity from the culture in which they live, the Bible itself warns repeatedly that we are not to live by the world's values, but by God's. As believers, we are instructed to be on guard against the spirit of this world—not to succumb to it. We are not to conform to the standards of "the nations" around us (Ezekiel 11:12) or to any other arbitrary, man-made standards, but are explicitly instructed to conform to the likeness of the Son of God (Romans 8:29).

Blaming society for our eating disorders is not an option. No matter how great the importance advertising places on thinness or what means women may use to achieve it, we cannot use societal standards as an excuse for our behavior. Using food in an unholy way is an individual choice one makes; not a collective crime. If the woman is a Christian, the Holy Spirit brings individual conviction over this sin.

Being controlled by other people, directly or indirectly, is a form of servitude. God's will for His people is freedom from this kind of enslavement. Accepting that God truly is all-sufficient and that our true needs were entirely met at the Cross enables us to move forward in victory. Seeking affirmation or unconditional acceptance from society is simply a manifestation of vanity and "fear of man" (preoccupation with others' opinion of one's self), a snare against which the Bible warns (Proverbs 29:25).

Political Prisoners or Slaves to Sin?
Wolf goes on to say:

> Women must claim anorexia as political damage done to us by a social order that considers our destruction insignificant because of what we are—less. We should identify it as Jews identify the death camps, as homosexuals identify AIDS: as a disgrace that is not our own, but that of an inhumane social order. Anorexia is a prison camp. One-fifth of well-educated American young women are inmates. Susie Orbach compared anorexia to the hunger strikes of political prisoners, particularly the suffragists. But the time for metaphors is behind us. To be anorexic or bulimic is to be a political prisoner.[5]

While a woman in the pit of an eating disorder may feel very much as if she were a prisoner, in reality, she is a prisoner only to her own sin nature. To compare self-destructive behavior, no matter how strong the addiction, to the concentration camps of Nazi Germany is a slap in the face to those who perished there. The prisoners in World War II Europe were innocent of any crime, did not provoke their attackers, and were held in the camps against their will. Tortured in the most inhumane ways imaginable, these millions of Jews, Gypsies and Slavs were true victims. Once a bulimic (or drunkard, or any other substance abuser) comes to view herself as a victim, her chances of meaningful recovery drop considerably. The "victim mentality" becomes a self-fulfilling prophecy. Rather than viewing ourselves as casualties who have unwittingly been immobilized by addiction, it is more accurate to see ourselves as sinners in need of a Savior extending the gift of repentance. Now true change can begin.

"But Don't I Have a 'Disease'?"
You may have heard that eating disorders are caused by genetics or some sort of non-specific "chemical imbalance." Low serotonin levels have been seen as the culprit for bulimia, despite the fact that no diagnostic tests or tissue samples have confirmed this hypothesis. Non-invasive "brain mapping" scans point to "hot spots," but the problem with this form of test is that areas of the brain display differently according to the patient's anxiety level or emotional state. The theory of "chemical imbalance" has prevailed for so long in the medical community that many accept it as iron-clad fact. Actually, in over twenty years of research, no evidence has been discovered suggesting that eating disorders are organic, and both psychotropic drugs and SSRI[6] inhibitors (anti-depressants) have been ineffectual in "curing" anorexics and bulimics. Renowned psychiatrists are now admitting that the chemical imbalance theory was just that all along—a theory.

So where do eating disorders come from? A biblical answer to that would be, in short, from our own deceitful hearts. Psychology has been trying to answer that question ever since bulimia and anorexia became household words back in the early 1980s, and has still come up short. It is human nature to always want to understand the "why" in our behavior. In fact, however, the "whys" are less important than recognizing that the behavior needs to change—and understanding the "how-to." How, exactly, do we rely on the Holy Spirit's convicting and restorative work within our souls to effect change? This needs to be our primary concern. Nevertheless, the old adage "know thy enemy" fits when battling an eating disorder, so we will look briefly at some contributing factors.

Gretchen Smith, a Washington-based biblical counselor, writes: "People with eating disorders and those who treat them have forever been trying to place the blame somewhere, typically outside the person with the disorder; we want to believe that our problem happens to us, rather than in us. Society loves and adores the victim model. Commonly, we are taught to blame our problematic behaviors on negative life experiences and the people who contributed to them, or on disease, or even on genetics. Personal responsibility is not too popular a concept in most circles." [7]

The Deadly Vice of Pride

We are all born with the same sin-loving Adamic nature. Sin is our "default" tendency, and encompasses every action, word or thought which is in rebellion to God. A sinner cannot keep from sinning (Romans 8, particularly verse 7). Andrew Murray said that pride is "the root of every sin and evil." Murray is right—pride is the beginning of every sin… pride is the epidemic vice.[8] Anorexia and bulimia are rooted in pride and many of its manifestations—including idolatry, lasciviousness (lust for pleasure, indulgence), gluttony, lack of regard for God's temple (the body), extreme vanity, envy, self-centeredness, selfishness, control, rage, fearfulness, dishonesty, and theft, to name a few.

Some of the primary forms of pride we need to consider are as follows (we will unpack these more fully in later chapters, and discuss how to repent of them):

1) Fear of man/insecurity

Often termed insecurity, fear of man can manifest itself in an eating disordered woman as self-abasement; self-abuse; self-absorption; self-pity and perfectionism. Being consumed with what others think of her is a common trait. A definition of insecurity is placing your faith, hope, trust, belief, or confidence in something or someone that can be taken away. Both a lean physique and the opinion of others represent transient "houses built on sand" with no eternal value, and trying to impress others rather than please God is sin (Galatians 1:10).

Fear of man can also lead to escapism (in which the bulimic engages each time she binges) and an unwillingness to be transparent with others. "[Anorexics and bulimics] spend an inordinate amount of time thinking about themselves and their problem. They may appear to be people pleasers, but their constant giving is often a control measure. The hope is that if they are just nice enough, good enough, helpful enough, they can, in effect, manipulate people into the desired response. They hope to establish a sense of security through the approval, respect, and loyalty "due" them by others. Knowing that someone is angry or upset at them, or otherwise disapproving, gives rise to feelings of fear of rejection or even abandonment."[9] Such women are typically very evasive and go to great lengths to deceive others by covering up their behavior. Their fear of others' reaction drives them to ever-greater extremes of lying and secrecy.

2) Vanity

Vanity, as the term is commonly used, may be seen as a form of self-worship. Everyone worships something; we are programmed for worship. Holding an exaggerated opinion of one's own appearance, abilities, gifts, talents or intellect idolatrously elevates one's own self and robs God of the glory due Him. In a sense, a vain person worships at the altar of "self." A woman preoccupied with her weight and appearance does not start out purging, starving or exercising to excess. Her vanity, left unchecked and unrecognized for what it is, leads to the sinful behavior.

"An eating disorder is first preceded by a thought. Then another thought, and then another. Eventually these thoughts become a meditation. The meditation sooner or later leads to an action. Very often, a person does not realize at this stage of the game how serious it all really is, and how "bound" she will soon become. The action is repeated, others are added, and soon habits are formed. Weeks, months, and years of thinking food-obsessed thoughts and performing eating-disordered behaviors go by and the bondage of sin becomes deeply entrenched."[10]

3) Idolatry

In its broadest possible sense, an idol is anything that has displaced or crowded out God in your heart. Unbelief that God is good, He is Who He says He is and will meet all our needs leads to idolatry. The Lord will not share His glory with another (Isaiah 42:8). Christ did not mince words when He noted, "…for where your treasure is, there your heart will be also." (Matthew 6:21b). Who (or what) is at the center of your life? Who (or what) do you worship? Another way of spotting an idol is anything you want badly enough that you are willing to sin in order to get it. How do you act when you cannot have or obtain something you value? By either definition, thinness is an "idol" in the heart of an anorexic or bulimic. What occupies the preeminent place in our hearts is what we treasure, or "idolize." The Bible refers to various types of passions and lusts, which in a metaphorical sense may be seen as "idols of the heart."

False beliefs that we harbor in our hearts lead to sinful behaviors. In a sense, all of us have some sort of "idols" in our hearts; the simplest way to spot them is by asking ourselves how we feel or act when we do not get what we desire. However, in a life-dominating sin such as anorexia or bulimia, the unbridled lust (for ever-increasing amounts of food; to be unnaturally thin) has become supreme. Biblical counselor Dr. Rick Thomas offers the following definition: "An idol is anyone or anything into which we invest an imbalance of time, energy, and resources. It is a longing, craving, desiring, wanting, must-have, only-happy-when, and want-so-badly-I-am-willing-to-disobey-God."[11]

4) Seeking control of and/or independence from others

More often than not, an eating disordered woman will concede in counseling that "[her] weight is the only thing [she] can control." The very premise behind this statement belies a prideful desire to be on top, calling the shots—whether in her own life, or that of others. Attempts to control others often take the form of manipulation, "guilt trips," or playing the martyr. Many eating disordered women come from families where the mother displayed some of these "high control" characteristics, and she has learned to imitate her mother's behavior. Although I believe it is rare for an anorexic or bulimic to consciously remain in bondage in order to manipulate or control another person, she typically resists any accountability in regards to her health or other "private" areas of her life. Proverbs is full of admonishments to those who are wise in their own eyes, and reject counsel or guidance from anyone.

Naturally, this illusion of "control" backfires once the individual slides deeper into the life-dominating sin of an eating disorder. Biblical counselor Ed Welch writes:

"On one side, you feel powerless. Your world feels out of control, and you are sick of it. On the other side, you think that your addiction helps you manage your life so you have more control. That's why you hate it and you love it."[12]

5) Lack of self-control/gluttony

I list these two sins together because the second is really a symptom of the first. The Bible always mentions "gluttony" in a negative light (Deuteronomy 21:20; Proverbs 23:21; Matthew 11:19; Titus 1:12) because it manifests slavery to one's passions. Christian author and counselor Martha Peace puts the issue succinctly:

Bulimia is wrong for two reasons: First, it can cause serious medical problems such as damage to your esophagus and your teeth. Second, it is a sin because overeating is gluttony, throwing up is a lack of self-control, and wanting to be thin so badly that you are willing to sin is idolatry.[13]

These were exactly the points on which God convicted me when I turned to Him for mercy, and reading someone as well-respected as Peace saying the same thing confirmed it.

An anorexic or bulimic woman typically forgets (or ignores) the fact that her body is not her own, but was bought at great price (1 Corinthians 6:20). When a woman with bulimia begins a binge, she may not even be hungry. It is certainly not a physical hunger she is trying to fill. There is something about God that Christians entangled in addictions either do not understand or do not like; therefore, they do not find true satisfaction in the Person and work of Jesus Christ. The bulimic uses food as a "drug" to seek instant gratification.

6) Perfectionism

A subtle form of pride often held up as a virtue, the perfectionist has her own system of "works righteousness." Much like fear of man, perfectionism takes one's eyes off of the finished work of Christ and onto the flaws of self. Thus, a performance-driven lifestyle with endless, often arbitrary rules and regulations mandates a score-keeping system in the woman's own mind. An anorexic's rituals (no food may be swallowed; must be cut into a certain number of bites; only "clean" foods are to be consumed) illustrate the perfectionist mindset.

Most anorexic and bulimic girls and women are known to their peers, teachers and co-workers as perfectionists, which the world considers virtuous. However, as we will see in a later chapter, the perfectionist mindset breeds an inflated view of one's own importance, leads to a low view of God, and mocks the Gospel. Hypocrisy, frustration, fear, worry and self-pity are the inevitable fruits of perfectionism.

7) Lack of prayer life/undisciplined thought life

Another commonality among Christian anorexic and bulimic women is lack of a consistent prayer life. Regular time reading the Bible also goes by the wayside. Usually, their guilt over what they know to be sinful behavior keeps them away from God. Spiritual apathy also sets in and motivation to be fed by the Word of God drops. This is a form of pride for two reasons: first, the woman will "run away" from God in shame (like the Prodigal Son of Luke 15, who was too proud initially to return to his father's house). The biblical solution is to confess her eating disorder as sin and repent. Secondly, indifference toward God's revealed will indicates an "I'll do it myself" mentality. Few individuals in the grips of self-destructive bondage want to admit that God's Word has the answers they need. It is far more difficult to humble ourselves under His hand than it is to wallow in self-pity and shame!

Prayerlessness and neglect of Scripture cause the eating disorder to become even more deeply entrenched. Repeatedly, a bulimic turns to the food—her drug of choice—to fill the spiritual void left by broken fellowship with God. Rather than seeking the intimacy she craves with her Father through prayer and the spiritual food of His Word, again and again she turns to a counterfeit. She needs to see Jesus Christ as more beautiful than her addiction in order to forsake it. Another problem arising from prayerlessness is failure to see sin as sin. Regular Scripture reading is necessary to discern thoughts and attitudes in opposition to God, and avoiding it quenches the Holy Spirit Who brings conviction (John 16:8).

The Bible tells us that we can control our thought-life. We will consider how to do so in our discussion on being transformed by the renewing of the mind. While a feeling of helplessness prevails in the eating disordered woman, at one point her behavior and thoughts were made by choice. Gretchen writes:

> People do in fact get to a point where the ability to choose seems completely spent, but originally, choices were available, and choices were made. Not only do people with eating disorders lack discipline to control their thoughts about eating or not eating, but a whole lot of other thoughts are raging out of control. Ungodly, and therefore unhealthy, obsessions run rampant. Untruthful, unproven, and otherwise destructive statements and ideas have been permitted to repeat again and again in their minds, becoming "tapes" which they play to themselves. This is how a faulty belief system is formed, and it influences both emotions and actions. We know from 2 Peter 1:3-4 that the person who has a spirit that is alive to God (born again) has access to every promise needed to overcome every evil desire she can possibly encounter. If you are overtaken in a sin, there is instruction from God that needs to be illuminated in your spirit by the Holy Spirit. For this reason, prayer and getting God's Word into your spirit are the crucial elements for overcoming an eating disorder.[14]

Additional sins that tend to go along with eating disorders (and worsen the problem) include:

Jealousy/envy. Also rooted in pride, envy breeds a competitive attitude towards others who may be thinner, more attractive, or more gifted. Additionally, an eating disordered woman is rarely happy for another's achievement or good fortune; her eyes are focused squarely on herself and her desires.

Anger. Lacking biblical communication and conflict resolution skills, women who abuse food typically avoid conflict, clamming up and internalizing irritation and frustration. This leads to bitterness and anger, which they again turn inward in self-destructive ways. While she would probably not state it in such blunt terms, a woman with an eating disorder is usually simmering a low-grade anger at God. Feeling cheated or not having received what she thinks she deserves, she returns to her pet sin in rebellion against Him.

Being unteachable/hypersensitive to criticism. Self-absorbed people often take any criticism, regardless of tone or intent, as a personal attack. Perfectionism, taken to its logical end, demands a façade of—you guessed it—perfection. Anytime a chip in that protective armor reveals a flaw, the anorexic or bulimic woman will panic.

Unforgiveness. Refusal to forgive is not only direct disobedience to God, it keeps a woman in captivity to her past. She keeps old wounds fresh in her mind, resulting in perpetually hurt feelings. This self-pity incites her to drown these painful emotions with eating (and perhaps drinking; there is a very high correlation between bulimia and alcohol abuse, perhaps for this reason). Alternately, she strictly controls the body through starvation and excessive exercise in an odd sort of penance to minimize the emotional pain resulting from her unforgiveness. Forgiveness is an extremely important part of the restoration process from an eating disorder, and I devote an entire chapter to it later in this book.While eating disorders are primarily a result of an internal condition, because we live in a sin-infested world there are external factors that play a more minor role in influencing us. There are several of these:

Media. We have mentioned in passing how unrealistic body images can influence girls' and women's thinking about their own bodies—breeding pride, vanity and envy. As Gretchen notes, "The body has become an idol for many, many people, and the pursuit of thinness or physical excellence a driving obsession."

Taste temptations. At no time in history has so much junk food been so readily available; nor has advertising been so rampant. Chips, doughnuts, fast-food burgers and salty snacks are addictive by nature; even people who do not have full-blown eating disorders struggle to limit their intake of these types of food. The bulimic has simply lost the battle.

Circumstances. Abuse, trauma, neglect, and adversity in life place pressure on people. Not all people respond to and cope with pressure the same way. Difficult circumstances combined with other factors previously mentioned can create the right conditions to favor an eating disorder. Some people "medicate" and anesthetize themselves with activities and/or substances, including food. Others gain a much-desired sense of power through rigid control of food intake, to the point of starvation. Still others find eating disorders useful for gaining attention, although usually at first they are not aware that this is what they are doing.

"For Where Your Treasure is, There Your Heart will be Also…"

Popular "wisdom" regarding eating disorders holds that while they begin with preoccupations with one's weight and body image, anorexia and bulimia are really complex issues that have little to do with food itself. Regardless of whether the obsession or preoccupation is about food, weight, or some ambiguous definition of "control," the Bible has given Christians clear instruction. Colossians 3:1-2 spells out what the preoccupation of our hearts should be: "Therefore if you have been raised up with Christ, keep seeking the things above, where Christ is, seated at the right hand of God. Set your mind on the things above, not on the things that are on earth." As we will see more fully in Chapter 6, if the initial thought or temptation to begin destructive eating habits is countered by Scripture from the beginning, the behavior will not develop. It will not take root in her heart. When a woman is caught up in anorexia, bulimia or chronic overeating it is proof that her mind is set on what her fallen flesh desires, and not "on the things of the Spirit" (Romans 8:5). By being on guard and recognizing thoughts that tempt us towards sinful eating patterns, we won't be seduced by the promise of "having our cake and eating it too."

A woman who is striving daily to be conformed into the image of Christ (Romans 8:29) and enjoys intimate fellowship with Him through prayer and His Word will not be lured by the empty promise of an addiction. However, none of us have completed the process to perfection, nor will we as long as we live on this earth and dwell in these temporal bodies. We can only pursue "Christ-likeness" and "press toward the goal for the prize of the upward call of God in Christ Jesus" (Philippians 3:14).

Addiction as Camouflage?

Let us assume that a young woman develops disordered eating habits primarily because she wants to be thinner. As she begins to lose weight in an unhealthy way, her desire completely engrosses her (thinness has become her idol) and her thoughts become increasingly food-obsessed (food is another idol in her life). She craves attention from the opposite sex, and secretly delights in the envious looks and comments from other girls that she is getting "too thin" (people-pleasing; vanity). She becomes increasingly unable to control her binges (lack of self-control). Concerned adults intervene at school, and she is furious (unrighteous anger), but is still driven to win her parents' approval by being "perfect" (fear of man; perfectionism). She despises her mother for her superficial value system and insistence on looks above all else (bitterness) and withdraws from friends (self-absorption; leading to brooding and self-pity). All of these forms of pride fueling her bulimia are heart issues, which will never be resolved apart from repentance and/or spiritual rebirth (if she is not yet a Christian).

The bulimia, then, is a symptom of a much more serious condition: sin. While every human who has ever walked the planet (with the obvious exception of the God-Man, Jesus Christ) has had this terminal condition, in the addict it is more pronounced only because we see the outward behavior to which she is enslaved. Jay Adams, the founder of the modern biblical counseling movement, sees some deviant behavior as a type of "camouflage":

What, then, is wrong with the 'mentally ill'? Their problem is autogenic; it is in themselves. The fundamental bent of fallen human nature is away from God. Man is born in sin, goes astray 'from his mother's womb speaking lies' (Psalm 58:3), and will therefore naturally (by nature) attempt various sinful dodges in an attempt to avoid facing up to his sin. He will fall into varying styles of sin according to the short-term successes or failures of the particular sinful responses that he makes to life's problems. Apart from organically generated difficulties, the 'mentally ill' are really people with un-solved personal problems. There is a mounting conviction that much bizarre behavior must be interpreted as camou-flage intended to divert attention from one's otherwise devi-ate behavior.[15]

In Lauren Greenfield's 2007 documentary"Thin," which follows four patients for a month at Renfrew inpatient facil-ity in Florida, the viewer is left with the overwhelming sense that the patients do not really desire to forsake their eating disorders nearly as much as they crave attention and sym-pathy. That may seem like a harsh assessment, but from ad-mission to discharge (when the women's insurance benefits expire), the patients appear intent on manipulating the staff just enough to ensure that they can continue their behavior (and lose weight) unperturbed. Despite the expense of inpa-tient treatment (often upwards of $1,000 per day), the young women featured in the film use verbal tactics (lamenting the disaster their lives have become), dramatic visual cues (heavy eyeliner applied at all hours of the day), and deliber-ately break rules (smoking in bathrooms; rushing out to get tattoos) in order to mask the real problem: their intentional abuse of food and the destruction of their bodies. Even had they been in a Christian facility offering biblical counsel, no change would come until the patients themselves desired an inward change. Attempts at modifying another person's be-havior, no matter how well intentioned, will always fail—and the addict will find inexhaustible means of camouflaging the real issue. Predictably, all four women Greenfield followed relapsed badly following discharge. One committed suicide. There was no evident change in any of their hearts.

The Abuse Factor

Poor role modeling and a lack of direction and discipline in the home rob children of the opportunity to develop the character and skills necessary for a healthy adulthood. While individual acceptance of responsibility is key to turning away from an eating disorder, it must be noted that often brutally painful childhood experiences can greatly increase a girl's predisposition to anorexia or bulimia. While the blame for the actual behavior cannot be placed squarely upon other people or circumstances that have wounded her, the painful scars that she is left with cannot (and should not) be overlooked. No biblical counselor should ever seek to minimize the damage done to a woman in her early life, but rather true healing through forgiveness should be sought through union with Christ Himself.

Lingering torment from verbal abuse (and otherwise being sinned against) is very real. It is not uncommon for mothers to justify criticizing their daughters' appearance and weight by pleading health concerns. If such women could only realize the far worse, long-term health toll of an eating disorder, they would put their vanity aside. In the 1980's, a well-known psychiatrist who specialized in eating disordered patients wrote, "Nearly every woman who has driven her daughter to an eating disorder has couched it in 'concern for her health.'"

While I appreciate her reluctance to gloss over the wounds inflicted by constant verbal abuse, again we need to take a step back and evaluate this statement in light of the Bible. The mothers in question harbor evil in their hearts, just like every other person in this fallen world. God knows their superficial and vain motives very well. Sinful motivations behind hurting the children He has entrusted to their care are exposed before Him. Proverbs 20:27 says, "The spirit of man is the lamp of the LORD, searching all the innermost parts of his being." God will judge and exact punishment on any who hurt or lead one of His children into sin (Mark 9:42) and feigning a righteous motive before His judgment for such evil will be impossible. 1 Corinthians 4:5 promises that God "will both bring to light the things hidden in the darkness and disclose the motives of men's hearts." Nothing can be concealed, and we may be sure God will vindicate all who have been abused. God takes mistreatment of His children very seriously, and likens it to touching the apple of His eye (Zechariah 2:8).

However, the problem lies with the premise behind the psychologist's phrase "has driven to." Biblically speaking, no matter what someone else has said or done to us, we are still responsible before God for our own behavior. We each unilaterally decide whether or not to sin. Therefore, we cannot duck responsibility by using our troubled past as the sole catalyst for our current condition. This is probably the hardest part of repentance to embrace, but we must "own" our sin as our own if we want to be forgiven, cleansed and freed from it. God will deal with the abuser in His own time; we are only responsible for repenting of our sin and moving forward. We cannot change the past or what people have done to us, we can only look at the biblical principles that God has laid out for us and allow Him to change our future.

As hard as it is to accept, an eating disorder is a chosen lifestyle. Addictive sins begin as deliberate behaviors, which become habits. Much of what we feel victimized by we actually played a huge part in bringing on ourselves because of choices we have made. We sin; we are sinned against. Still, no one physically forces anyone else to starve or binge and purge. A drug addict can became "hopelessly" addicted after the first shot, but he/she was doomed to become a junkie when he/she made the succession of choices that led to a willingness to try that first hit of the drug. It works the same way with unhealthy eating habits.

We choose our actions, our thoughts, and our beliefs, and these choices directly influence our emotions. If someone says, "you are stupid" or "you are fat" you have a choice to believe or reject that statement. Granted, if a person hears this repeatedly, it is a difficult message to reject, especially for a vulnerable and immature child, but it still is a personal choice. God-honoring changes also can bring about the reversal of fallout from such damaging choices.

Many people who have suffered terrible tragedies in their lives believe that people or events caused their eating disorders. A person with a lust for food, for instance, will find something to eat over; it might be a big thing, it might be little things—it might be almost everything. A Slavic joke about drinking goes, "Some drink from happiness; some drink from sorrow; some drink from the time they get up in the morning." Much like a drunkard's tendency to always find some rationale for a drink, a bulimic will similarly rationalize her "need" to binge. Stress, rejection, and failed interpersonal relationships are all common ways we excuse using food to "comfort" ourselves rather than seeking God's solution.

"If We Confess Our Sins, He is Faithful and Just…"

Apart from Christ, it is impossible to have a God-honoring attitude towards sin committed against us. Nor is it possible to maintain a God-centered hope in our circumstances. As a young person, I did not know how to cope with my unhappy home situation. Since I had never heard the Gospel, I was without the Holy Spirit for guidance. Even so, I believed in the existence of God and knew He was a protector. While I certainly could not have given a Bible reference, the small bit of knowledge I had about God was enough to realize intuitively that if I had pursued Him, He would have revealed Himself to me (Hebrews 11:6). If I had trusted in Christ, Who even then I saw as a Hero and Rescuer, He would never have driven me away (John 6:37). Even in my spiritual blindness, I knew enough to know right from wrong. I certainly knew that deliberately vomiting was wrong, and I knew that I shouldn't begin. Even with this pricked conscience, I gave in to the powerful temptation to lose weight "painlessly." It wasn't strictly about the food, or a way to "punish" myself for some infraction, real or imagined. It was simply easier to keep quiet, let the anger build up inside, drop by drop, and keep crossing the days off my calendar than it was to take it to God. Sin always seems to provide the 'easier' route. Having an abusive past seems to provide a ready-made excuse.

Understanding that the roots of addiction are sin—I have listed the primary ones above—frees us to embrace the solution. 1 John 1:9 proclaims that "If we confess our sins, He is faithful and righteous to forgive us our sins and to cleanse us from all unrighteousness." We will discuss this verse and similar ones more fully a little later, but for now linger over the logical implications that your food addiction is sin. All sin can be forgiven, and put "as far as the east is from the west" (Psalm 103:12). There is no sin from which the Christian cannot repent, and axiomatically, there is no sin so great that God will not pardon it. God would not hold you responsible for something over which you are helpless (such as a disease or victimization). Therefore, the realization that an eating disorder A) is a sin which B) can be forsaken and therefore C) utterly forgiven and abandoned, should bring you great relief and hope. You are not doomed to a lifetime of failure, if you truly desire to forsake this destructive lifestyle. Restoration and healing is God's promise to the repentant (2 Chronicles 7:14; James 5:15-16).

During the years I was bulimic, shame kept me from going to God and confessing this sin. Fear kept me from telling others. Both are tools the enemy uses to keep us from the foot of the Cross. Before we can walk in victory, as with any sin, we must learn to repent.

Let's start by looking at what repentance really is, and then how to walk in it as we apply the Gospel to each of the areas of sin listed above.

Chapter 3
What is Repentance?

First off, repentance is a gift. A gift, you say? Isn't repentance facing the music; letting yourself in for punishment when you've done wrong? The word used to conjure up images of my sixth-grade teacher forcing pupils to stay in from recess and write "I will not forget to cover my books" dozens of times on the classroom blackboard. I never thought of repentance as a positive thing, until I experienced grace.

In Acts 3:12-24, the apostle Peter is preaching to a group of astonished onlookers who have just witnessed John and himself heal a crippled beggar. Many of these spectators were in the same crowd that demanded the release of Barabbas and the execution of Jesus. Midway through Peter's witness to the power of Christ's resurrection, he concisely states God's will for everyone's life: "Therefore repent and return, so that your sins may be wiped away, in order that times of refreshing may come from the presence of the Lord" (Acts 3:19). That is God's exhortation to all who have "ears to hear": repent and return.

Repentance literally means to "change one's mind" about sin. Hatred of sin and a sincere desire to turn from it is necessary for salvation, but after conversion there is still an ongoing repentance necessary to restore broken fellowship with God. God provides both the conviction over sin, and the grace to repent—it is impossible for us, in our fallen nature, to generate repentance apart from the Holy Spirit. My pastor describes repentance as making a spiritual U-turn. Whenever our life is walking away from the Cross, God commands us to make a U-turn toward the Cross. He calls this change of direction "fruit." Once you change your mind about sin, it will inevitably show up in your actions. True Christians will fall, and will need to continuously repent—not for a subsequent salvation, but for restored fellowship with the Lord.

Repentance vs. Regret and Remorse

The Bible talks about a "worldly sorrow" and a "godly sorrow," the latter of which characterizes a truly repentant heart. 2 Corinthians 7:10 says, "For the sorrow that is according to the will of God produces a repentance without regret, leading to salvation, but the sorrow of the world produces death." Repentance leaves no regret—what freedom! When we repent, God completely forgives us, blots out the sin, and tells us our conscience should be completely clean (Hebrews 9:9, 14; Heb. 10:22; 1 Peter 3:21). But first, when the Holy Spirit convicts us of sin, we sorrow over it. Accurately seeing our sin saddens us, because it hinders our intimacy with God. Max Lucado wrote, "There is no creature on earth more miserable than a disobedient Christian." This is so because we realize we have forfeited our fellowship with our Father. The unhappiest people tend to be Christians who are not walking with God and continue grieving the Holy Spirit. The conviction He sends is to call us back, never to condemn us (Romans 8:1). God graciously offers us an opportunity to return to Him, admit that we've sinned, and ask for His forgiveness—which He is always faithful to provide (1 John 1:9). All we have to do is humble ourselves to receive it, and turn from our behavior. He provides the strength we need. This truly is a gift, because on our own merits, we deserve nothing.

A "worldly sorrow" may be simply regretting the immediate consequences of the sin, or hoping to avoid punishment. So often, women with known eating disorders will act as if they want help, but really what they want is to get people off their backs and leave them alone so they can still indulge the addiction. I know of women whose families have spent tens of thousands of dollars on inpatient therapy, and they're no better when they come out than when they went in. They had a "worldly sorrow," but had no real desire to repent of their behavior. There are many dangerous physical consequences of anorexia and bulimia, including electrolyte imbalances, cardiac arrhythmia, enamel erosion, ruptured esophagus, amenorrhea and infertility. While the physical risks of anorexia and bulimia are not really the focus of this book, they are very real and serious. A woman might be scared enough of these disastrous side effects to seek treatment, but fear of these is still not the motivation that will drive her to true repentance.

Remorse is sorrow because one's actions have hurt others. Any addiction ultimately affects many people, and many eating disordered women are guilt-ridden over the toll it has taken on their families. They may want to "get better" for the sake of others. Repentance, however, is produced by the sobering knowledge that we have rebelled against God. It is a heart-issue, motivated by a desire to obey God for His sake alone.

The Greek word for repentance is "metanoia," with "nous" meaning "to change" and "meta" meaning "mind," but the full sense of the word involves more than an intellectual assent. Puritan writer Thomas Watson outlined six aspects included in biblical repentance:

1.) Seeing your sin—1 John 1:8-10.
2.) Sorrowing over your sin—We must do more than admit it. We must internally engage with it. Psalm 51:17; Isaiah 57:15; 2 Corinthians 7:9.
3.) Confessing your sin—We must put our sin into words and agree with God that what we did was wrong. Psalm 51:4; Hosea 14:1-3; 2 Corinthians 7:11; 1 John 1:9.
4.) Being ashamed of your sin—Watson: "blushing is the color of virtue." Jeremiah 6:15; 31:19.
5.) Hating your sin—Job 42:5-6.

6.) Turning from your sin—Watson: "Reformation is left last to bring up the rear of repentance. It is not the heart of repentance, but the fruit of repentance." Matthew 3:7-8; Acts 26:20.
a. At the very least, this means removing yourself as much as possible from places of temptation (Proverbs 4:14-17).
b. If your sin was against other people, then you must go to them and ask their forgiveness (Matthew 5:23-24).
c. If the sin involves stealing, then restitution must be made (Luke 19:8).
Repentance is necessary for God to forgive us (Acts 2:38; 3:19; 8:22). [16]

Agreeing with God

If you are habitually purging or starving, this may sound frightening. In the back of your mind, you may be thinking, "But I've tried that before! I know this behavior is wrong; I want to stop, but I just can't." Yes, you can, if you decide that you truly want to. Agreeing with God that bulimia (or anorexia) is sin is the first step. Hopefully, we all agree that self-destructive behavior is sin, and all sin is rebellion against God. I have seen 1 Corinthians 6:19, "Or do you not know that your body is a temple of the Holy Spirit who is in you, whom you have from God, and that you are not your own?" taken out of context and used to argue against everything from body piercing to eating potato chips, but I don't think it's a stretch to apply it to eating disorders. In the following verse, Paul goes on to say, "For you have been bought with a price: therefore glorify God in your body…" Later in the same letter he says, "Whether, then, you eat or drink or whatever you do, do all to the glory of God" (1 Corinthians 10:31). Does bulimic behavior honor or glorify God? Does it manifest self-control? God is glorified when we are in service to Him. When we use food as God intended, we will be healthy—and this glorifies Him because we are productive servants. You can't be glorifying Him if you are purging or starving. Ask yourself honestly: do I consider my behavior (bingeing, purging, starving or eating to excess) sinful? If so, are you really okay with continuing on in it?

Before continuing, I want to clarify: I stand in judgment of no one. I myself ignored feelings of guilt, rationalized the sin, and told myself it was a "disease" for years. I alternated between ignoring the problem and praying about other things while running away from God when guilt overwhelmed me. This went on for over a decade whilst I was a professing Christian. Until we allow ourselves to feel conviction over this sin, (abusing the bodies that God created), we can run away and pretend it doesn't matter. When we face it as sin, we have to ask ourselves the question: do I really want to keep enjoying this sin more than I want to enjoy the fellowship of Christ's presence, and blessing, in my life? Do I want to hold onto it at the expense of Christ's friendship? The fact that He would even condescend to call sinners His friends (John 15:13-15) is astonishing. This truth alone should motivate a heart change.

The Motivation for Repentance: God is Holy

The fear of physical consequences wasn't enough to make me stop. Ironically, the fear of divine punishment wasn't, either. When I thought, "God's angry at me; He hates me" (which was not true), it didn't drive me to repentance. It drove me to want to hide. Romans 2:4 "Or do you think lightly of the riches of His kindness and tolerance and patience, not knowing that the kindness of God leads you to repentance? came to have real meaning to me. Once I realized He loved me, even while I was abusing myself by purging, it strengthened me to turn to Him in confession, and then gradually to find strength to overcome it. God was extremely patient with me, tolerating my weakness for fourteen years until I finally made up my mind to forsake the cycle. Repentance is not a negative thing at all, and conviction is the tool God uses to bring us there. God is infinitely gracious, but He also takes sin very seriously.

One thought that made a difference to me when I was struggling with "I want to repent, but I don't think I can overcome this" was the following: If I had given my life for someone, I would be pretty hurt if I saw her abusing her body by bingeing and purging (or cutting, or starving). As I began immersing myself in the Bible and listening to sound preaching, it became apparent how much Jesus really does love us. How could I go on doing something as if His sacrifice meant nothing? The writer of Hebrews pulls no punches: he says that we are 'crucifying Him all over again'. In context, he was writing about apostasy, but the entire Bible points to the fact that continual, unrepentant (not even feeling sorry) sin is doing just that. Grace is God's smile on those who are too weak to help themselves. But if we call ourselves His disciples, He expects us to do our part growing in obedience. In Romans 6:1, Paul asks us the rhetorical question, "What shall we say then? Are we to continue in sin so that grace may increase?" Of course not!

All sin grieves the Holy Spirit (Isaiah 63:10; Ephesians 4:30). In fact, Scripture tells us that God weeps over His children's rebellion (Isaiah 16:9; Luke 19:41). He is the very personification of compassion. The early Church father Augustine attested to the personal nature of Christ's atonement, and the 19th century theologian Charles Spurgeon preached several sermons on this important truth. Most tellingly, the apostle Paul, writing under the inspiration of the Holy Spirit, tells us: "the life which I now live in the flesh I live by faith in the Son of God, who loved me and gave Himself up for me." (Galatians 2:20b; emphasis mine). While Jesus died for all who would come to Him, at the same time, His sacrifice is highly personal and individual. The awestruck joy of the spiritual rebirth is mainly from realizing just this: Christ loved me so much, that even though I am a wretched sinner, He still went to the Cross on my behalf to display God's infinite goodness and love.

Genuine Repentance is Generated by True Holiness

A true change of heart is caused by holiness. In itself a gift of God, true holiness will always result in a changed life. The understanding that we are, in ourselves, incapable of living the righteous life that God requires produces a sincere humility and dependence on God to complete the work of sanctification He began (Philippians 1:6). In 1692, Presbyterian minister Walter Marshall outlined several biblical principles on true holiness in his book "The Gospel Mystery of Sanctification." Lasting, God-honoring change in your life blooms from a pure heart. Marshall observes that true holiness…

…is produced in someone who has received from God a heart that is freely willing to live a godly life (Psalm 19:8; he must fight against sin and hate it; Galatians 5:17; Psalm 36:4).

…is produced in someone who is assured that she is forgiven and reconciled to God (Romans 4:5-7; John 8:36; Philippians 2:13; Romans 8:7-8) and is assured that God loves her (1 John 4:19; 1 Timothy 1:5).

…understands that God will not help one live a holy life unless one uses the means God has provided to pursue this holy life—salvation and sanctification that will give Him all the glory (2 Timothy 2:5).

…is shown in the lives of those who have sufficient strength to will and to do what God enables and calls them to do. "Your real goal is not simply to change some bad habits. Your real goal is to put to death your corrupt, sinful desires which give rise to those bad habits. Also, you are called not only to stop fulfilling your sinful lusts, but also to become filled with holy love and holy desires" (Emphasis mine).

…means that one delights in doing God's will; he longs to do it more than he longs to do anything else.

…bases the Christian life upon God's love for the believer, and not upon the believer's ability to love God, legalism or "easy believism."[17]

I wrestled with the personal aspect of Christ's love for years. Eventually I realized that not only was His love for me real, but even doubting it must grieve Him because it puts limits on His love. Questioning whether He "really loves me" is an affront to God's character, as He does not ever tire of His children. If you really believe in your heart that Christ paid the ultimate price for your redemption, yet you have no desire to turn from your eating disorder, you are essentially saying to Him "thanks very much for dying for me; but I think I'll just do what I want." This is the epitome of pride.

Humbling Yourself Under God's Hand

Most of us think we're actually pretty humble already, but pride is sneaky. Whether we want to admit it or not, we anorexics and bulimics are a prideful bunch. Self-loathing is not humility; it is actually "inverted pride" because we are still focused on ourselves instead of God. We are actually so self-absorbed that preoccupation with how we appear, what others think of us, and how vile we are (the truth we must "hide") crowds out thinking on whatever is true, noble, pure and lovely (Philippians 4:8). Further, we are often prideful enough to think that we can stop this compulsive behavior on our own. Even when we stop deceiving ourselves and recognize our desperate plight, pride still keeps us from running to God. Fear of what He "thought" of me kept me from the Father for years.

Like the Prodigal Son too proud to leave the pigpen, we often stay stuck in our own destructive cycle far longer than we need to. Why? Do we honestly think God doesn't know about our "secret" binge/purge episodes? Perhaps if we don't face our shameful habit in His presence, we can pretend it doesn't exist. So we continue to put concealer on under our eyes to hide the dark circles and burst capillaries, and apply 'lipstick smiles' before church. If we look the part of pulled-together, mature believers, maybe the people at church will believe that that's what we are. Maybe we will even half-believe it, too. God, however, isn't buying into our act. As long as we continue this prideful masquerade, we are distancing ourselves from God.

Both the apostle Peter and Jesus' younger brother James cited Proverbs 3:34 to remind us that "God is opposed to the proud, but gives grace to the humble." (cf. James 4:6 and 1 Peter 5:5). If we were to try pigeonholing repentance into one or two verses, this might be the first one. We might follow up this thought with James 4:10: "Humble yourselves in the presence of the Lord, and He will exalt you," (cf. 1 Peter 5:6). Until you truly humble yourself before God, you will not be able to repent (turn from the sin in your heart that drives the addiction). Ultimately, repentance will play itself out in your changed behavior. Thus, humbling yourself before God is the first step.

So how do we do it? A good definition of humility is seeing who you are in relation to Who God is. True humility is not so much thinking less of yourself as it is thinking of yourself less. It is seeing yourself realistically in light of God's perfection. He is holy; we are not. We often carry an inflated sense of our own importance, forgetting that our chief end is to love, obey and glorify our Lord. Realize that you are a desperate sinner in need of a Savior—not just once for salvation, but in the ongoing battle against indwelling sin. Humbling yourself before God means coming to Him on His terms, with no agenda.

This is not as terrifying as it might sound. God is not going to smash you (Luke 20:18); you are simply "breaking" your own will voluntarily in submission to His, because you know His way works best. Humbling yourself involves coming to Him with open hands, knowing that in yourself you have nothing to offer Him, and on your own merits have no claim to mercy. You agree with God that you have failed and without His intervention, your life will only yield more failure.

It takes humility to accept grace, because our flesh screams to "earn" favor—to prove that we are somehow worthy. A humble person approaches God like the tax collector of Luke 18:13: "But the tax collector, standing some distance away, was even unwilling to lift up his eyes to heaven, but was beating his breast, saying, 'God, be merciful to me, the sinner!'"

Sometimes therapists talk about hitting "rock bottom," but when you are truly humbling yourself under God's mighty hand, you are standing on the only solid Rock there is. Knowing how unworthy we are before God (and how loved we are, as His adopted children, in spite of this) should cause us to feel great humility and thankfulness. Nehemiah 9:17 provides a wonderful revelation of God's character: "But You are a God of forgiveness, Gracious and compassionate, slow to anger and abounding in loving-kindness." He does not scorn or chastise His children when they return to Him.

Ed Welch says this about God's gracious acceptance of the repentant sinner:

> When we listen to God after difficult self-examination, God reveals Himself as the Welcoming One. No "I told you so." No time-outs in a spiritual isolation room. Instead, God rejoices that we have turned to Him in a more whole-hearted way. God promises the repentant person, "None of the offenses he has committed will be remembered against him." (Ezekiel 18:22) …your own sins, no matter how big, are not bigger than God's pleasure in forgiveness.[18]

When I was struggling to continuously get back up and repent of bulimia, a verse that really encouraged me was Matthew 12:20, which quotes the prophet Isaiah: "A battered reed He will not break off, and a smoldering wick He will not put out." This verse speaks to the fact that Jesus mends broken lives. He's not harsh, but He wants us to turn from that ugly sin that's an offense to God and is destroying our lives.

So often we Christians sing about the Cross, wear necklaces, and put fish on our cars, but we overlook an important message: He didn't suffer and die just to give us salvation (huge in and of itself), but also to free us from the bondage of sin in our daily lives. That's a crucial truth to a Christian anorexic or bulimic. You're not still a slave—you can choose freedom. Whether or not you want it is another story. Can you willingly continue to hurt (with your behavior) the One Who loved you enough to die for you, so you could be free from the very behavior you now choose? This is what it comes down to.

Being Broken before God

Being "broken" simply means you are staying in that place of humility before God. As a broken vessel, you are chastened enough to realize self-reliance is futile. Sometimes, even overcoming certain areas of sin in our lives or attaining some spiritual "achievement" can become a source of pride. Such arrogance demands to be dealt with. Any fruit of the Holy Spirit developing in our lives comes solely from Him; it was never of our doing. Not only do we fail Christ in many ways every day, our own particular weaknesses and habitual sins are our own doing—we cannot shift them to anyone else. If we are too proud to admit our own guilt, God will not help us. If we cannot concede our own complete helplessness, He may leave us in the pit until we are sufficiently broken. We need to be able to see our own depravity so we can hate it as God does. Mark Buchanan, author of "Your God is Too Safe," wrote that brokenness "molds our character closer to the character of God than anything else."

Moreover, all sin is ultimately against God. It is an affront to His holiness. This is why in Psalm 51:4 King David cried: "Against You, You only, I have sinned and done what is evil in Your sight, so that You are justified when You speak and blameless when You judge." This was the heartfelt cry of a broken man. Until we see the seriousness of our own wrong actions, we cannot be truly broken. The Gospel is clear that the penalty we deserve for our sin is an eternity of separation from God, Who is too holy to allow sin into His presence. Praise God that in His abundant mercy He has provided a way out—through the sacrifice of His Son on Calvary. Throughout the entire biblical account, we see a God Who rejoices in forgiving and is always the initiator of reconciliation.

While our human instinct is one of self-preservation when we've been wronged, the biblical illustration of Hosea's wayward wife and his steadfast pursuit of her prove that God is not like us. His intense compassion for His people reveals the steadfastness of His will to redeem and restore them. Once forgiven, God never brings sin up again. His focus is not on the pain of betrayal, but rather on the joy of restored fellowship. Welch writes, "Moreover, this is not a stoic faithfulness. It is vulnerable and passionate. It is a faithfulness so intense that God describes it as tearing at His insides."[19] (Hosea 11:8-9). Understanding what sin cost God and how much He loves us in spite of what we have done with our lives should break our hearts. If it does not, we don't really understand grace.

Further down in his prayer of contrition, David continues: "The sacrifices of God are a broken spirit; a broken and a contrite heart, O God, You will not despise" (Psalm 51:17). This passage is not saying that God wants us to walk around depressed and miserable because we can't change ourselves. David is rightly observing that a repentant, humble spirit when we approach God is of far more value in His sight than the animal sacrifices Old Testament Israel was required to make in atonement for sin. Furthermore, notice how God promises to respond to the heart that sorrows over its sin: He will not despise. Merriam-Webster defines the verb "despise" as: *to look down on with contempt or aversion <despised the weak> 2 : to regard as negligible, worthless, or distasteful.*

God promises never to do this when our hearts are broken over our sin and we come before Him with empty hands.

"I'm Repentant…Now What?"

The best way to start moving forward toward repentance is to make time with God a priority, and follow through on it. Talking about your struggle with other people (while not wrong, in and of itself) will not help you to resist temptation, although a mature Christian may be able to give you godly counsel. However, often when we are discussing our particular besetting sins with other people, we have a tendency to minimize or even rationalize our behavior. Sometimes, we even avoid going to God because we are so busy hiding behind other people. If you want God to forgive and restore you, sooner or later you will have to get alone with Him and face this sin squarely.

Make a point of getting uninterrupted time by yourself to seek God. (Some people call this "closet prayer." It doesn't have to be in the closet. The bedroom or the living room couch works just as well). Tell God exactly what's in your heart; He already knows about it, anyway. Be honest with Him about how you feel. You may feel so ashamed that you don't want to face Him; alternately, you may just feel numb. If you are not even sure you want to change, tell Him that, too. Sometimes, when we are in rebellion and know this deep down, it's okay to pray a "help me want to want to" prayer. For example, I have sometimes had to ask for the desire to forgive somebody, simply because I wanted to be obedient to God, but could not produce any love for the offending party on my own.

Facing an eating disorder can be similar. To see our sin the way God sees it, we have to look at it objectively through the lens of His Word. We need to agree with God about what He says. There's just one problem: our flesh (depraved human nature) is in the way. Paul records his ongoing struggle with the flesh: "For I know that nothing good dwells in me, that is, in my flesh; for the willing is present in me, but the doing of the good is not. For the good that I want, I do not do, but I practice the very evil that I do not want." (Romans 7:18-19). One of the Doctrines of Grace is called total depravity. This does not mean that we are as bad as we possibly can be, but it does mean that no aspect of our soul or motivation of our heart has been untouched by sin. We can only see the evil tendency in our own hearts when God supernaturally opens our eyes to it.

Asking God for the will and desire to obey Him is mandatory, or we will follow our own evil impulses every time. Keeping a journal to record your thoughts, prayers, and relevant Scriptures may be helpful. Record your victories, as well as any verses God brings to your attention which particularly speak to you. You may also find that using a specific Bible study helps you to be consistent. Relatively few people are able to simply sit down and read the Bible from Genesis to Revelation, although there is nothing wrong with doing so. However, this may not be the most effective way of letting God's Word speak to you.

Getting to Know the Lover of Your Soul

A critical first step in repenting to God is truly getting to know Him. Once we truly know Him, we come to realize that we can trust Him. Learning to see God for Who He really is (rather than Who we may have imagined Him to be—angry, distant, or harsh) is the first building block in our relationship to Him as Father, Lord, and Savior. Studying all that the Bible has to say about His compassion and mercy, I was able to gain the confidence I needed to approach Him in prayer. Whether or not you use a Bible study or concordance to supplement your time alone with God is a personal choice. The most important thing is that you get into His Word, and commit to letting it teach you about God and how to obey Him in your specific situation.

When God granted me repentance back in 2003, I used a study called "Experiencing the Heart of Jesus" to get to know Him better. It is the type of workbook from which newer Christians could benefit. Broken down into ten weeks' worth of five-day lessons, Lucado examines different aspects of God's character, as revealed in the Person of Jesus Christ. For a week, the reader studies what the Bible has to say about the grace of Christ; then a week on the freedom of Christ; the forgiveness of Christ; the joy of Christ, and so on. Using passages from the entire Bible, the student is engaged in cross-referencing and Scripture memorization. Arthur Pink's "The Attributes of God" and J.I. Packer's "Knowing God" are also good resources for those better versed in theology.

While I was able to repent and let God restore me without the aid of counseling, this is not necessarily the best way to proceed. God created us to be in relationship—not only with Him, but with each other, as well. He may lead you to a godly counselor who can walk with you through this trial. A trained, biblical counselor's role is to help you in your struggle by pointing you to Christ and illuminating what Scripture actually says about indwelling sin. She will also hold you accountable and discuss how to apply this truth practically. A counselor may have insight into areas where your heart is deceived which you lack the objectivity to discern. Pray about seeking outside help. Be sure and look for a biblical counselor, so that the exhortation you receive is God's wisdom rather than man's. (See Chapter 9 and the Addendum for more information about biblical counseling).

How Many Times a Day?
If you have been bulimic for any length of time, you are probably bingeing and purging at least once a day. Even when you are not bingeing, much (if not most) of your time is consumed by thoughts of food. This is especially true if

you alternate your purging with starving. If your mind is as enslaved as mine was, at any given moment you are most likely either A) in the middle of a binge; B) planning your next binge; or C) feeling shame and despair over your most recent binge. The very nature of this addiction feeds into a vicious cycle: for reasons we don't fully understand, we are driven to the food. Panic then sets in; we must get rid of it at all costs. Purging is followed by intense guilt and self-hatred; we resolve never to do that again—that was the Very Last Time. Subsequently, circumstances, emotions or stress trigger us to revert to this habit for "comfort" and the cycle starts all over again. Each time we repeat this self-defeating pattern, the bondage gets a bit more deeply entrenched, our faith that God can or will forgive us erodes further, and Satan laughs. He has been watching you for a long time, and knows exactly how to bring you down.

Ed Welch accurately calls addictions "worship disorders." In his book, *Addictions: A Banquet in the Grave*, he asks the rhetorical question, "Will we worship ourselves and our own desires or will we worship the true God?"[20] Mankind was made for relationship with the Creator, and we will worship instinctively—even adopting forms of self-worship flowing from the intrinsic evil that we all possess (Jeremiah 17:9; Luke 6:45).

Habitual, besetting sin can be especially hard to repent from because we feel like such hypocrites. How can I tearfully tell God I'm sorry and resolve never to purge again on Wednesday, only to do the same thing again on Thursday? Adding to our bewilderment is the fact that when we cried out for mercy, we truly were sorry, too. We truly hated our sin; this slimy, muddy pit of bulimia. So why do we feel compelled to jump back in...sometimes for no apparent reason? Why should we expect God to forgive us when we're 'serial repenters'?

Because He said so, that's why.
It is so important to understand what the Bible says about repentance and pardon. In 1 John 1:9, we have one of the most plainly-stated promises in Scripture about God's promise to forgive when we confess, no strings attached: "If we confess our sins, He is faithful and righteous to forgive us our sins and to cleanse us from all unrighteousness." Paul follows that promise up by reminding us that God is faithful, even when we are not (2 Timothy 2:13). He is well aware of our weaknesses, and knows ahead of time what we are going to do. This applies to eating disorders, as well. Each and every time you succumb to the temptation, get back up and determine to repent, regardless of how guilty you feel. As the grace of the Gospel becomes a reality to you, you will begin to turn from your former enslavement to grace-motivated obedience.

Repeat Offenders…Enough is Enough!
Unlike drugs or alcohol, you cannot abstain completely from food. This is one reason that eating disorders are much more difficult to overcome than other addictions, even when true sorrow and repentance are present. You still have to take that tiger of temptation out of the cage several times a day and stroke it. In the beginning, you may fail. When I first got serious about repentance, for a few months I had probably no more than a 60% success rate at keeping my food down and resisting the urge to purge. I failed in resolve almost as often as I succeeded, and I realized after the fact that my failure was a result of ignoring the Holy Spirit's warnings. Also, I would forget or be "too busy" to pray—seeking God before, during and after every meal. We will discuss specific ways to deal with temptation in this book, but the point is that initially I would often wind up back in the pit, covered in sin. I had two choices: to give up and stay there, or to humble myself before God once more. I chose to trust that Christ would

have compassion on me yet again. And again....and again. And He was faithful to do just that.

As you probably do, I felt like I was letting God down. During this season, one promise that really blessed me was Luke 17:3-4: "...Be on your guard! If your brother sins, rebuke him; and if he repents, forgive him. And if he sins against you seven times a day, and returns to you seven times, saying, 'I repent,' forgive him." Of course, Christ never commands anything of His followers that He doesn't do Himself. Regardless of what your feelings may be telling you, you have not used up your "allowance of grace." When I think of how patient the Lord was with me during the months of turning from the bulimia, it just completely bowls me over with gratitude. When you fall and repent with a truly humble and broken spirit, no matter how many times, He rejoices and holds you up. You're not a disappointment to Him.

I don't know that I've ever had someone sin against me and then come back contrite, only to do it all over again....but hypothetically speaking, how would I react? Having been on the receiving end of this kind of mercy myself, I can easily concur with Dr. John Macarthur on this point:

> Someone might ask, "Who in the world would commit the same offense seven times in one day and then profess repentance after each time?" Here's the point: this sort of behavior is precisely how we sin against God. We sin; then we express sorrow for our sin and seek God's forgiveness; then we turn around and commit precisely the same sin again. Anyone who has ever been in bondage to a sinful habit knows precisely what the routine is like.
>
> Does God forgive under such circumstances? Yes, He does. And since His forgiveness sets the criterion by which we are to forgive, the standard is set blessedly high. What may seem at first like an impossibly unfair and unattainable standard is in fact wonderful news for anyone who has ever

needed to seek the forgiveness of God for repeat offenses. Jesus is teaching here that the forgiveness we extend to others should be as boundless as the mercy of God we desire for ourselves. That shatters all the limits anyone would try to place on human forgiveness.[21]

Since it is an ongoing process, it helps to keep reminding ourselves of what the Bible says about repentance and God's promise of forgiveness. When we fail God by giving in and using food instead of turning to Him, we are prone to believe what our emotions are telling us rather than what His Word says. It is God's nature to show mercy upon the repentant sinner, no matter how many times you find yourself at His feet. Here is a sampling of some of the verses that speak of God's great mercy. It is by no means exhaustive, but you may find it helpful to look them up and write them in a notebook or prayer journal for situations when you doubt God's grace:

Lamentations 3:22-23	**Psalm 69:16**	**Romans 15:9**
1 Kings 8:28	**Psalm 116:1**	**Ephesians 2:4**
2 Chronicles 6:19	**Micah 7:18**	**Titus 3:5**
Nehemiah 9:31	**Mark 5:19**	**Hebrews 4:16**
Psalm 6:9	**Luke 1:50**	**James 5:11**
Psalm 25:6	**Luke 18:13**	**1 Peter 2:10**
Psalm 28:6	**Romans 9:16**	**Jude 1:21**
Psalm 51 (one of the great penitential Psalms)	**Romans 11:30**	

The struggle of a Christian anorexic or bulimic is not usually sorrowing over her sin. If we are saved and indwelt by the Holy Spirit, we know when we have grieved Him. A true Christian feels the conviction He brings (John 16:8). The problem, as you probably discovered long ago, is actually turning away from the behavior. This is the very nature of an addiction—while we may hate our sin passionately, consistently rejecting it and walking in obedience seems elusive.

How do we get from being repentant sinners stuck in the mire to having victory over this bondage and walking in freedom? In the next chapters, we will examine the importance of knowing your true position in Christ and what it means to "be transformed by the renewing of your mind" (Romans 12:2).

Chapter 4

Your Position in Christ—A Slave No Longer

For several years after college, I worked for an international business association in Bulgaria. Communism had only recently been relegated to the ashbin of history, and the concept of a market economy was still difficult for many Bulgarians to grasp. The president of Shell Petroleum related how he had been trying to explain the concept of product value to his secretary by saying, "Something is worth whatever someone is willing to pay for it." She vigorously disagreed, insisting that a product was worth whatever its set market price happened to be. He held up his ballpoint pen, and insisted that if someone were willing to pay $200 for it, that pen was worth $200. The secretary was utterly bewildered. A pen, at that time, cost no more than 2 leva (about $.10). She knew what the pen had cost, because she herself ordered the office supplies! There was no way that pen could be worth $200. "It would be worth $200," her employer countered, "if there was anyone willing to pay $200 for it."

In economics, supply and consumer demand largely determine product cost. An item's value is determined by the price consumers are willing to pay. For years, I mistakenly believed that the same principle holds true in Christianity. Although we are not worthy, many well-meaning books and Bible teachers insist we became "worth" when Someone was willing to pay for us. This teaching, that Christ saved us because we are of "value," is related to an upside-down view of the atonement which holds that because Christ went to the Cross on our behalf, we must be worth a great deal. In fact, the Bible maintains that God redeemed us despite the fact that we were His enemies and in opposition to Him (Romans 5:10; Colossians 1:21). To claim that God saved us because we have intrinsic value is a humanistic (and therefore heretical) position. Stuart Scott writes:

What is an appropriate view of self? We are so very far beneath God and totally unworthy before Him (Psalm 8:1-4). We are no better and no worse than others, because we are all desperately wicked and totally incapable of anything worthwhile in God's sight on our own (John 15:5; Romans 3:10-18). There is nothing that anyone has accomplished or possesses that they should take credit for themselves (1 Corinthians 4:7). We basically have no worth in and of ourselves, but God has given us (believers) a place we do not deserve and has set His love on us anyway (Ephesians 2:4-7).[22] (emphasis mine).

Completely on His own initiative, God chose to reconcile us to Himself in an unprecedented display of grace (unmerited or undeserved favor). His impeccable nature does not allow sin into His presence. In the greatest transaction that ever was or ever will be, Jesus went to the Cross, in perfect obedience to the Father, because He is gracious and chose to redeem sinners. At Calvary, God judged Christ as if He were judging sinners like us (even though He was sinless), so that He might treat sinners as if they were perfect (even though they were sinful). To "impute" means to credit to the account of another. If you have recognized Jesus as King and Ruler over your life, turned from sin (rebellion) and to Him in repentance, you have been "credited" with the spotless standing of Christ in exchange for His taking your sin-debt.

God, in His infinite mercy, created you in His image for His own pleasure. He will love and rejoice over His redeemed forever. He knows that He is your greatest need, and only true source of joy. Only in Him could you ever hope to find peace. Furthermore, He offers us the assurance that His covenant children are, indeed, precious to Him because He has chosen to make us His own: "Are not five sparrows sold for two cents? Yet not one of them is forgotten before God. Indeed, the very hairs of your head are all numbered. Do not fear; you are more valuable than many sparrows….. Do not be afraid, little flock, for your Father has chosen gladly to give you the kingdom." (Luke 12:6-7; 32)

This extravagant grace glorifies God by revealing His own holy and infinitely generous character. It is not a reflection upon us, the undeserving objects of His mercy.

What it Means to Be in Christ

When you first came to the Lord, whether it was twenty years or five minutes ago, you were washed clean of your sin and given a new nature. The miracle of the new birth is God's infusion of a new, eternal, life-giving spirit into you. This is why Jesus said so emphatically in John 3:3 that "…unless one is born again he cannot see the kingdom of God" (emphasis mine). When you responded to God's sovereign call and repented of your old self-driven life, you became a child of God. The Bible tells us that God "rescued us from the domain of darkness, and transferred us to the kingdom of His beloved Son" (Colossians 1:13) and "seated us with Him in the heavenly places in Christ Jesus" (Ephesians 2:6). Paul reminds us in Romans 8:37 that "…in all these things [trials and persecution] we overwhelmingly conquer through Him who loved us." Notice that all of these statements speak of present realities for the believer; they are not futuristic, theoretical promises.

Throughout Scripture, there are many spiritual benefits available to Christians from the moment they turn to Christ and forever thereafter. Why? Because of our position. Whereas once we were enemies of God, we have now been brought near, by the blood of His Son. We are in the family—in fact, we are co-heirs with Christ (Romans 8:17). Truly knowing in the very marrow of our bones who we are in Christ, not merely assenting to it in our minds, is life changing. God loves you even as He loves His Son, Jesus (John 17:23).

There is much talk in Christian circles today about our "identity in Christ," but the Bible never uses that terminology. The fascination with "finding one's identity" actually arose from the theories of psychoanalyst Erik Erickson. Christian counselors may try to legitimize seeking one's "identity" by qualifying that it is to be "in Christ," but to do so shifts the focus off of God and His greatness and onto ourselves. The Bible does not uphold the notion that we need to validate ourselves by seeking our "identity"; rather, we are to seek only God's glory and ascribe all honor to Him. Martha Peace explains:

> Erikson's theory of personality development is also the Christian psychologist's model for teaching that your "identity" is in Christ. If we can just understand who we are in Christ, we will realize our identity and no longer be depressed or anxious or feel badly about ourselves....this is a perversion of the true biblical teaching that Christians are "in Christ." Our union with Christ is a precious truth. We should love it and believe it, but not twist it into something God never intended—a formula to solve emotional problems or make man feel worthy.[23]

Because all of our focus must be on the glory and worthiness of God, rather than seeking to have our carnal "identity needs" met, it is more accurate to refer to our position in Christ rather than our identity in Him. To help solidify your understanding of this subtle, yet important distinction, I suggest reading 1 John carefully. Note how often the term "in Christ" (or some variant thereof) occurs. Everywhere John uses the description, it is in reference to obedience and personal holiness (vvs. 2:5; 2:28; 3:24; 2:28; 5:20; etc.) Needless to say, John is not talking about viewing our position in Christ as a way to meet our emotional needs. "In Christ" clearly refers to our justified position, and carries with it the implication of obedience and being conformed to the character of Christ—not seeking to find "meaning" or personal fulfillment. It is because of our position in Christ that our inheritance—eternal life—is ours. Both throughout Scripture and in this one little epistle it is clear that if we truly are "in Him," we will walk in the light (1 John 1:7), overcome the evil one (1 John 2:14, 4:4), and have fellowship with God and our fellow believers (1 John 1:3-7).

The Power of the Cross

The Cross did more than secure our entrance to Heaven when we leave this earth (although our salvation is the greatest gift of grace we will ever receive). If He had never done another thing for us, Christ deserves our eternal praise and gratitude just for making us righteous before God, and in so doing, saving us from the torment of hell. But by dying in our place, Jesus also broke the power sin holds over us. At Calvary, Christ defeated death. In reality, we are no longer slaves to sin.

In addition to justification, the Cross is also about sanctification—the outworking of holiness in the lives of God's adopted children. John Calvin wrote, "Let believers, therefore, learn to embrace Him, not only for justification, but also for sanctification, as He has been given to us for both these purposes."[24] If we consistently acted as our true position as "more than conquerors" and "co-heirs with Christ" indicates, the battle we face against sin might not seem so insurmountable. Remember how Jesus said the devil came to "steal, kill and destroy" (John 10:10)? Because you are made in the image of God, Satan and his demons will do everything possible to steal your joy, kill your spirit, and destroy your life.

Whether we believe it or not; whether we feel like it or

not; whatever our emotions may be telling us, God's Word is clear: if we have been born again, we have a new nature. We do not have two separate natures dueling it out; we have gone from being spiritually dead to our inner "spirit man" being united with Christ through His Holy Spirit. This intangible part of you, your "spirit" or "soul" (the Bible uses the two Greek equivalent terms in different contexts to refer to the "inner man"), is made up of the mind (controlling thoughts), the will (controlling decisions), and the emotions (feelings—which often control you!). It is on the basis of this present reality that Paul instructs us to "consider [our]selves to be dead to sin, but alive to God in Christ Jesus" (Romans 6:11). Other translations tell us to "count" or "reckon" ourselves dead to sin.

Paul discusses at length the inward battle the Christian faces. Even though his spirit has been reborn, he still struggles against temptations and "lusts of the flesh." Even Paul was still a work in progress. While positionally justified before God, our sanctification will not be complete until we go to be with the Lord and all temptation has disappeared. We will spend the rest of our lives trying to get our inner man to conform to the image of Christ.

Why, if God has given us a new nature, do we still do battle with the reality of indwelling sin? The Bible usually refers to our old, evil nature as the "flesh." When Paul talks about the sinful passions we had when we were "in the flesh" (Romans 7:5), he means governed by our old nature—before we knew Christ. He is not saying that the day we were saved those unrighteous desires and appetites magically disappeared. That is why he instructs believers to "Put on the full armor of God, so that you will be able to stand firm against the schemes of the devil" (Ephesians 6:11). No one just rolls out of bed in the morning and into her armor; we must consciously and deliberately discipline ourselves to take up the shield of faith, and put on the breastplate of righteousness. As Christ did when physically present with His disciples, Paul fully anticipated the ongoing struggle between conquering indwelling sin and walking according to our true nature as redeemed, blood-bought children of God.

Pastor Tony Evans compares the Christian's conflicting natures to a car factory that has been shut down. Cars produced by the old manufacturer are still in circulation, fully operational. All makes and models did not become non-functional the minute they stopped rolling off the assembly line. Likewise, even though our "sin factory" has been put out of business by the Holy Spirit, with a lifetime of practice sin's "products" are very much engrained in our lives. This is especially true of a life-dominating sin, such as bulimia. It should come as no surprise that we are utterly incapable of "shutting off" sin's influence, because throughout Scripture we are told that we cannot change our nature on our own. Evans writes:

> When you come to Jesus Christ, He transports you immediately to the heavenly places and seats you with Himself.… But you still carry the residual effects of the trip, because you are still in your body where sin has made itself at home.… .The more you did something, the more it developed into a pattern. The more you thought about something, the more you thought yourself into a pattern. That's why merely trying harder doesn't solve your problem.[25]

Who's Your Daddy?

In John's Gospel, right before the crucifixion, Jesus tells His disciples that they need to live in vital union with Him if they hope to do anything worthwhile to God. The flipside of this exhortation is that it's impossible to accomplish anything without Him. "I am the vine, you are the branches; he who abides in Me and I in him, he bears much fruit, for apart from Me you can do nothing" (John 15:5). This most certainly includes overcoming sin on our own strength. Previously, Jesus had stated that no one can even come to Him unless the Father draws Him (John 6:44). Now, a few verses later in John 15:16, Jesus again makes it crystal clear that He chose His disciples (and by extension, us). We didn't initiate our relationship to Christ. From beginning to end, we need God to will, desire, or accomplish anything (Philippians 2:13).

We are also reassured continuously of who we are—God's adopted children. There is no reason to question that we are His. We're in the family; God does not consider us the red-headed step-children. We're his "own possession" (1 Peter 2:9). Twenty-six times in the four Gospels, addressing believers, Jesus Himself referred to God as "your Father." Romans 8:16 says, "The Spirit Himself testifies with our spirit that we are children of God," and again in Galatians 4:6 Paul reminds Christians, "Because you are sons, God has sent forth the Spirit of His Son into our hearts, crying, "Abba! Father!" The Father-son (or daughter) relationship is permanent and ir-revocable (John 8:35). While sin blocks our intimate fellow-ship with God, there is nothing you can do to sever that cov-enant relationship. He has promised to complete the work He began in you (Philippians 1:6). You are, and will always be, His daughter. That is why Jesus is not ashamed to call you His sister (Hebrews 2:11).

Your true identity is that of a child of God, a joint-heir, a saint, a sister and disciple of Christ. Your identification with Him, however, is based on your position in Him—rather than being used as an excuse to spiritualize "self concept," your standing with God is to "the praise of His glory" (Ephe-sians 1:12); not your own glory. Your position as God's child is not meant to be an abstract, theological concept. It must determine who you "count" yourself to be. Consider your anorexic or bulimic lifestyle through the lens of this truth. You may never have thought about it in these terms before, but if you belong to Him, Jesus died for this sin as well. In eternity past, before He even created you, He knew that you would offer your body as an instrument to sin (Romans 6:13). While the particular battle varies (some people struggle with pornography, others with stealing, others with greed and compulsive shopping), one constant remains: we are sinners in desperate need of a Savior.

Once you are in Christ, His blood covers every sin you have ever committed: past, present, and even future. While you may be utterly ashamed to approach God, let me assure you, He deals with this sin in His daughters all the time. There is no spiritual condition the Great Physician hasn't seen, and nothing is beyond His healing touch. Because of our relationship to Him, He has promised to supply all we need for holiness if we rely on His strength and not our own. The writer of Hebrews boldly proclaims, "Let us then approach the throne of grace with confidence, so that we may receive mercy and find grace to help us in our time of need" (Hebrews 4:16).

As my pastor often says, there is no sin a non-Christian can commit that a Christian is incapable of committing.[26] Even if you are currently stuck in the miry pit of bulimia, you are still His daughter. Whether or not you realize your true position in Christ is a factor in how long you will stay there. The enemy of your soul, the devil, has used this particular addiction to ensnare you in his lies, that you are beyond hope; God has not truly redeemed you; your sin is too vile and disgusting for you to have a place in the Kingdom. Like his original lie to Eve in the Garden of Eden, he causes you to question by planting doubts in your mind about what God has declared to be true. "Does God really love me? Has God really said…?" is a tactic to open doors of doubt.

There is no question that the behavior is offensive. We know that even as we mechanically go through the rituals. The anorexic intuitively knows that her starvation is neither noble nor virtuous. She knows that it is self-destructive and therefore wrong. No bulimic needs to be told that gorging on copious amounts of food (only to later purge it by vomiting and/or laxative abuse) is shameful and abusive of the body God created. It is not necessary to exegete Bible verses to understand this—bulimia flies in the face of common sense and decency (Romans 1:19-20). The Bible warns against excesses and rebukes those "whose god is their stomachs" (Philippians 3:19). However, to claim that a "true child of God" is immune to life-dominating sin (as the pastor mentioned in the introduction did) is to say more than the Bible does. Nowhere are we told that we will not fall; only that we are not slaves to the old nature because we have the Holy Spirit within us. Christians are certainly capable of living like slaves in practice; even though positionally we have already been made righteous. Only when we realize Satan truly has no power over us because of what Christ has done can we ever hope to walk out of our self-made prisons.

Why does God even choose to redeem messy sinners like us? Have you ever wondered why He loves His children so much? We have no intrinsic value of our own—the Bible states that we are dust (Genesis 3:19; Psalm 90:3, 103:14;) and were natural enemies of God by our rebellion (Romans 5:10; Colossians 1:21). If, then, we are nothing in and of ourselves and have no inherent goodness, doesn't that make us worthless? Utterly contemptible to a holy God? Actually, no. In Genesis 1:31, God looked at His handiwork and saw that it was "very good." Man was His masterpiece, created in His own image and bearing the divine imprint. Ephesians 2:10 calls us God's "workmanship," but the meaning of the word *poeima* in Greek is actually closer to "work of art." It was when sin entered the world that we became innately corrupt. Although we have no inherent value (something naturally ours which would recommend us on the strength of our own merits), we do have imputed value, only and because God has chosen to bestow it on us. As utterly undeserved as it is, it is real and as His child, you are loved. Does this seem paradoxical?

The Father loves you as He loves His Son, Jesus (John 17:26). God has made you precious to Him, for no other reason than His good pleasure and for His glory. Often, I grab my youngest child, who at the time of this writing is four years old. I munch her cheeks and tickle her, teasing her: "How come I love you so much?" Natalia's confident retort is always the same: "Because you do! I'm your baby!" What is the deep, theological reason that God loves you so much? Because He does. We can be as confident as a four-year-old of that fact when we come before His throne.

If you have trouble accepting that God loves you, look up the following Scriptures and record them in a journal or notebook:

Psalm 18:9; 16	**Isaiah 54:10**	**Romans 8:35, 38-39**
Psalm 34:19-20	**Jeremiah 31:3**	**Galatians 2:20**
Psalm 103:11	**John 3:16**	**Hebrews 13:5**
Isaiah 43:2-4	**John 15:13**	**1 John 3:1**
Isaiah 49:16	**Romans 5:8**	**1 John 4:10**

Getting Love Settled in Your Heart

There are many more passages in Scripture that speak of God's love and rejoicing over His children. Speaking from experience, I can assure you that really getting it settled deep down in your heart that the God of all the universe really, truly loves you, His daughter, and invites you to turn to Him in repentance is crucial to your walking free from an eating disorder. Why would you want to spend time with a person who you believe is angry with you, or at best, only grudgingly tolerates you? Sadly, this is how many struggling Christians view God. Yes, God hates sin and He wants to make you holy. He knows you cannot do this on your own and wants you to realize it, too. He does not dole out love based on your performance.

As long as you hold yourself back from Him, (whether out of fear, pride, or both), His love will not touch you deep down inside where it will effect change. Your behavior will never change, as long as your heart is not melted and encouraged by confidence in the Father's love. You will stay in the cycle of defeat, and this grieves the Holy Spirit. God will not force His way into your life; you must respond to Him and allow yourself to believe in His enduring love. No matter how much rejection you may have suffered in the past at the hands of other people, Hebrews 13:5 promises that God is with us: "I will never desert you; nor will I ever forsake you." Have you ever stopped to ask yourself, "How does this affect the way I live my life?" Is it just a warm, fuzzy catch phrase? Are you convinced that God loves you tenderly and personally, or is this just an endearment?

Seeing this verse in the King James Version provides a clue that the assurance of His presence is individual, and not just collective. This translation uses the you-singular term "thee" here, rather than the plural "ye," which is faithful to the original Hebrew. Many of God's promises are, in fact, "singular" and therefore personal words to us, but we often miss that in the newer translations. What an amazing thought, that we are not simply one of countless faces to the Almighty; but He is faithful to sustain each one of His children in exactly the way that he or she needs.

If you look up the verse's cross-references, you see that the author of Hebrews was quoting from Deuteronomy, then Joshua. The context in Deuteronomy 31:6 reveals that the Israelites were going into battle. Where was the Lord leading them when He gave this promise? Into Canaan, the Promised Land. First He says to them, "Be strong and courageous. Do not be afraid or terrified." He promises to go into battle with them, and assures their victory.

This is not simply an endearment; it's much more than that,

if we learn to apply the illustration. What are our "enemies"? Or, put another way, what do we do battle against? Sin: especially our most ingrained, besetting sins (in the current context, anorexia or bulimia). We feel like we are fighting a war, and fast losing ground. In Romans 7:23, Paul specifically says the carnal desires "wage war against" the spirit and law of God. Yes, we're dead to sin, but even the Spirit-filled New Testament writers acknowledged that the holy life is a continual battle. God promises not only to fight the battle with us, but He won't abandon or forsake us when we're in defeat. He won't leave us at the mercy of our sin. Can you imagine God shaking His head and exclaiming to the angels, "Oh, she did that again. I can't believe that hopeless reprobate turned to food again instead of Me. I've got better things to do than contend with her."

While the immediate, historical context was literal battle in the Old Testament, the application is spiritual for us. Spiritual warfare also conjures up Paul's allegory of "putting on the full armor of God" in Ephesians 6:11. The whole idea of fighting a battle against sin and being soldiers is common in the New Testament. Paul refers several times to his fellow evangelists as "soldiers" of Christ, again comparing the spiritual battle to a military one. Soldiers on the battlefield never leave their fallen or wounded brethren behind, and God is assuring us in this simple promise, repeated three times in Scripture, that neither will He abandon His servants when we struggle and fail in our sin. Looking at that promise in its original context forced me to see it in a whole new light. Many times, when we sin, our first instinct is to run and hide. This promise is that He is an Ally, ever fighting by our side. The following verse confirms that: "We confidently say, 'The Lord is my helper; I will not be afraid. What will man do to me?'"(Hebrews 13:6).

As Jesus illustrated in the parable of the Prodigal Son, the Father never gives up on us. He sovereignly awaits His wayward daughters to take the first faltering step towards His warm embrace. He meets you when you turn to Him, and will carry you much of the way. Once you allow yourself to trust in His enduring love, you can't help but be changed by it—He calls us to repentance through His loving kindness (Romans 2:4). As our Father, He wants our best. God is not holding some sort of punishment over your head as retribution for all the times you've abused food or abused your body; His will is for you to be joyful and have peace. This involves re-evaluating your priorities, beliefs and values (what truly governs you, after Sunday's praise music fades) in light of what God's are, and then committing to having the mind of Christ.

In the next chapter, let's look at how we develop faulty, emotionally-based beliefs and convictions, and how to repent of them.

Chapter 5

Your Convictions: Fact or Feelings-Based?

By the time unhealthy eating habits have taken root, an anorexic or bulimic has already developed an unbiblical way of thinking about food. We have already looked at where some of these attitudes and tendencies originate back in Chapter 2. While the ultimate responsibility for our actions lies with us, it is safe to say that eating disorders do not occur spontaneously, or in a vacuum. Girls who have weight problems incorporate the notion that eating is a weakness, and associate it with morality. Therefore, consuming fattening food is seen as sinful; while subsisting on celery and lettuce is somehow "virtuous." This is vanity. Denying hunger in order to become slim, to be socially accepted or aesthetically desirable, becomes the "good works" the girl or woman must achieve. This is legalism, a form of self-righteousness. The instant gratification of eating, to satisfy physical hunger, social expectation, or craving, is considered giving in to the weakness of the flesh and causes shame (even if she is not overweight and is not overeating). This may sound logical to a thinness-obsessed woman preoccupied with food, but is it biblical?

The "Starvation as Virtue" Lie

In and of itself, eating is not morally wrong. Paul explains this to the Roman and Corinthian Christians in his epistles. The recipients in Corinth were divided over whether a believer in Christ could legitimately consume meat that had been sacrificed to pagan idols and then sold at a discount in the marketplace. The issue was not the food itself or animal cruelty. The question raised a "gray area" of personal conviction, and Paul was warning the more mature Christians not to do anything that might cause a weaker brother to stumble (many of the believers felt they should abstain, as eating meat might send the message that they condoned idol worship).

Several times, Paul lays out the principle that Christians should be motivated by love, and therefore ought to voluntarily avoid any activity that (while not inherently sinful) might lead another believer to rationalize the same behavior, which in their life brings conviction. A modern-day application of this principle would be abstaining from alcohol simply to avoid tempting those who might have problems with drunkenness; not because all drinking is necessarily a sin. Ultimately, Paul is clear on the issue of food: "But food will not commend us to God; we are neither the worse if we do not eat, nor the better if we do eat." (1 Corinthians 8:8). Later, in his pastoral letter to Timothy, he again points out that there is to be no moralistic connection made with eating: "But the Spirit explicitly says that in later times some will fall away from the faith, paying attention to deceitful spirits and doctrines of demons, by means of the hypocrisy of liars seared in their own conscience as with a branding iron, men who forbid marriage and advocate abstaining from foods which God has created to be gratefully shared in by those who believe and know the truth. For everything created by God is good, and nothing is to be rejected if it is received with gratitude" (1 Timothy 4:2-4).

Aside from the hang-ups different ascetic or legalistic groups like to associate with eating, what is God's view of food? After all, He created it and commanded man to use it for his own benefit back in Genesis 1:29: "Then God said, "Behold, I have given you every plant yielding seed that is on the surface of all the earth, and every tree which has fruit yielding seed; it shall be food for you." After the Flood, in

Genesis 9:3 God explicitly condones an omnivorous diet for mankind: "Every moving thing that is alive shall be food for you; I give all to you, as I gave the green plant."

Does Scripture declare cheesecake or lasagna inherently sinful? If your Bible has a concordance, I encourage you to look up all the references to food, eating, and feeding. You may be surprised to learn that God ordained it as a positive thing. You "feel" dirty if you eat, but what does God's Truth say? He created food for our bodies, to nourish us. Actually, there are many places in Scripture where the metaphor of feeding is used in a spiritual sense. It speaks of parental nourishment. If being fed or fullness were bad, wouldn't God have used a different metaphor? Check out Psalm 81:10: "I, the LORD, am your God, who brought you up from the land of Egypt; open your mouth wide and I will fill it. Elsewhere, God's Word is described as "honey" and we're told to "eat and be filled." Throughout the Bible, while gluttony is condemned, food is seen as a gift from God to be enjoyed.

References to food or feasting are found over one thousand times in Scripture, and the image of the "feast" is always celebratory. The symbolism of Isaiah 25:6-8, which alludes to the removal of sin, is preserved in the Lord's Supper. God wants us with Him for the final, consummate feast: the wedding supper of the Lamb. The believer is right to look forward to this final chapter of redemptive history, and the connotation of food symbolizes both physical and spiritual sustenance. Starvation is not a fruit of the Spirit; joy and thanksgiving are.

Much of the battle with disordered eating is based on irrational or emotionally-based thinking, which must be recognized for what it is. As you let God renew your mind, you have to learn to stop and say, "Wait. I am not going to believe a lie; I will choose to believe what God's Word says about (*fill in the blank*). Also, remember this: feelings are subjective. They are fickle. Basing your faith, your decisions, or convictions about anything important in life on your emotions is wrong—because feelings change. They cannot be trusted; whereas objective and absolute Truth (God) can be.

Let me give you a few examples. You "feel" you are overweight, but know intellectually you are not. You must choose to believe the facts over your feelings. Evaluate how you feel (food is bad; purge good) and hold it up to the light of what GOD says. You have to choose, by an act of the will, to believe His Word and act on it. You also need to pray constantly for strength to be able to do this; you simply can't reverse these wrong thinking patterns in a day.

"But I Feel Ugly!"

Another idol women with eating disorders have set up in their hearts is closely related to the pursuit of thinness—physical beauty. None of us is so naïve as to pretend to ourselves that looks simply don't matter at all. After all, we never go to work in pajamas or with our hair in curlers! However, an unhealthy preoccupation with how we look is what the Bible calls vanity (Job 15:31 2 Peter 2:18), and it is a form of pride. In her book about redefining our perceptions of beauty, Regina Franklin notes:

> Women strive to shape their lives after that which popular culture tells them is beautiful, and Christian women are no exception. When we are obsessed with physical attractiveness, we assert that the world's standards of beauty matter more than God's, and we begin to reflect the values of a world that Jesus said we are not a part of even though we remain in it.[27]

Time for a heart-check: do you deliberately dress in such a way as to call attention to your lean physique? When at your "low weight," do you don shorter skirts and stretchy, figure-clinging jerseys to show off your slim figure, or post pictures of yourself on social networking sites modeling your new bathing suit? Or, perhaps you have been keeping down a few meals lately and are self-conscious about the few pounds you have re-gained. Do you try to hide them in baggier clothing, or constantly seek reassurance from other young women that you aren't "getting fat"?

There is nothing wrong with wanting to look pretty; this is a natural, instinctive desire that all women have. Men are attracted to beauty, and it is appropriate and good to try to look our best. One of the ways a married woman can show love for her husband is to take care of herself and look good for him.

On the flip side, convincing ourselves that we are terribly ugly and sliding into self-pity over what we see as our extreme unattractiveness is also wrong, and is a sign of pride just as surely as preening is. How is being obsessed with our own perceived "ugliness" pride? Any preoccupation with self indicates self-absorption (self can be an idol, as well) and a mind not set on things above. When we think, "I am so pathetically ugly; there is none as ugly as me," who is at the center? Me. Again, we need to consciously reject these thoughts and lies that tell us we are hideous, and choose as an act of the will to believe what God says. When you find yourself sliding into self-pity, you need to find ways to love and serve others. This is an important way you can glorify God, and demonstrate His sacrificial love—regardless of how you feel.

What does God say about true beauty? Quite a lot; as He is the source of all beauty. God says you are fearfully and wonderfully made (Psalm 139:14) and, in fact, you are made in His very image (Genesis 1:26-27; 1 Corinthians 11:7). God does not look at outward appearances; nor does He judge by superficial standards: "God sees not as man sees, for man looks at the outward appearance, but the LORD looks at the heart" (1 Samuel 16:7). Physical beauty is transient at best: "Charm is deceitful and beauty is vain, but a woman who fears the LORD, she shall be praised" (Proverbs 31:30). Peter tells us that in God's eyes, beauty comes from our spiritual condition. Listen to what the married apostle has to say to Christian wives: "Your adornment must not be merely external braiding the hair, and wearing gold jewelry, or putting on dresses; 4but let it be the hidden person of the heart, with the imperishable quality of a gentle and quiet spirit, which is precious in the sight of God." (1 Peter 3:3-4).

While we know from Scripture that Paul was celibate, and scholars are in general agreement that the apostle John was probably a bachelor as well, several references in the New Testament affirm that Peter was married (see Matthew 8:14; Mark 1:30). Peter's wife accompanied him on his missionary journeys (1 Corinthians 9:5). Although Scripture does not record her name, the testimony of Peter's wife must have been as powerful as that of the apostle himself. She was probably extremely grateful to the Lord Jesus for changing Simon from a brash, outspoken fisherman into the mature and devoted disciple we see in the book of Acts.

As a Christian husband and an early Church leader, Peter was able to speak both prophetically and experientially about what makes a woman beautiful. Furthermore, his wife must have been of extremely noble and courageous stock to endure the hardships of a first-century evangelistic mission. One early tradition says that she, too, was crucified along with Peter under the Emperor Nero, encouraging him to the end to stand strong for Christ. This was not likely a woman preoccupied with how wide her rear end looked in a dress. She had been with the Lord, and her mind was on higher things. When we women let the mind of Christ prevail in areas even as personal as our appearance, we will be about our Father's business. If you are seeking God and using your gifts to serve Him (as the women of the Apostolic age did), you will find yourself preoccupied with your appearance less and less.

How Emotions Interact with our Mind and Will

What exactly are "emotions"? Are they the same thing as thoughts or concerns? Not exactly. Emotions may be best defined as "organic bodily responses that are largely involuntary and are triggered by behavior, thoughts, and attitudes."[28] Examples of emotions would be fear, anger, resentment, worry, and feelings of guilt. Because of the way we have "programmed" ourselves to think, over time certain places, people or circumstances evoke such strong emotions in us that we react on the basis of those feelings. The presence and availability of food evokes an intense emotional and physiological response in a bulimic—both excitement (in anticipation) and anxiety (guilt feelings of knowing the binge/purge cycle is about to begin). Have you ever smelled pizza, or thought about what you would eat later, and felt your pulse increase and the back of your knee start to sweat? That is an emotional reaction. Going shopping for a bathing suit will likewise produce a certain emotional response in an anorexic or bulimic.

While emotions are not wrong in and of themselves, too often these feelings become the dominant force in decisions we make, how we live, and how we perceive ourselves and others. We should be constantly training our minds to think God's thoughts (more on this process in the next chapter), which will ultimately influence our feelings and our will. When I was in college, my small group leader in Campus Crusade used to say, "Faith should always be based on fact; never on feelings." This is absolutely true, as feelings are subjective and outrageously fickle. As nearly anyone can testify, our moods and emotions can vacillate day to day, with or without a change in our circumstances. In a similar way, we should be on alert for when our thinking about food, our bodies, or weight-related issues starts to reflect a worldly value system rather than a biblical one. Your goal is to be singular: to obey God, whether you feel like it or not.

If our relationship with God and others in the Body of Christ is emotionally driven, it will be superficial and we will never mature as Christians. It is important to stick to the habit of reading the Bible every day, regardless of how you happen to feel. Putting solid truth into your mind and believing it as an act of the will is the surest and most authentic way to deal with your emotional state. Godly ways of dealing with your anger, depression, frustration, self-pity, unbelief and despair are all addressed in Scripture. When your beliefs influencing your emotional state stand in contradiction to what God's Word says, that, too, is clarified.

For example, we have already looked at how God's emphatic promise never to leave nor forsake us counters our feelings of aloneness and abandonment. For most of my life, I believed I was not good at anything. 1 Corinthians 12:12-25 confirms the indispensable function of each and every member of the Body, and states that I have been given gifts to use to build others up and glorify God. I was thinking only in terms of how to benefit myself. Another lie that has often seized my emotions is that God is distant and disinterested in me. This is the sin of unbelief, which needs to be replaced by faith. Psalm 145:18 says, "The LORD is near to all who call on him, to all who call on him in truth." Furthermore, Jesus says that He is gentle and promises to give rest to all who are weary and come to Him (Matthew 11:28). Peter, who was one of Jesus' closest friends during His earthly ministry, reminds us that "the eyes of the Lord are on the righteous and his ears are attentive to their prayer, but the face of the Lord is against those who do evil" (1 Peter 3:12). What great reassurance!

It is possible to "know" something with certainty, and yet be dead wrong. When I weighed less than 100 lbs. and could not find clothes to fit, I "knew" I was fat. I have "known" that my husband didn't love me; likewise I have "known" that God is rejecting me. On all counts I was deceived. Emotions are powerful and we humans (especially women) are vulnerable to believing them, but we need to re-train our minds by allowing God's Word to overrule our faulty belief system.

Personalized Encouragement from God

One of the most exciting parts of the journey with God as you get to know Him happens when the Holy Spirit makes a particular verse or passage an absolute reality to you. Of course, all Scripture is God-breathed, and it is the way in which He always speaks to us. Occasionally, however, as you continue to uncover truth in the Bible, something may seem to leap off the page and straight into your heart. It may be that the verse convicts you in a deeply personal way. Other times, it may be a particular encouragement so clear to you that you are amazed something written thousands of years ago could have so much relevance. In either case, the Holy Spirit has illuminated something specific from His Word to your heart that completely surpasses an intellectual understanding. The light bulb comes on, and you suddenly "get it" on a deeper level.

I'll never forget the first time God encouraged me in this way. During the euphoric first months of freedom from bulimia, I developed a voracious appetite for reading the Bible, and generally took it with me everywhere I anticipated having "down time." Still battling the occasional temptation to purge, I also struggled to believe that God had really forgiven me and I was completely clean. Although intellectually I believed God's promise that in Christ I am a new creation (2 Corinthians 5:17), I could not forget the many wasted years of frenzied purging. I felt as if I needed to do something by way of penance; that God could not fully accept me until I somehow "made it up to Him." It is pride that tells us God's acceptance is based on our performance, rather than Christ's righteousness. God brought me to repentance for doubting His mercy through a particular passage of Scripture.

Since I am an interpreter, I spend a lot of time sitting in courtrooms and hospital waiting rooms. On one particular day, I sat reading Isaiah while the court was in recess, waiting for the client's case to be called. When I came to the words, "Therefore the LORD longs to be gracious to you, and therefore He waits on high to have compassion on you: for the LORD is a God of justice; how blessed are all those who long for Him"(Isaiah 30:18), I nearly fell off my chair! It was as if a lightning bolt had shot that incredible message of grace straight into my heart. My pulse speeded up as I suddenly realized, "He means me. He actually longs to be gracious to me. He rises to show me compassion." It was so unexpected and so totally undeserved that I was, once again, amazed by the tenderness of the Father's heart. In context, this verse was talking about God's promise to the exiled Israelites, who had abandoned Him and repeatedly run after other gods. They didn't deserve His mercy or compassion either, yet He swore it to them on oath. He does the same thing with His wayward children today.

Conviction, Never Condemnation

God's Word often encourages us in such specific, personal ways by illuminating truth. The Holy Spirit also uses His truth to convict us in this way—He helps us repent by uncovering unconfessed sin we may be harboring in our hearts. As I mentioned, another sin I carried for many years alongside bulimia was alcohol abuse. Most of the women I have counseled also report struggles with drunkenness as well as bingeing and purging. (I use the biblical term "drunkenness" rather than "alcoholism." As a well-known biblical counselor says, Jesus didn't die for any "isms.")

I started drinking in my early twenties, and from the first sip it was as if a switch had been thrown in my brain. As time went on, I realized my behavior was not normal or healthy, but the temptation to keep drinking until I was "buzzed" eventually developed into a besetting habit that I could not break once I started to drink. Unwilling to admit I had let myself become a slave to sin in this area, I would alternately rationalize my imbibing as "social drinking" and vow to cut back in order to "moderate" the amount I drank. While I certainly didn't drink every day, (Friday and Saturday nights were the norm), each time I had any kind of alcoholic beverage in my hand I felt incapable of stopping. The mind-altering "high" of the experience was too exhilarating; at the very least, it provided a temporary escape from the guilt and shame I carried around when sober.

I have noticed that God tends to work on one thing at a time in His children's lives. Although there are no verses specifically dealing with tobacco in the Bible, I was convicted that smoking was a chemical way of stuffing my tension and aggravation down inside rather than turning it all over to Him. Giving up cigarettes was relatively easy. Once that vice was gone, the Holy Spirit began to bring individual passages to my attention that dealt with excessive drinking. It was uncanny! Every time I opened the Bible from about 2001 until I finally surrendered in the fall of 2003, (further witness to the limitless patience of God), it seemed the Spirit was driving home the evils of too much wine. Easily able to polish off a bottle by myself, this made me uncomfortable.

I knew enough about the Bible, even at that point, to realize we cannot simply tear out the parts we don't like. "All Scripture is inspired by God and profitable for teaching, for reproof, for correction, for training in righteousness," (2 Timothy 3:16). It certainly seemed that God was rebuking and correcting me! Sprawled on the couch with a dog-eared Student Bible, I would no sooner get comfortable than I'd read, "Wine is a mocker, strong drink a brawler, and whoever is intoxicated by it is not wise" (Proverbs 20:1) or, a little further on, "For the heavy drinker and the glutton will come to poverty, and drowsiness will clothe one with rags," (Proverbs 23:21; emphasis mine). "Great," I'd think. "We covered both drinking and bulimia right there, Lord."

I was not "feeling" too good about myself, as the saying goes. Moving to the New Testament for some comforting words, my eyes would fall upon "Older women likewise are to be reverent in their behavior, not malicious gossips nor enslaved to much wine, teaching what is good," (Titus 2:3). I knew this was not a coincidence—the Holy Spirit was getting my attention. Once He had it, I was miserable until I repented. Illuminating specific Scriptures to you is one way that God cleanses you with water of the Word (Ephesians 5:26) and helps you renew your mind.

The Purpose of Emotions

Thus far we've considered how to combat unbiblical emotions with the sword of the Spirit. These include feelings of doubt, anxiety and perfectionism that arise from a skewed understanding of God, or of our relationship to Him as daughters. But what about the legitimate role of emotions? Unlike computers, which can assimilate enormous amounts of information and produce accurate results based on the programming data, we have subjective feelings. These can indeed guide us toward truth and appropriate behavior. God gave us emotions for a reason—not to be controlled by them, but in order to be fully human and relate to one another and Him on a level unknown in the animal kingdom. Over the centuries, innumerable philosophies and theories about how we think and the connection between the mind and our physical bodies have been proposed, but for our purposes it is enough to acknowledge that: 1) emotions exist and are a valid, even vital, part of being human; 2) God has given us emotional capacity to serve as a guide, but not to rule us; and 3) negative emotions can be an indication that something is wrong spiritually.

Bulimics in particular usually have intense emotions,

which they try to suppress and numb with food. Once the "high" of the binge has worn off and the shame of the purging sets in, her depression worsens. The cycle and interplay between the emotionally-driven behavior and "sedative" is fairly common to all addicts, and is well represented by the following diagram: [29]

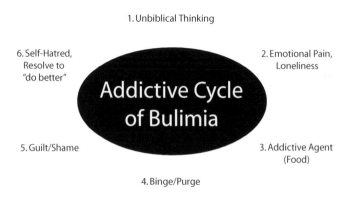

1. Unbiblical Thinking

6. Self-Hatred, Resolve to "do better"

2. Emotional Pain, Loneliness

Addictive Cycle of Bulimia

5. Guilt/Shame

3. Addictive Agent (Food)

4. Binge/Purge

The addiction itself, as a sinful activity, will draw the addict into a depression that can only be explained spiritually. The root problem is not the emotion itself; it is her behavior, which is causing the painful emotion. When the Holy Spirit controls our consciences, we know that we are grieving Him by our sin (even if we choose to suppress this knowledge). In the case of eating disorders or other addictions, depression and shame are simply indicators that something is wrong. This is why antidepressant drugs, which are aimed at relieving the emotions directly, don't work for anorexics and bulimics. They simply treat the symptom (depression) without getting at its root (the patient has been voluntarily gorging and vomiting her food every day for years).

Vernon Grounds, a preacher and biblical counselor, described the emotional effect of sin this way: "Psychic pain is inflicted by the Holy Spirit as He creates the conviction of sin, a conviction that God's law has been broken."[30] Biblical counseling pioneer Jay Adams compares emotions to a warning light on a car dashboard:

> What must one do to set his conscience at rest? The same thing he does to extinguish the red light on the dashboard. He doesn't take a hammer and smash the red light. Instead, he gets out and lifts the hood to see what is wrong. His problem is not with the light on the dashboard. He is thankful for the light; it has warned him early enough to do something about the real problem. Likewise, one's problem is not with his conscience. It is his friend, warning him that there is something wrong with his behavior. There is no emotional problem. One should not try to smash his conscience then. He will not want to put it to sleep by pills or any means that would anesthetize it.[31]

Thus, emotions serve a useful purpose in helping us root out underlying sin. This is not to say that all grief, sadness, or anxiety is caused by latent sin, but in general we do well to take spiritual inventory when these affections overtake us. When stuck in the bondage of an eating disorder or other addiction, it is a near-certainty that the addiction is the cause of these negative emotions. Depression does not drive anyone to bulimia, but bulimia will certainly cause depression in a woman whose conscience is still sensitive enough to perceive the conviction of the Holy Spirit.

The flip side of knowing that our sinful behavior destroys our joy and produces painful emotions is that righteous behavior results in good emotions. Obeying God truly is its own reward. The peace of which Christ speaks in John 14:27 is a deep and abiding peace in our relationship with God. The Lord has made it clear that love for Him cannot be separated from obedience to Him (Matthew 28:20; John 14:23), and obedience to God in turn produces joy. When the world is our master we will always end up feeling inadequate; when we learn to root our thinking in Scriptural principles, we will discover joy and peace. In the next chapter, we will examine how to "be transformed by the renewing of your mind" (Romans 12:2).

Chapter 6

Renewing your Mind with the Washing of the Word

Several years ago, I was counseling a young Canadian woman through e-mail. "Emma" had been purging daily for several years, and could no longer get through a meal without panicking over the calories she was consuming. The image of a successful, trim and attractive woman was highly valued in Emma's family, and she could not help comparing herself to her svelte, professional cousins. She began seeking solace in the very food she feared, gradually becoming enslaved to the binge/purge ritual. She wrote: "I just really want to stop thinking that purging is even an option- it should not be on my mind as I am eating!" Her comment pin-points the basic struggle that every bulimic constantly faces. Every sin begins in the mind, with what we think in our hearts.

I heard from Emma again recently. Her eating disorder was completely in the past, and she was working towards a Master's Degree. This time, she wrote: "It's been so long since I purged, I really can't even imagine doing it anymore. It's hard to believe that was such a big part of my life back then….." What had changed? Emma was transformed by the renewing of her mind.

Paul exhorts believers: "Therefore I urge you, brethren, by the mercies of God, to present your bodies a living and holy sacrifice, acceptable to God, which is your spiritual service of worship. And do not be conformed to this world, but be transformed by the renewing of your mind, so that you may prove what the will of God is, that which is good and acceptable and perfect."(Romans 12:1-2). We are not to use our bodies to serve the kingdom of darkness, but rather to offer their use in God's service. (cf. Romans 6:13). Resisting the constant lure to sin with our bodies requires vigilance and self-control, both of which are cultivated by prayer and reading God's Word. The process requires an internal shift in thinking—deliberately turning away from ungodly and destructive thought patterns to true, biblical ones.

If you are trapped in the cycle of bulimia or anorexia, nothing is going to change until you let God renew your mind. God has chosen to reveal His mind, priorities and desires for His children through His Word, the Bible. If you have been born again, this is probably not a new concept to you—the inerrancy of Scripture is, after all, one of the fundamentals of the Christian faith. However, even sincere believers often buy into false conclusions about truth, themselves, the world's standards, and even God. How does this happen?

For one thing, our own human nature is inherently dishonest. "The heart is more deceitful than all else and is desperately sick; who can understand it?" (Jeremiah 17:9). We are masters at fooling ourselves (through rationalization) and others (by hypocrisy) in more ways than we realize. We have a propensity to see things the way we want to and to play by our own rules if we can get away with it. This is the whole basis on which "doing your own thing" is accepted by many. Refusing to agree that there is absolute truth (and that God determines it; we do not) has led to the climate of moral relativity in which we now live. Unfortunately, this tendency to invent our own truth often leads people into unbiblical beliefs about God.

Knowing God as He Is
Since Christ is no longer with us physically, without a dynamic relationship with Him and a solid grasp of His re-

vealed nature, there is a temptation to "remake" Christ into our own image. This is why it is so important to stay grounded in the Word of God. To allow God's thoughts to truly become your own, you must commit to spending time each day reading the Bible in order to let His Word seep into your soul. Books about the Bible, while you may glean much from them, are not a substitute for the Bible itself. A study Bible with a concordance will help you get the most out of your devotional time. The best way to start, especially if you have never read the Bible before, is to first read the Gospel of John and then the book of Romans. These two books nail down the essentials of the Christian faith, establish Christ's deity, and reveal God's sovereign plan of election and salvation by faith in Christ alone. As we saw in the last chapter, study of the Bible is crucial in order to know God and the attributes of His divine nature.

Next, I suggest reading the Synoptic Gospels (Matthew, Mark, and Luke) to become thoroughly acquainted with the Jesus we proclaim as Lord. Both His compassion and hard-hitting attitude toward sin are unmistakable throughout the pages of the New Testament. Moving forward, the Acts of the Apostles is a fast-paced lesson in Church history, building the "bridge" between the nuclear group in Jerusalem and the spread of the Gospel over the known world. As we survey the unfolding story in Acts, we observe how the coming of the Holy Spirit changed both the course of redemptive history and individual lives. Next, the remaining letters of Paul, Peter, John, Jude and James encourage, convict and exhort the believer to worship, live and relate to other people God's way.

As you read the Old Testament, (the Hebrew Scriptures consisting of the Torah, Law and Prophets), you will learn how to see it through the lens of the New Testament. God's covenants with His people make more sense if you see their ultimate fulfillment in the coming of Christ. Genesis may bring back memories of Sunday school stories heard long ago; the other books of the Pentateuch, traditionally ascribed to Moses, cover forty years of Israel's desert wanderings. The long history of Israel and Judah's evil kings and cyclical slides into corruption may not seem very edifying, but it is a testimony of God's faithfulness and unending patience with His undeserving people. Reading the prophets, you will see allusions to Jesus Christ on every page. By the time you reach the account of the Archangel Gabriel's visit to the aging Zachariah at the beginning of Matthew, you will be well familiar with the mind and workings of the Lord Jesus Christ.

If it all seems overwhelming to you now, relax! You have a lifetime to get to know your Redeemer. He isn't going anywhere. There are different ways to approach reading the Bible, and you can go at your own pace. The important thing is that you study, not how or how fast you read. If you choose to read only one chapter per day, you will have completed the Bible in about three years. If you read three chapters per day and an additional two on Sunday, you will finish in one year. Using a Bible study to concentrate on a particular book or theme in Scripture is also a great way to learn (the Macarthur Study Library, for example, has many excellent resources available).

Throughout history, the further people have strayed from the supremacy of Scripture, the more removed they have become from their Creator. In our corrupted human nature, we love to create our own god. A safe god; custom-designed to suit our tastes. Let's face it, we all have our own desires and agendas. If we can just get "god" (however we may conceive of him) to back us up…well, now that's really a "higher power" we can worship! The Jesus of the Gospels is not the non-confrontational, infinitely tolerant, impotent idol the liberal church has molded Him into. Such a "revised" image of Jesus may not threaten willful sinners, and they may stay comfortable in whatever lifestyle they please. A selective reading of Scripture may yield a very different deity; not a true representation of the One True God.

Conversely, Jesus is not the harsh, ascetic taskmaster the Church of the Dark Ages portrayed Him to be. The Christ of the Bible is a gentle Shepherd, not a drill sergeant. Still, He takes sin very seriously. It cost Him greatly. A perfectly holy God cannot wink at sin and still be just. In order to fully grasp God's unfathomable love for His people, His infinite mercy, and His hatred of sin (as well as His definition of what "sin" is; not ours), you must go straight to the source. The Bible is the only direct revelation humanity has from the lips of God. As you pursue knowing Him, God will reveal His heart to you (Jeremiah 29:13; James 4:8).

What does this have to do with eating disorders?
Remember how I said at the beginning of the chapter that nothing would change until you allowed God to renew your mind? As you fill yourself with God's thoughts, you are going to learn to agree with what He says and allow His "opinion" to become your own. If you are deep in despair over an addiction you've carried for a long time, regardless of how you got there, it should come as no surprise that something is off base in your thinking. Will you choose to agree with God, and reject your old thought patterns? He has much more to say on some very personal issues than you may have thought. If you can change your obsessive thoughts about food, weight, beauty, control, or whatever else may vex you, you are well on the way to changing your behavior. Remember, you are not doing this alone—the Holy Spirit is providing the strength you need. All you have to do is submit to Him and choose to obey, no matter what your emotions may be telling you.

Let's start with your obsession with thinness. If you are anorexic or bulimic, this is definitely the overriding passion that drives you. While there is some disagreement among biblical counselors as to whether an unhealthy obsession or "lust of the flesh" can properly be termed an "idol," Ezekiel 14:4 and 14:7 condemn "idols of the heart." Additionally, in Colossians 3:5 Paul states, "Therefore consider the members of your earthly body as dead to immorality, impurity, passion, evil desire, and greed, which amounts to idolatry." (emphasis mine). In Ephesians 5:5 he pronounces any immoral, impure or greedy person to be an idolater, so clearly idolatry has at least a metaphorical implication beyond the worship of inanimate objects. Idols are not necessarily wooden or stone knick-knacks you may enshrine in your home. The issue is not a few Hummels or the odd Precious Moments figurine.

Biblical counselors David Tyler and Kurt Grady write:

> The gradual descent into idolatry begins somewhat innocently until eventually the idol serves more and more purposes in a person's life. It takes a focal point or center stage and becomes the axis of everyday living. The tendency of our psychologized culture is to talk about the uncontrollable characteristic of "addiction." People talk about the external thing controlling them. The Bible brings in the crucial element of the heart. The heart controls man. Man is responsible. We desire and pursue the behavior or substance. The tantalizing call to sin is rooted in the heart, and as it is practiced over a period of time becomes a habit. That is the fundamental nature of sin.....the problem is not God or the circumstances; it is the individual himself. Lust, not biology or genetics, is the principal problem. [32]

Are you willing to agree with God that an obsession with thinness at all costs is idolatry? If you are ever to win the battle against an eating disorder, you need to recognize the dichotomy you place between God's standards and the world's. Next, you need to resolve to re-program your mind with a biblical definition of beauty in order to replace the world's superficial definition.

Let's look at how God feels about idolatry in His children's lives. It will be helpful to have a concordance in the back of your Bible to scan for "keywords." I counted one hundred and seventy-nine verses that speak of idols or idolatry, and not one of them casts it in a favorable light! Here are just a few to give you the idea of how seriously God takes this sin:

"They will be turned back and be utterly put to shame, who trust in idols, who say to molten images, 'You are our gods.'"—Isaiah 42:17

"Those who fashion a graven image are all of them futile, and their precious things are of no profit; even their own witnesses fail to see or know, so that they will be put to shame."—Isaiah 44:9

"Bel has bowed down, Nebo stoops over; their images are consigned to the beasts and the cattle. The things that you carry are burdensome, a load for the weary beast."—Isaiah 46:1

"For anyone of the house of Israel or of the immigrants who stay in Israel who separates himself from Me, sets up his idols in his heart, puts right before his face the stumbling block of his iniquity, and then comes to the prophet to inquire of Me for himself, I the LORD will be brought to answer him in My own person."—Ezekiel 14:7

"Now while Paul was waiting for them at Athens, his spirit was being provoked within him as he was observing the city full of idols."—Acts 17:16

"I wrote you in my letter not to associate with immoral people; I did not at all mean with the immoral people of this world, or with the covetous and swindlers, or with idolaters, for then you would have to go out of the world. But actually, I wrote to you not to associate with any so-called brother if he is an immoral person, or covetous, or an idolater, or a reviler, or a drunkard, or a swindler—not even to eat with such a one."—1 Corinthians 5:9-11

"Therefore, my beloved, flee from idolatry."—1 Corinthians 10:14

"Little children, guard yourselves from idols."—1 John 5:21

What can we see about idolatry from the passages above? Holding onto metaphorical "idols" in our heart, whatever they may be, will lead to shame. It provokes God, Who is to be pre-eminent in the believer's life, to anger. The idol (in this case, being unnaturally thin at any cost) is worthless in God's eyes. Not only does emaciation have no eternal value, it is burdensome. Vanity, another manifestation of pride, is behind this obsession. The food-obsessed Christian is wearied by her own self-destructive, vain pursuit. The relentless binge-purge cycle is detestable and has caused her to go astray. This idol she has set up in her heart has separated her from God's fellowship and has stymied her growth in holiness. Do you recognize yourself in this picture? Just as the idolatry of our culture at large distresses God, so does your consuming passion.

We are to keep ourselves—and even flee—from idols, at all costs. As your Father, God's will is that you would be sheltered from the devastating consequences of serving anything but Him alone. The eating disorder has caused you to lose sight of His priorities, and it grieves Him. Intimacy with God is inextricably linked to obedience (John 14:21; 15:7-10). If you will agree with Him that weight has become an idol in your life, you can decide to repent of this way of thinking. Ask yourself the following questions: Am I willing to strive to be thin at all costs? Even at the cost of disobeying God? Would I be willing to gain weight if God removes this idol from my heart? Is staying a size two worth forfeiting my fellowship with God? Keeping a journal as you work through these difficult personal questions may be helpful.

Restoring Food to its Appropriate Place

To either an anorexic or bulimic, food has become an idol as surely as thinness has. For the anorexic, extreme deprivation of what God provides to sustain life has become an all-consuming obsession. While food has become an object of both fascination (worship) and revulsion, starvation is a means to wield power (over herself and others). Denial of her appetite is the passive-aggressive technique an anorexic will use to call attention to her spiritual or emotional emptiness. While claiming she is not hungry, there is rarely a waking moment that she is not thinking about food.

A bulimic is also so preoccupied with food that she has trouble concentrating on everyday tasks and responsibilities. She is anxious when in the presence of other people for very long, as she is unable to binge without restraint. Desperate for affection and close relationships, paradoxically she must keep other people at a distance in order to maintain her frenzied habit. As a drunkard might describe being "in love" with the bottle, a bulimic is "in love" with food, although not for nourishment. Spiking and plunging blood sugar levels aggravate her cravings. While expelling it from her body, the bulimic has exalted her drug of choice to an exceedingly great position of importance. Bulimia is the ultimate "dysfunctional" relationship.

While those who have never experienced eating disorders may only ruminate about food when hungry or as mealtime approaches, for the anorexic or bulimic it is impossible to "turn off" these thoughts. Being addicted to food is an all-day, every-day passion. Driving by a doughnut shop or Kentucky Fried Chicken spurs cravings and overpowering, immediate urges to binge. The strength of these compulsions rivals those of a heroin addict about to shoot up. Daydreaming about high-calorie, starchy or fatty recipes becomes a constant cassette that loops in the mind. In a very real sense, the continual desire for food and insatiable craving for greater quantities is one of what the Bible lists as lusts of the flesh (Ephesians 2:3; Titus 3:3; 1 Peter 2:11; 1 Peter 4:2).

Lust is not just sexual in nature. Overpowering urges and

uncontrollable desires for what gratifies the flesh are varied in nature, as the many types of addictions attests. All lusts are unhealthy and go directly against the pursuit of holiness, which is why believers are warned not to "indulge the desires of the flesh and of the mind" (Ephesians 2:3). Romans 13:14 commands us to make no provision for such passions. In his letter to the pleasure-loving Corinthians, Paul points out that, in fact, not everything is spiritually beneficial. He counters the argument that there is no moral connection between satisfying natural lusts and a person's spiritual condition with the simple statement, "I will not be mastered by anything" (1 Cor. 6:12b).

The nature of lust is that it leads to an ever-increasing desire for more (Ephesians 4:19). Individuals who have given in to viewing pornography will testify to how what started as an "innocent habit" gradually took over their lives and, in many cases, culminated in infidelity and destroyed their marriages. The same is true of bulimia. What initially appeared as a "Plan B" option to avoid the consequences of unwanted pounds inevitably becomes an uncontrollable compulsion to consume and purge vast amounts of food. The binges get larger and more frequent. By the time the bulimic realizes she cannot stop on her own, she is already trapped. This is how the devil operates: by making the object of one's lust appear attractive and benign, then confronting the sinner with condemnation and despair.

Whereas self-control is a fruit of the Spirit, unbridled lust is a trap of Satan. These obsessive thoughts attached to food, sex, wine, or other objects clearly reveal a bastardization of their original purpose. Sex is holy and fulfilling when enjoyed as God intended—within the marriage relationship (Hebrews 13:4). Wine and other alcoholic drinks may be enjoyed in moderation (Psalm 104:15; Ecclesiastes 9:7), and all food is given to people to enjoy with thankfulness (Genesis 9:3; Romans 14; 1 Timothy 4:4). However, like everything good God has created and given man to enjoy, Satan tries to pervert food's original, legitimate purpose of nourishing our bodies by turning it into an object of lust. This attitude clearly does not come from God's hand, but from the world: "For all that is in the world, the lust of the flesh and the lust of the eyes and the boastful pride of life, is not from the Father, but is from the world" (1 John 2:16). Jesus refers to Satan as "the prince of this world" three times in John's Gospel.

Renewing your mind with the Word, in the context of repenting of an eating disorder, means first making a conscious, deliberate decision to remove food from the position of "idol" or "lust" it has become. It also means rejecting the vanity that allows you to take pride in your concave stomach, or sets a goal weight lower than the norm. It then means relearning to eat and view food the way God intended. This renewal in your "inner man" will not happen immediately or automatically, but rather takes persistence and a commitment on your part. If you agree that what God says is right and true, you will learn to counter the lies Satan brings against you with Scripture. In time, you will find that God's words become deeply engraved on your heart.

Establishing Godly Thought Patterns—The "Y" Chart
A helpful visual aid to realigning unbiblical thoughts is the "Y" chart. Biblical counselors often use such a diagram to help counselees see precisely where their thoughts diverge from what the Word teaches. As a negative, unscriptural thought enters the mind, there is a point at which we choose either to let it take root, or to reject it and replace it with God's truth on the matter. For example, a bulimic woman may brood over childhood criticisms for being chubby, and anger may surface. As she ruminates and dwells on the memory, resentment at her past tormentor may lead to unforgiving thoughts, self-pity, and shame. Growing increasingly agitated, she automatically begins planning her next

binge to "comfort" herself.

If she had paused at the moment the unpleasant memory (and accompanying emotions) had entered her mind, she would have recognized she had a choice: to let her own flesh-based thought patterns spiral out of control; or to ponder what God's thoughts might be on the matter. She might have brought to mind any of the passages that discuss God's unconditional love for the believer and His definition of beauty; likewise, she might have consciously determined to "cast all [her] anxiety on Him, for He cares for [her]" (1 Peter 5:7). Considering a right response to her critic, she would have undoubtedly recognized God's requirement to forgive anyone against whom she is holding a grudge. She would remember the Holy Spirit's warning against allowing a defiling, bitter root from taking root (Hebrews 12:15).

The "Y" chart simply provides a visual tool to demonstrate the pattern of replacing destructive, sinful thoughts with biblical, Christ-honoring ones. Having Scripture memorized for instant recall makes the process more automatic, although it takes discipline to routinely pause and recognize the point of decision. Will we choose to go our own way, or God's way in our minds? What we meditate upon will ultimately play out in our words and actions (Luke 6:45).

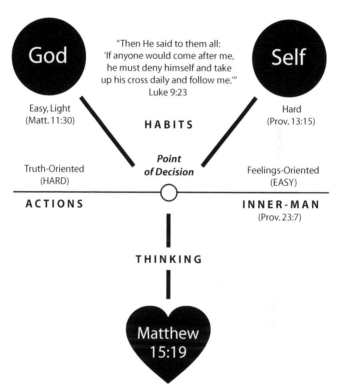

God

Self

"Then He said to them all:
'If anyone would come after me,
he must deny himself and take
up his cross daily and follow me.'"
Luke 9:23

Easy, Light
(Matt. 11:30)

Hard
(Prov. 13:15)

HABITS

*Point
of Decision*

Truth-Oriented
(HARD)

Feelings-Oriented
(EASY)

ACTIONS

INNER-MAN
(Prov. 23:7)

THINKING

Matthew
15:19

"For out of the heart come evil thoughts,
murder, adultery, sexual immorality,
theft, false testimony, slander."

Chapter 7

"Little Miss Perfect"

In 1976, fourteen-year-old Nadia Comaneci made history at the Montreal Summer Olympics by scoring the first ten ever awarded in women's gymnastics. Even the electrical scoreboards were unprepared to bear witness to perfection, initially displaying a "1.0." Thrust into the spotlight, the girl from a coal-mining town in Transylvania suddenly became an icon. It would be difficult to overstate the impact Nadia had on the sport. Her name became synonymous with excellence, and the press dubbed her "Little Miss Perfect." But as she grew, Nadia now faced an ironic obstacle: living up to her own name. Younger, smaller girls arrived on the scene who were capable of performing increasingly difficult feats. What was considered "perfect" in 1976 would be considered outdated by the ever-changing FIG Code of Points a decade later. Nadia's "perfection," although impressive in its time, was temporary and short-lived.

Gymnastics is extremely subjective by the standards of nearly every other sport, with the possible exception of figure skating. Form, precision and execution of skills matter as much as technical difficulty. No matter how explosive the dismount, a gymnast may expect at least a tenth of a point deduction if her toes are not pointed or she takes a step on the landing. She knows the value of training, and that she will not win medals for looking cute in her leotard or having a nice personality. Years of arduous work come down to a two-minute performance on a four-inch balance beam. At the elite level, one tenth of a point can make the difference between a gold medal and an eighth-place finish. However, the key fact to remember is that it's a performance. Once she washes the chalk off her callused hands and leaves the gym, the Code of Points is no longer in effect. She's just another sinner in need of God's love for her in the Gospel.

Never Believe Your Own Press

The perfectionist mindset, in our spiritual lives, is a form of self-righteousness. It ignores the power of the Gospel to sanctify us. When we talk about "the Gospel," we are really referring to a Person—the Lord Jesus Christ. The Gospel is the Person and work of Christ; all that Jesus was, is, and shall ever be; all He has done and will do. This is important to get straight in our minds, because many Christians tend to see the Gospel as only having application for salvation. Until you are rightly affected by the Gospel in your day-to-day life, you will not be rightly motivated to live for the Lord Jesus Christ. Evangelist George Whitefield referred to self-righteousness as "the last idol taken out of our heart," because in our pride we secretly want to do something or achieve some accomplishment that will commend us to God.

Christian counselor Rick Thomas writes:

> Perfectionism is the fear-motivated response of people who are not comfortable with who they are. They realize that something is wrong with them. They sense their own "internal awkwardness." They are not comfortable in their own skin. Rather than fleeing to God to fix what is wrong, their solution is a "do it yourself" attitude.

> Their path to wholeness is through a performance-driven, perfectionist mindset. This is spiritual madness, the mind

gone mad. Perfectionism is not only untenable, but it is il-
logical. And it is a blatant denial of the Gospel.[33]

Rather than bringing them to the Cross, the perfectionist
tries to "atone" for her very real flaws by covering them up
under achievement, service, performance, and rigid self-discipline. She is self-reliant and self-punishing with her self-imposed code of "righteousness points." This leads unavoidably
to self-righteousness when she "performs" well; self-loathing when she does not. I hope you have noticed a pattern
here: her eyes are constantly focused inwardly, on self, rather
than upwards, towards her Savior. Certain that others would
think less of her if they "really" knew her perceived flaws, she
cultivates a mask of perfection—and then strives tirelessly to
live up to it. This is hypocrisy, and it leads inevitably to defeat
and crushing sadness. Pride over our accomplishments or
self-generated spiritual growth can only last until the next
time we fall—and then guilt sets in.

This moralistic mindset of self-improvement sets us up for
failure, because it takes our eyes off of Christ and fixes them
on ourselves. Remember how in Chapter 4 we discussed how
our position in Christ means we are now "dead to sin and
alive to God," even though we still struggle against sin daily?
God commands us to believe it. We forget so easily that our
position in Christ is because of His perfect righteousness,
only by being motivated by His abiding love can we truly be
at peace with God: "He made Him who knew no sin to be sin
on our behalf, so that we might become the righteousness of
God in Him" (2 Corinthians 5:21).

His Will; His Strength; for His Glory

At the 2000 Olympic Games in Sydney, Australia, American
diver Laura Wilkinson defied the odds by winning the gold
medal only a few short months after breaking three bones in
her foot. Almost immediately after her winning scores were

posted, an interviewer asked the tearful young athlete about her accomplishment. "I can do all things through Christ Who strengthens me," (Philippians 4:13) Wilkinson replied. Notwithstanding the long hours of training and sacrifices she had made to earn her place on the podium, she reflected the glory back onto Christ—Who had given her both the talent and the perseverance to train, win, and glorify Him.

Still competing at national championships a decade after her Olympic win, Wilkinson trains hard but holds a proper, biblical view of her accomplishments. How, as an Olympic medalist constantly in the public eye (and under a certain amount of pressure to win), does she avoid the twin snare of perfectionism and fear of man? "I feel like I can face any situation," she says. "Sometimes I come out victorious, sometimes I am defeated. But I know that God has plans for my life and I trust Him. My value and his plans for me do not lie in my score at the end of the meet. He uses both wonderful and difficult moments to mold me into the person he wants me to be. There is nothing more important than our relationship with God."34 Realizing God's sovereign purpose in our lives—both in victories and trials—is vital to glorifying Him in all situations. Wilkinson, by exercising self-control and competing in the Games, was able to win and enjoy "a perishable wreath" (1 Corinthians 9:25), but without losing sight of the imperishable prize—her true reward.

Whether you are an Olympic athlete or a homemaker facing mountains of laundry, your ultimate goal must be singular: to glorify God. He is not glorified when you allow yourself to believe you can gain "merit points" with Him based on what you achieve that day. The perfectionist's conscience accuses her for her failings, but her solution is to "try harder" rather than realize that Christ has already made her a new creation and will bring her sanctification to completion (Philippians 2:13). Genuine faith, which motivates obedience, is generated by an appreciation of Christ's deep, abiding love—and that His grace is greater than our ability to mess up. Nothing pleases Him more than when we believe that His ability to forgive and cleanse is greater than our sin.

The "Perfect" Body

Perfectionism is one of the besetting forms of pride spawning eating disorders. As her fixation on attaining "the ideal weight" grows, the anorexic castigates herself if she eats more than her self-allotted ration. She considers herself a failure, and if pressed, might admit she's fallen a few notches in God's eyes. A bulimic instinctively feels that God loves her less if she overeats or purges. An anorexic develops elaborate rituals to "atone" for eating—cutting food up into miniscule pieces; not letting it touch her lips; exercising to exhaustion. A bulimic, devastated by the guilt of her last binge/purge episode, resolves to stick to a "perfect" diet—no fat; no junk; no white starches. Diet soda only; and only cereal with "bran" in the name. Exercise every day. Only weigh yourself first thing in the morning, before you've had even a cup of coffee. And no matter what, absolutely no sweets in the house.

How many of these "rules" sound familiar? And how did you feel when you broke one of them, or failed to live up to your own standard of "righteousness"? When we harbor a particular sinful attitude in our hearts, such as perfectionism, it generally affects all areas of our life. In anorexia and bulimia, the obvious manifestation of perfectionism is attached to your preoccupation with weight. We have already seen how idolatry and vanity need to be repented, but eating disordered women tend to be perfectionists in other areas of life, as well. They tend to be high achievers in school, recognized as bright and conscientious workers, and are frequently accomplished musicians, athletes, or dancers.

Of course, there is nothing wrong with getting good grades or working hard—in fact, God commands us to do so: "Whatever you do, do your work heartily, as for the Lord rather than for men, knowing that from the Lord you will receive the reward of the inheritance. It is the Lord Christ whom you serve" (Colossians 3:23-24). Sin enters the picture when we start to believe our own hype: that we are something because we have done (performed) or accomplished something—whether it be make straight A's; lose enough weight to be the thinnest at school; or win an Olympic gold medal. No matter how "perfect" we try to appear on the outside, our hearts testify to the truth: we will never be righteous on our own. We need grace daily; even hourly—and we need the Giver of grace to change us.

In His Eyes

Because of this works-based mindset, a common anxiety anorexic and bulimic Christian women share is the thought, "What does God think of me?" I remember often fearing He was disgusted with me and that I was beyond His grace. The behavior creates such powerful feelings of guilt and shame within us that we actually doubt God's love for us. Since we see ourselves as disgusting, unloved, and presumably unlovable, how could a perfect and righteous God love us? This may be a deep fear you have as well, but do not want to admit. As I shared in my testimony, I suppressed these nagging doubts by studying apologetics and theology, teaching Bible studies, and even going on a missions trip. I may have been saved, but no amount of evangelical activity could convince me that I was right with God.

In her book, *Because He Loves Me,* Elyse Fitzpatrick shows how this cycle of trying to "score points" with God drives us further away from the Cross:

> If we're not completely convinced that His love is ours right now—fully and unalterably ours—we'll always hide in the shadows, focusing on our performance, fearing His wrath…If we don't consciously live in the light of His love,

the Gospel will be secondary, virtually meaningless, and Jesus Christ will fade into significance. Our faith will become all about us, our performance, and how we think we're doing, and our transformation will be hindered. [35]

Accepting that God truly is all-sufficient and that your true needs were entirely met at the Cross frees you to move forward in victory. He is your eternal Father; your heroic Savior; your protective elder Brother; the Lover of your soul; your Mighty Fortress, Healer, Deliverer and Redeemer; your beloved Master; the Friend Who sticks closer than a brother. He is your Advocate; your Counselor and Comforter; your Paraclete and Heavenly Bridegroom. Through the relationship of the three Persons of the Trinity, God is all this to you and much more. Don't try too hard to understand the workings of the Trinity; theologians have been doing mental gymnastics for two millennia and have given themselves a collective headache. Just accept it as a mystery and rejoice in the indescribable love God has lavished on you and poured out in your heart through faith (Romans 5:5). You don't have to fight, strive, or earn points with God to secure His approval—if you belong to Him, the Lord Jesus has already secured that for you. This knowledge should inspire you to "...Love the Lord your God with all your heart, and with all your soul, and with all your mind" (Matthew 22:37). True obedience flows out of a heart broken by seeing its helpless estate, and motivated by loving gratitude to the Savior.

Don't Think You Can Redeem Yourself to the Redeemer

One woman battling bulimia wrote me: "I am studying to be a dietician and nutritionist so I can help girls and hopefully redeem myself in GOD'S eyes..." (emphasis mine). I responded, "So, you're going to redeem yourself to the Redeemer? Good luck with that! Colleen, I used to think the same way as you. Here's a bubble-buster: you can't redeem yourself. Only Christ's shed blood on the Cross can redeem you, which thankfully He's already done. It strikes at our pride to realize this....there's nothing you can do to redeem yourself, but the amazing thing is, GOD will redeem your past in the future. How He'll do that specifically in your life I don't know, but you'll know clearly it had nothing to do with your own efforts. But by all means keep studying; just be sure and point the girls you counsel to the Great Physician!"

While aiming to become a nutritionist is certainly an admirable goal, avoid the pitfall of thinking you can do "penance" or something to "make it up to God." You can't and you spurn His grace when you try. Jesus doesn't give "do-overs." He simply forgives and redeems—it's all Him and no us. What He does call us to do is to find rest in Him, rejoicing that His complete sacrifice covers our every flaw, and receiving His forgiveness. "It is hard for the performance-driven person to admit his wrongness. It is counter-intuitive to his worldview. His life has been shaped in such a way that acceptance from others is dependent on his behavior. To say, "I have sinned" is the worst possible scenario for the self-righteous performer. But it is the only true path to freedom."[36]

Redemption was never about us or our self-designated righteousness—it was always, and eternally will be, about His mercy, grace and perfect righteousness covering what we never could. "But by His doing you are in Christ Jesus, who became to us wisdom from God, and righteousness and sanctification, and redemption, so that, just as it is written, 'LET HIM WHO BOASTS, BOAST IN THE LORD'" (1 Corinthians 1:30-31). Perfectionism allows us to boast in ourselves. The Gospel shows us the folly of even trying to do that.

Fear of Man and People-Pleasing

Closely related to the sin of perfectionism is what the Bible calls "fear of man." This does not necessarily refer to craven fear or the fright of impending attack, but rather reflects an inordinate concern with what others think of you. Sometimes labeled "insecurity" or "people-pleasing," this attitude elevates other peoples' view of you above God's. Whereas perfectionism is primarily concerned with performance-based living to attain personal goals of perfection, fear of man dictates a performance in order to impress or live up to the expectations of others. Of course, people around us may not really expect the same perfection we demand of ourselves, but we are convinced they would like us just a little more if we were "better."

Weight loss for the anorexic or bulimic often starts out as a way to earn approval (primarily from the young woman's mother, but sometimes from another authority figure, such as a coach). Soon, she finds herself attracting compliments on her weight—perhaps for the first time in her life—and "feeds" on the attention! If losing some weight is good, then more is better. When anorexia gives way to bulimia (as it often does—bulimia is ten times more common in the United States than anorexia), she is paranoid about the possibility of gaining a pound. Having given in to her powerful cravings, she fears losing her "thin" status. The idea of being the "fat girl" is more than she can bear. Again she purges.

My mother's statement, "Boys don't date fat girls" was an unambiguous statement to a pre-pubescent child: "You must change in order to be loved. You must look a certain way to be attractive, and right now you don't measure up." Are you concerned that people think highly of you, and believe it is connected to your weight? That, like it or not, is fear of man.

Although many Christians are loath to call it sin, attempts to make ourselves look good, insecurity in its many forms and preoccupation with others' opinions is something of which we're all guilty. When I lived in Bulgaria, I used to be amused at all the young foreign investors and embassy staff trying to impress each other at cocktail parties with their great importance. And yet, I was no better. Bulgarian women, who are known for being quite beautiful, are exceptionally thin (even by European standards). This did not escape my notice, and I did not want to be a "fat American"—which is how I thought they saw me.

Comparison Breeds Jealousy

Constantly comparing ourselves to others is also a way we can be entrapped by the fear of man. Measuring our own looks, weight, abilities or talents against those of our friends generally leaves us feeling we come up short. This is an affront to God's generosity, as He has given us all different gifts to exercise (Romans 12:6). What we are actually saying to God when we measure our assets against someone else's is that we are dissatisfied with how He has created or blessed us. Brooding over what we perceive to be lacking in our lives (a goal weight; a boyfriend; athletic ability) leads to the twin sins of envy and self-pity, and is ingratitude. Galatians 5:26 warns against both bragging and envying, both forms of pride: Let us not become boastful, challenging one another, envying one another.

How do we "turn off" the natural tendency to compare ourselves to others? Ever since we were little girls on the playground, we've checked each other out to see who had the prettiest pink shoes. It is hard for some women to resist evaluating other women and coveting a slimmer figure or more toned legs. The antidote is not to focus on own assets or attributes; it is to cultivate a heart of thanksgiving to the Father. Regularly praise Him for Who He is, and what He has done in your life.

"Rejoice always; pray without ceasing; in everything give thanks; for this is God's will for you in Christ Jesus." (1 Thessalonians 5:16-18)

Praise-seeking

Another way in which fear of man can drive our motivations is through service. Many eating disordered women, particularly anorexics, fall into this snare. Serving others should flow naturally out of a heart grateful for God's mercy, and eager to show the same grace to His people. When we start to think, "maybe they will accept me if I do more for the church" or "I can't say no to another shift in the nursery—the pastor's wife will think I'm selfish!" we need to check our motives: this is subtle manipulation, and it is rooted in a desire for approval. The motivation for serving must always be rooted in the Gospel—in other words, out of sheer gratitude to God for all that He has done for you through Christ (Ephesians 4:32), with no thought of self-advancement.

The Lord Jesus was the only one obeyed God perfectly, and His motives were always driven by pure love and a desire to glorify His Father—never to cause others to speak well of Him (John 5:41). Christ had some pointed words for the praise-seekers of His day:

"Woe to you, scribes and Pharisees, hypocrites! For you are like whitewashed tombs which on the outside appear beautiful, but inside they are full of dead men's bones and all uncleanness. So you, too, outwardly appear righteous to men, but inwardly you are full of hypocrisy and lawlessness" (Matthew 23:27-28).

Christ sees the unlovely parts of our heart and tells us not to whitewash it or cover it up with "good deeds." Like Adam and Eve in the Garden of Eden, we know we have done wrong and are ashamed, so we sew "fig leaves" to cover up our shame. These "fig leaves," such as service, accomplishments and achievements may look nice, but God looks at our motives to be seen in a better light than we deserve. Humbling ourselves under His hand means allowing Him to gently strip off the fig leaves—and there, we find grace.

Paul, also, in warning the Church against legalism (judging one another by moralistic standards), reminds us that we are to seek the approval of God rather than men:

"But he is a Jew who is one inwardly; and circumcision is that which is of the heart, by the Spirit, not by the letter; and his praise is not from men, but from God" (Romans 2:29).

When you are relying on your own "good performance" either so other people will esteem you or to placate your inner feelings of guilt and condemnation, you are not trusting God. You cannot solve your own sin problem by over-compensating in another area, lying, manipulating the opinions of others, or rationalizing your shortcomings even to yourself. The only solution is to repent of your "whitewashed" image, stop hiding in the shadows, and trust completely in Christ's perfect work and perfect love for you.

Chapter 8

Tempted Beyond What You Can Bear?

Repenting of this addiction to food takes time, but steadfast faith and ongoing practice of the spiritual disciplines (prayer, reading the Bible, meditating and memorizing Scripture, worship) are the means God uses to break the chains that bind you. Ask yourself, "Do I really believe this?"

During the years I was controlled by bulimia, I desperately wanted God to free me but deep down didn't really believe it was possible. When I finally got serious about seeking Him, I remember often struggling with doubts…would He really be so gracious as to remove the chains I had put on myself? I knew even then that God could heal me, (after all, He can deliver anyone from anything, in any way He so chooses); it was more a question of would He.

Many Christians…do not consider overeating to be synonymous with the "gluttony" spoken of repeatedly in the Bible. Such a Christian may be doing very well spiritually and taking dominion over her flesh in many areas, but she's hardened her heart when it comes to her eating habits. Similarly, an anorexic Christian may not equate her unnatural thinness with the destruction of God's temple. Rationalization plays a key role here, as the glutton says to herself "God made food for His people to enjoy!" and the anorexic extols the virtue of self-control and a "fasted life." Yet another scenario is the backslidden Christian or one who has a very shallow relationship with the Lord. This person is walking most (if not all) of the time in her flesh rather than in the spirit. Every attempt to overcome an eating disorder is purely under her own steam. Failure is her trademark.[37]

Whether the sin is adultery or gluttony, the answer is the same: only Christ forgives and cleanses.

In Matthew and Mark's Gospel accounts, there is a touching story of an outcast leper who comes to Jesus for healing. "And a leper came to Jesus, beseeching Him and falling on his knees before Him, and saying, 'If You are willing, You can make me clean. Moved with compassion, Jesus stretched out His hand and touched him, and said to him, 'I am willing; be cleansed'" (Mark 1:40-42). These three verses are loaded with significance. Those infected with leprosy had to stay clear of others, isolated from friends and family, and dressed in rags. Most humiliating of all was the warning bell they sounded, shouting "Unclean! Unclean!" when it was necessary to enter a town. They survived by begging for scraps.

The leper in this account, so aware of the revulsion his condition evoked in "decent folk," wasn't sure the Lord would even condescend to heal him. How well I can relate; perhaps you can too! More than once, I repeated his heartfelt plea through tears as I sought God's intervention (usually after a binge). How we long to be freed; but will the Lord be willing this time? For us, the unclean? Enslaved by the life-dominating sin of gluttony?

Jesus leaves no doubt in anyone's mind, least of all the unfortunate leper's. He could have healed him from a distance. Missionaries who have served in Asian leper colonies describe the stench as overpowering; few Westerners are capable of getting close enough to directly minister aid. No one could be faulted for tactfully shrinking back, but that was never Jesus' style. Breaking both with convention and Mosaic purity laws, Jesus "reached out His hand and touched the man." Rather than being defiled by it, the Author of Life could touch death and turn it to life. Mark's note that Jesus was "filled with compassion" is superfluous—we can see how gentleness, empathy and compassion emanates from His very being as His mercy covers this leper and makes him whole. The word "compassion" was "splanktazoa" in Greek, a term coined by the Gospel writer Luke. The term alludes to being moved deeply, in the heart or very seat of one's being, in an almost physical way. There are numerous verses that describe the Lord Jesus as "feeling compassion" (cf. Luke 7:13).

Take comfort in the fact that the same Lord Who was willing to heal the lepers of Judea is also ready, willing and more than able to cleanse you. In fact, as He works in your heart, you will conquer this sin because He has already conquered it. However, when you are confronted with the intensity of temptation, this precious truth may seem like merely an abstract, theological concept. Even as you spend time in God's presence, letting Him feed you from His Word daily, you will still have to deal with the excruciating reality of temptation. As a former bulimic, I understand this particular battle all too well. Fortunately, the Bible tells us that Christ understands temptation and sympathizes with us in our weaknesses (Hebrews 4:14). He also teaches us the importance of discipline in establishing righteous habits: "...Discipline yourself for the purpose of godliness" (1 Timothy 4:7).

Enticement in the Break Room

Allow me to set a scene all too familiar to a bulimic. Sue has been bulimic for seven years, purging daily and sometimes several times per day. She was born again last year, but this secret vice is the one thing she cannot seem to kick. After responding to an altar call at church a few months ago, she has been trying to surrender her food addiction to God and walk in the power of the Holy Spirit. Her friends from church make it look so easy; Sue imagines everyone else has the "joy of the Lord" that seems to elude her.

Sue has been striving for self-control and has not missed her morning quiet time in weeks. She knows the right verses and reminds herself daily that because of her position in Christ, she is "more than a conqueror" (like most addicts, Sue feels more like a slave than a saint most of the time). She has even been conscientiously avoiding places of temptation as much as possible. Lately, she has begun practicing good nutritional defenses like eating complex carbohydrates for breakfast, in order to help keep hunger and cravings at bay. She even had a great devotional time with the Lord this morning, got into the car and listened to worship CDs on the way to work. She thanked the Lord for getting her through a full week without a binge—the longest period she has abstained in over two years. As she arrives at her office job, Sue feels on top of the world. She has even begun thinking of herself as "cured." Then, at 10:30 am, she spots the chocolate layer cake in the break-room. A dozen bagels are sitting unsupervised in the conference room, left over from the morning's meeting. Her brain goes haywire. There's no time to think; no chance to pray. She sees no option out of the inevitable binge (even if it's only one piece of cake; to a bulimic, there's no turning back). She panics. She is not thinking of the past weeks' victories; the man who loves her; the children who need her. She's not even mentally rehearsing her Scripture memory verses or calling out to Jesus for strength. Her brain has literally gone into overdrive, and then blanks out everything but the binge. She has known no other mechanism for so long that initially, she feels helpless in some situations to respond differently. It won't always be this way, but it is right now.

Sound familiar? Certain "binge food" triggers, which definitely include cake, doughnuts and pizza, almost set the bulimic up for failure. The compulsion to binge is incredibly strong and rational thought vanishes. The bulimic will do anything to get her fix. Then, after purging, numbness temporarily sets in because to give way to the feelings of remorse would devastate her. Within a short time, shame and hopelessness consume her....and that is when the guilt/self-hatred/temptation/binge/purge cycle starts all over again.

"So, What Do I Do with Temptation?"

First of all, anticipate it. We all know that temptation will come; it's inevitable. All temptation to sin is prompted by the world, the flesh, or the devil. It would be nice if God would simply remove the temptation so you would no longer have this battle, but He has allowed it in order to sharpen and mature you. With no temptation, there would be no refining of the Christian's character, and consequently, no spiritual growth. You already know that your area of greatest weakness is food, which is something that we all have to confront and make choices about several times each day. Now, honestly evaluate yourself: do you really want to stand strong and resist the urge to binge on the food you will only purge afterward? Obviously, for this behavior to become so ingrained, there is some sort of "reward" inherent in it.

While intellectually you may know how wrong and dangerous bulimia is, you are, in some way, getting something out of it—else the compulsion would not be so strong. This is the way addictions work. Something about it attracts you. If you were not getting gratification (however fleeting) from the binge, the vicious cycle would not have continued for this long. In "Deceptive Diagnosis: When Sin is Called Sickness," addiction is thus defined:

> The question is: If addiction isn't disease, then what is it? An addiction is a habitual response and a source of gratification or security. It is a way of coping with internal feelings and external pressures…"[38]

Don't be afraid to take a hard, long look. People generally stay stuck in sin for a long time either because they don't really believe they can change, because deep down they don't want to give up their pet sin, or both. How badly do you want to repent from bulimia? Badly enough to actually stop bingeing?

In his book "When the Enemy Strikes," Pastor Charles Stanley cites five common excuses people offer to justify why they give in to temptation:

1) Somebody made me do it;

2) God made me do it (in essence faulting God for not preventing the temptation in the first place);

3) God knows I'm weak;

4) This situation is different (belief that one is being tempted in some unusual way, such as saying, "I don't know anyone else who has ever faced this."); and

5) I've thought about it so I might as well do it.

Excuse number four is one most bulimics have probably entertained, if we're honest. Stanley writes,

> The temptation of Jesus in the wilderness gives us the pattern of response we are to use when the devil tempts us... there is no substitute for knowing the Word of God. The less you know, the more susceptible you are to the devil's temptations. It is vitally important that you read, study and memorize the Word of God so you have verses of Scripture already planted in your heart and mind when temptations arise. If you have done this, the Holy Spirit can bring those verses to your remembrance quickly. They become a powerful reply to temptation.[39]

I completely agree. The weapon of offense in the Christian's arsenal against sin and the devil's schemes is the sword of the Spirit; the Word of God (Ephesians 6:17). Spending time in prayer and reading the Word will not only give you the mind of Christ (1 Corinthians 2:16), it will also help shore up your defenses for the next time temptation inevitably strikes. If we accept what God says, we know that relying on our own strength or determination, apart from His Word, will fail us every time. However, we have a responsibility to use the resources He has given us in order to stand against temptation—namely, the full armor of God.

This Means War!

Paul gives very solid instruction regarding temptation in the following passage, comparing our standoff with the devil to a battle: "Put on the full armor of God, so that you will be able to stand firm against the schemes of the devil. For our struggle is not against flesh and blood, but against the rulers, against the powers, against the world forces of this darkness, against the spiritual forces of wickedness in the heavenly places. Therefore, take up the full armor of God, so that you will be able to resist in the evil day, and having done everything, to stand firm" (Ephesians 6:11-13).

The time to put on the armor of God is not when we are in the middle of temptation. We need to methodically plan how we will respond before we are standing, plate in hand, at the buffet table. In addition to internalizing what the Bible says about how to flee temptation, resist the devil and stand strong, constant prayer is our ongoing defense.

We have consciously rejected the sin (repentance), but we are still enticed and caught off-guard. What do we do? Paul goes on in the next few verses to define the Christian's "suit of armor": "Stand firm therefore, having girded your loins with truth, and having put on the breastplate of righteousness, and having shod your feet with the preparation of the Gospel of peace; in addition to all, taking up the shield of faith with which you will be able to extinguish all the flaming arrows of the evil one. And take the helmet of salvation, and the sword of the Spirit, which is the Word of God" (Ephesians 6:14-17).

In the epistle bearing his name, James tells us plainly "Submit therefore to God. Resist the devil and he will flee from you" (James 4:7; emphasis mine). The Greek word for "resist" (anthistemi) means to set one's self against; to withstand; resist; oppose. When our allegiance is to God alone, we are not to even give the temptation time to take root in our minds. The longer we entertain the possibility of giving in, the less likely we will be to simply "flee."

Several years ago, my manager sent me to a local wholesale club to pick up a sheet cake for the company's employees. I was still in the early stages of facing my bulimia as a spiritual issue, and although I was repentant, my struggle was still marked by more failure than success. I recalled reading and reflecting on Paul's repeated pleas for God to remove his "thorn in the flesh" in 2 Corinthians 12:7-10, and God's patient response, "And He has said to me, 'My grace is sufficient for you, for my power is made perfect in weakness.'" As I walked through the bakery section of the store, I whispered his paradoxical statement to myself, "When I am weak, then I am strong." I was beginning to learn how to turn to God in my moment of greatest weakness. Whether the "thorn" is a trial, a physical condition, persecution or a besetting temptation (such as bulimia), the principle still applies: His grace is sufficient for us. He truly will supply the supernatural strength we need to resist, if only we remember to ask Him for help and then put it into action.

A Way Out

You are probably familiar with 1 Corinthians 10:13: "No temptation has overtaken you but such as is common to man; and God is faithful, who will not allow you to be tempted beyond what you are able, but with the temptation will provide the way of escape also, so that you will be able to endure it." Here, Paul recognizes the reality of temptation, and promises that God will provide recourse so that giving in to sin is not inevitable. Let's look at it in context. Paul has just explained for twelve verses how, throughout Israel's history, the people were collectively and individually inclined to sin—even when God Himself was present with them in the wilderness. While enjoying an intimacy with Yahweh unprecedented in the patriarchal period before Moses, the very people God led out of Egypt turned to idolatry—right under His nose, so to speak.

Paul is warning the Corinthian believers not to see themselves as immune to sin. If the Israelites were so prone to idolatry that God made an example of them by slaying them in the desert, what makes Christians think they are somehow superior? Much like the message of Proverbs 16:18, "Pride goes before destruction, and a haughty spirit before stumbling," Paul tells the believers in the preceding verse, "Therefore let him who thinks he stands take heed that he does not fall!"(1 Corinthians 10:12). There is a lesson in there for us, too. Often, just when we think we've got a particular sin or temptation beaten, it blindsides us again. Before we know it, we've landed flat on our backs in the mud. A binge can follow weeks of careful eating, just when you tell yourself you've got this stubborn bulimia beaten. Admitting your weakness and depending totally on God to help you stand strong when tempted is your only hope of coming through unscathed.

Additionally, Paul is reassuring us that no temptation we face is in any way unique. Lust, in all its various forms, has been around since man first walked the planet. Satan and his legions have been around even longer than that (Luke 10:18), so he has had ample time to study your weaknesses, anticipated reactions, and ways to exploit them. If you have been born again, however, you are never at his mercy—Paul's whole point in this passage is that God will never leave you in a situation where demonic plots, worldly influences or internal vices have the upper hand. The Heidelberg Catechism states:

> I trust Him so much that I do not doubt He will provide

> whatever I need for body and soul, and He will turn to my
> good whatever adversity He sends me in this sad world. He
> is able to do this because He is almighty God; He desires to
> do this because He is a faithful Father.[40]

God will always provide a way out of the situation in which you find yourself tempted; moreover, He will provide the strength you need to take the opportunity to flee. The responsibility is then on you, believer, to take it. As John puts it in his first epistle, "greater is He who is in you than he who is in the world" (1 John 4:4). The One Who is in us is the Holy Spirit, and John states in the same verse that we are from God and have already overcome evil spirits. It is a settled, final reality.

What are some of the ways out a bulimic might take when tempted with "binge" food, or when experiencing that agitated, nervous feeling of craving a "fix"? We have already looked at the most important—turning immediately to God in prayer. Seeking solace in a Bible study or Christian book to set your mind on spiritual things is also a good option; if you can remain on-task for fifteen minutes, you will probably not go through with the binge. Some women report that turning on praise music and spontaneously worshipping helps them greatly; others choose to leave the house and go for a walk, or to write in a journal.

All of these are good examples, and if you are alone at home, I would stress the importance of getting out of the kitchen and away from food so that you can focus your thoughts on God. If you are at work, discipline yourself to flee temptation by getting back to your desk or cubicle as soon as possible. No one will know that you are silently praying or rehearsing Scripture. Your thoughts are just as loud in heaven as your shouts; God can meet you anywhere you happen to be. If you are at home or somewhere that enables you to have privacy when tempted to binge, consider having an accountability partner or mature Christian friend whom you can call in such moments (We will discuss the importance of accountability in chapter 14). While it is God alone Who sustains you through the trial and ultimately will empower you to forsake sin, often He will use someone else to come alongside to encourage and hold you up. While the Lord cultivates the fruit of self-control within you, others in the Body of Christ can help you develop it.

Jesus Himself understood our human propensity to be easily tempted. In the Garden of Gethsemane, He said, "Keep watching and praying that you may not enter into temptation; the spirit is willing, but the flesh is weak." (Matthew 26:41; Mark 14:38). More than just demonstrating once more the Lord's compassion on sinners, this statement contains a basic blueprint for how we are to deal with temptation: watch (be on your guard for ways you are likely to be enticed; be aware of your own personal weaknesses and have a game plan ready to deal with temptation when it comes); and pray (acknowledging that we rely on God's strength; not our own). Prayer and knowing what God's Word says about how to respond are ultimately our best and only defenses against the enemy's snares.

As you prepare your own "game plan" to deal with the temptation to abuse food, look up the following verses and record any that seem especially applicable or poignant to you:

Matthew 4:1-11 (cf.	**Luke 22:40**	**1 Timothy 6:9**
Mark 1:12-13; Luke	**1 Corinthians 7:5**	**Hebrews 2:18**
4:1-13)	**1 Corinthians 10:13**	**Hebrews 4:15**
Matthew 6:13	**Galatians 6:1**	**James 1:2**
Matthew 26:41	**1 Thessalonians 3:5**	**James 1:13-14**
Mark 14:38		

Take Every Thought Captive

You may have been taught that it is impossible to control what you think about. An illustration to support this theory is the instruction: "Try not to think of a pink elephant." Of course, now the listener will have the image of a pink elephant firmly embedded in his or her mind. While it is true that we have no control over what thoughts enter our minds, we do have a choice over whether or not to dwell on a particular thought. This is the principle illustrated by the "Y" chart. What we habitually think or brood over becomes what the Bible calls a meditation.

James writes: "But each one is tempted when he is carried away and enticed by his own lust. Then when lust has conceived, it gives birth to sin; and when sin is accomplished, it brings forth death" (James 1:14-15). In our natural, human nature, corrupted by sin, we have evil desires. Even the "good" things that we want—good relationships; security; love—are partially tainted by selfish motives. Our "evil desire," in the context of our addictive struggle, is to use food in an unholy way. We have been comforting ourselves with excessive amounts of food, and purging it to avoid the consequences of weight-gain. We've done this so often for so long that we don't even typically stop to think of it as sin anymore. When we do, we recognize the struggle for what it is—a battle between our old, sinful nature with all of its lusts, and our new, regenerate nature that strives to please Christ. We desire these two mutually exclusive things simultaneously—to binge and purge (thus temporarily pleasing our flesh); and to abstain and eat moderately (thus pleasing God).

For so long, we have succumbed to the powerful lure of those thoughts that tell us, "You really can have your cake and eat it, too. This pleasure is yours. Indulge all you want. It's so easy to get rid of it afterward." Now, those very thoughts set off a craving and desire so intense we don't really believe we can resist it. The very prospect of purging and the desire to eat uncontrollably masters us. Bulimia, for its part, very often 'gives birth to death', as James put it. The cycle must be broken as soon as the thought passes through the mind—don't even let it take root.

You have probably discovered that you cannot change your attitudes on your own. This is a supernatural work of the Holy Spirit. As we have already discussed, He lives within you and never leaves—even when you grieve Him with your behavior. The Holy Spirit does not decide to leave just because you chose to vomit that day, but what very often happens is that the shame associated with the bulimia causes us to run and hide from God, rather than immediately repent and ask His help in battling these consuming thoughts. The sin effectively breaks our fellowship with Christ until we repent, as we have seen.

In her book, *Because He Loves Me,* biblical counselor Elyse Fitzpatrick emphasizes the importance of focusing on Christ's infinite love in order to allow the Gospel to transform our attitude toward sin and temptation. When tempted to rebel, a godly thought to rehearse is as follows:

Jesus loves me and this love is so intentional, committed and powerful that it caused him to die in my place. But He has also been resurrected, which means that right now, as I'm tempted….I can refuse this evil desire because he has conquered sin in my life. I don't have to live for myself any more…instead I can remember that I live for him.41

Christ is Lord of Our Minds

In his second letter to the Corinthian church, Paul is combating heresies and various worldly philosophies that were creeping into the Church at the time. The Hellenistic world was known for its many philosophical schools of thought, such as the Epicureans and the Ascetics. Teachings of aberrant mystical groups, including the Gnostics, threatened to infiltrate the early Church. Just as in our day, Christians were being led astray by worldly "wisdom" which blatantly contradicted God's wisdom. He wrote: "We are destroying speculations and every lofty thing raised up against the knowledge of God, and we are taking every thought captive to the obedience of Christ" (2 Corinthians 10:5). His exhortation to this impressionable, young church is general enough to apply to any type of "wrong thinking" that clamors for our attention and competes with God's Word. Just as familiarizing ourselves with sound doctrine helps us spot a counterfeit, knowing what God's marching orders are helps us spot sin. We already know bulimia is wrong; we need to stop the temptation at the very door of our minds. The longer we entertain a thought, the more likely it is that we will give in to it.

"Taking a thought captive" might be thought of as running it by Jesus. Nothing that doesn't get past our elder Brother may be allowed to enter and take up residence in our minds. A major role of the Holy Spirit is your sanctification, including in your thought-life. Naturally, many thousands of thoughts enter our minds every day that we do not consciously stop, examine or bring before the Throne. The more you pray about and anticipate a temptation, the more strength the Holy Spirit gives to resist it (in this case, the temptation to purge). Using a visual such as the "Y chart" may help you spot the moment of decision where you determine which direction to take in your thought life.

Make a conscious decision to yield your mind and will to God's. Ask Him to give you God-honoring thoughts and desires, as you seek Him in prayer and become better acquainted with Him through reading His Word. You are only asking God for what He delights to give, and this is a prayer He will always answer. Make it a habit to pray before, during and immediately after every meal, thanking Him for His presence, strength, and the self-discipline that the Holy Spirit is working in you. Taking captive those insidious thoughts of purging will become more automatic, and gradually they will subside. As you continue to navigate re-learning to eat and prayerfully resisting those temptations, a time will soon come when those thoughts have disappeared completely. You may not believe this from where you are right now, but the power of the Holy Spirit in a believer's life is stronger than any power or force on earth. He pours Himself into every humble and contrite heart that is submitted to Christ. The same power that raised Christ from the dead is bringing you up out of the pit into a new life of freedom, but it all starts in your mind. Jay Adams writes:

> Because of Adam's sin—and their own—human beings do not think straight! …Constantly, in the Scriptures, we discover God correcting the results of sinful human thinking. The problem is so serious that He sets it forth in the sharpest terms of contrast when He reminds us, "My thoughts are not your thoughts, neither are my ways your ways…again and again, in the Scriptures, we are confronted with the fact that sinful human thought reverses God's thought.[42]

"But this bulimia has such a grip on me….the devil must be controlling me!"

Let's be clear: Satan does not and cannot control your mind. Neither can he control your behavior. He can, however, throw such intensely powerful messages at you that you may feel you are controlled by them. That is another weapon in his arsenal—making you think you are powerless. Left to our own devices, we are—but how easily we forget the power that is available to us through our Advocate with the Father. The enemy of your soul will exploit your weakness at every opportunity. Knowing this in advance and anticipating his evil intentions is important to gaining victory over him.

Sometimes, women with anorexia or bulimia will talk about their disorder as if it were a separate entity—a "monster" with a life of its own. While I can passionately testify that a bulimic truly feels as if she has no choice while in binge mode, God assures us that there always is a choice. We need to remind ourselves of our true position—in Christ (permanently) and therefore freed from the power of sin. The belief that the eating disorder is completely beyond your control and, as such, can be labeled a "disease" is a misconception prevalent even among Christian women who truly desire to turn around, but have been conditioned to believe they are powerless to do so.

I received the following comment from a woman I had counseled for several years, with no improvement on her part: "I don't know what it will take….this ED has such a grip on me…the devil won't leave me alone." I replied: "No. Addictions and other sins don't have a grip on people; people have a death-grip on them. Bulimia is an intangible object. It's not a disease; not an "issue"; and not an entity with a will or grip of its own. It's a learned behavior. By God's grace, it can be un-learned."

The idea that an eating disorder "has its claws into me deep" (another claim I have received) reminds me of a program on drug addiction I once watched on NBC's "Dateline." A journalist was interviewing a crystal meth addict, who, despite a privileged upbringing and affluent marriage, wound up sleeping on the streets and selling herself to get high. Noting that she had been offered rehab and ultimately lost her children, the journalist observed, "Still, you chose the drugs." The woman quickly replied, "The drugs chose me." The interviewer dryly countered, "Drugs don't choose people."

I am empathetic to how powerful those cravings are. I realize first-hand how incredibly difficult it is to repent of an eating disorder and how strong that bondage can be. However, you must strongly reject the temptation to blame the addiction itself, or feel victimized by your own sin. Seeing how the cycle starts—by allowing the thought of bingeing to take root—is crucial in order to learn how to break the pattern.

When we consciously reject entertaining an evil thought, a basic principle in renewing our minds is to replace it with a God-honoring one. For example, let's say you're at a party where you don't know anyone, and out of habit you are drawn to the ample buffet table. You know from experience that you will seek solace in the food, only to disappear later into the ladies' room. As tempting as the rich appetizers and glistening shrimp are, you resolve to stand firm. "God is with me," you tell yourself; "gluttony will not get the upper hand tonight!" You have taken the first step: the thought of bingeing and purging seized you, but you immediately 'took it captive'. Now, you must replace it with a godly alternative. This is where memorizing Scripture becomes very practical. When faced with a temptation, we are very often called to make a split-second decision, not to linger over the thought and essentially debate with ourselves over it. When Jesus was tempted in the wilderness, three times He quoted Scripture to Satan: 'It is written'. As you learn to do the same, you will find your thoughts reflecting God's point of view more often.

The Bible constantly tells us that our thoughts do matter. When you categorically and forcefully reject even the very option of purging, learn to replace it with some of the verses you have committed to memory. Paul affirms this practice of getting our thought life under control: "Finally, brethren, whatever is true, whatever is honorable, whatever is right, whatever is pure, whatever is lovely, whatever is of good repute, if there is any excellence and if anything worthy of praise, dwell on these things" (Philippians 4:8).

Putting On and Putting Off

As a bulimic begins to practice taking her obsessive thoughts captive to Christ, gradually they will decrease in frequency and intensity. Her behavior will begin to change. True repentance always leads to a steady (if sometimes gradual) decline in sin and improved behavior. As we turn from the old thought patterns that led us into slavery in the first place, the

Holy Spirit imparts both the will and the strength to change our behavior. Paul describes this process as "putting off the sinful nature" (NIV, Colossians 2:11) or "lay[ing] aside the deeds of darkness and put[ing] on the armor of light" (Romans 13:12). In Ephesians 4:22-24 he tells believers to "lay aside" ("put off" in other translations) the old self and "put on" the new self—which, he goes on to say, "in the likeness of God has been created in righteousness and holiness of the truth." In the likeness of God? Sounds like a tall order! But remember, He has equipped us and will help us grow. A couple of chapters later, Paul twice exhorts Christians to "put on" the armor of God. Clearly, Paul originated what biblical counselors call the "put off/put on" principle.

Jay Adams says this about the practice of putting on the new, Christ-like self:

> These two factors ["putting off" and "putting on"] always must be present in order to effect genuine change. Putting off will not be permanent without putting on. Putting on is hypocritical as well as temporary, unless it is accompanied by putting off.... Sanctification continues as the believer daily turns from sin to righteousness.[43]

Likewise, avoiding old patterns of behavior (such as using food for emotional reasons) will not bring about true, inward change unless those old habits are replaced with new, godly ones. Nature abhors a vacuum. Allowing God to pull up the roots of our besetting, habitual sin is the first step—but the next is to fill in the hole that remains with Christ-like behavior and thoughts. Of course, developing these God-honoring practices does not happen overnight, but they are cultivated as the Holy Spirit changes our hearts. If you are persistent in seeking God, He will give you the strength and desire to obey Him. Our behavior changes, because God's love has first transformed our hearts and altered our thinking.

Paul gives us concrete examples of how we must consciously discard old tendencies and deliberately replace them in Ephesians 4:25-32. Let's look at a few of the sinful habits he tells us to stop doing, and what we are to start doing instead:

"Put Off"
"Put On"
(v. 25) Lying
Speaking truthfully
(v. 26) Unrighteous anger
Resolve disputes immediately
(v. 28) Stealing
Honest work
(v.29) Unwholesome talk
Edifying/beneficial speech
(v. 31) bitterness, rage, anger, slander
Kindness, compassion, forgiveness

Now, let's take this principle and apply it to eating disorders. Most of the warnings and exhortations the Bible gives us are general enough to apply to any sin, because all sin ultimately is a heart issue. While Paul did not specifically have gluttony or self-abuse in mind when he penned his epistles, Romans 8:13 is a goal all repentant anorexics and bulimics can share: "…if you are living according to the flesh, you must die; but if by the Spirit you are putting to death the deeds of the body, you will live."

What specific attitudes and thought patterns can you identify which need to be "put off"? What actions? I mention thoughts and attitudes first, as they determine your outward behavior (Luke 6:45). As you prayerfully identify areas of your thought-life that are contributing to your eating disorder, ask God to show you biblical attitudes to "put on" in their place. I have listed a few suggestions to get you started:

"Put Off"
"Put On"

Number on scale determines my value
I am made in the image of God (Gen. 1:26) and my purpose is to glorify Him (Ps. 86:9; Isa. 60:21)

Counting calories
Food is necessary to sustain life; receive with gratitude (1 Tim. 4:4)

Fear of gaining weight
God created my body; I can trust Him as I eat the way He intended (Psalm 139:13)

Some foods are forbidden or "dirty"
No particular food is unclean (Acts 10:15)

No one cares about me; I may as well comfort myself with a binge
God cares about me, and I can turn to Him (1 Peter 5:7)

"Putting off" and "putting on" in order to renew the mind is a major premise in biblical counseling. In 2008, when I began researching the field, I was surprised at the similarity between Adams' writing on this method and the insights I myself had gleaned as I sought counsel in the Word. The Bible's instruction in overcoming sin and disciplining our thought life is simple, really—I don't claim it is easy, but it is indeed simple. God doesn't offer us convoluted models and complex interplays between "hidden chambers" in our souls or our "subconscious" (a completely unbiblical concept). He exposes our sin for what it is, and offers us Himself as the means to overcome. Why muddy the waters with the world's "wisdom" when the Great Counselor has made Himself freely available to you?

If you are considering seeking a counselor to help guide you through the process of repentance and restoration from your eating disorder, it is vitally important that you seek out someone who handles the Word of God correctly and will give you solid, godly exhortation. We will discuss the field of biblical counseling and compare it to secular, psychology-based counseling in the next chapter.

Chapter 9
What About Counseling?

Most of the Christian women with whom I have corresponded have, at one time or another, sought counseling or therapy of some sort to assist them in overcoming their eating disorders. To be sure, the Holy Spirit is our Counselor; the Greek term "paraclete" means advocate, intercessor or One Who counsels. In John's Gospel, the Lord Jesus Christ refers to the Holy Spirit several times in this way (John 14:16; 16:7). Christ sent Him to dwell with His people in order to convict, encourage, and help them to remain faithful. I firmly believe that God is abundantly able to grant us repentance and heal us from any and all addictions, including anorexia and bulimia, without outside help. This was my own experience. However, the Bible encourages us to avail ourselves of godly counsel and accountability, and so the subject of counseling deserves discussion.

My purpose is not to convince you that you must seek counseling apart from going directly to God in repentance, but rather to encourage discernment in choosing a counselor if and when you decide to go that route. The most important consideration is, of course, whether you will be given godly advice that is in harmony with Scripture. Without the Holy Spirit's illumination, sin will never be exposed as such—and consequently, cannot be dealt with properly. You would benefit from meeting with a trained biblical counselor who will handle the Word responsibly and hold you accountable. The Apostle Paul's words in Colossians 1:28 provide the "mission statement" of counseling, with the God-glorifying end in sight: "We proclaim Him, admonishing every man and teaching every man with all wisdom, so that we may present every man complete in Christ."

Why Biblical Counseling?

Scripture is sufficient. The field of biblical counseling, (or "nouthetic" as it is sometimes known—from the Greek work noutheteo, meaning to "rebuke, exhort, encourage and equip)," presumes that the Bible contains all the answers we need to deal with matters of soul-care. Biblical counselors are convinced that "His divine power has granted to us everything pertaining to life and godliness, through the true knowledge of Him who called us by His own glory and excellence" (2 Peter 1:3; emphasis mine).

If we claim the Bible as our source of truth, we have to accept all of it—including the uncomfortable passages that tell us things about ourselves that we would really rather not hear. Rather than drawing from man-made, man-centered theories of human behavior, biblical counselors do not venture further than the revelation God has given us to understand why we act as we do. For example, when facing an addictive sin honestly, 2 Timothy 3:4 unmasks us as "...lovers of pleasure rather than lovers of God." Besides helping us identify the problem, God's Word provides the solution: to turn from idolatrous desires, and become as much like the Lord Jesus Christ as possible.

Hope is restored. Very few women with eating disorders maintain any hope whatsoever that they will ever be free of this bondage. You may have had this dark secret for so long and the pattern has become so deeply entrenched in your life that you truly do not believe you will ever walk away from it. You may even begin to see yourself as a victim of a "monster" or an external force beyond your control. Current 'wisdom' maintains that fully overcoming anorexia or bulimia is not even possible. The Bible, on the other hand, teaches that "with God all things are possible" (Matthew 19:26). An important task of the biblical counselor (arguably the most important one) is to give the counselee hope.

Throughout His Word, God assures His children that if they will change their thinking and attitudes toward sin, He will enable them to turn around and change their ways. The following verses demonstrate God's willingness to restore His wayward children:

"…and My people who are called by My name humble themselves and pray and seek My face and turn from their wicked ways, then I will hear from heaven, will forgive their sin and will heal their land." (2 Chronicles 7:14).

"…He Himself bore our sins in His body on the cross, so that we might die to sin and live to righteousness; for by His wounds you were healed." (1 Peter 2:24).

The basis of hope is clear: if we repent, God will heal us Himself. Will we be let down, after getting our hopes up again? Not if we persevere, says Paul:

"And not only this, but we also exult in our tribulations, knowing that tribulation brings about perseverance; and perseverance, proven character; and proven character, hope; and hope does not disappoint, because the love of God has been poured out within our hearts through the Holy Spirit who was given to us" (Romans 5:3-5; emphasis mine).

The goal is total transformation. A biblical counselor must also help you realize that the goal of true Christian counseling is change—progressively into the image of Christ (Romans 8:29). Sometimes an individual will approach counseling as an opportunity to talk, not really wanting to change her behavior. I once heard a pastor say, "A lot of people don't really want help—they just want someone to feel sorry for them. But that's not love." That is not the goal of biblical counseling, either. The purpose of truly Christ-centered counseling is a totally transformed life, not just "clean and sober" living. This kind of radical, inward change towards Christ-likeness glorifies God, which must be your primary desire.

"But we all, with unveiled face, beholding as in a mirror the glory of the Lord, are being transformed into the same image from glory to glory, just as from the Lord, the Spirit" (2 Corinthians 3:18).

Because it presupposes the sufficiency and inerrancy of Scripture, biblical counseling is only appropriate or effective if the counselee has been born again. If not, the starting point for the counselor is to present the Gospel and explain the seriousness of sin. It is necessary (as in any evangelism encounter) for the problem of sin to be accepted as a personal, concrete dilemma separating the individual from God. Sin is not simply as an abstract concept; it is a concrete, personal malady we all share. Only when an individual sees and comprehends the full horror of her sin can she grasp the extent of lavish grace that is extended to her through the Cross. As the "Prince of Preachers" Charles Spurgeon put it, "until we have felt the noose of sin around our necks, we will not weep with joy when Christ cuts the rope."

What the Bible calls "repentance unto salvation" is the prerequisite to the true holiness which we discussed in Chapter 3. A desire to obey and please God is the catalyst for any deep, enduring, abiding change within the spirit—anything else is just "cleaning the outside of the cup" (Luke 11:39). Once the heart which has been previously hostile toward God has been reconciled to Him through faith in Christ, the Holy Spirit's work of sanctification can begin (John 15:5; 1 Peter 1:2). The outside will begin to match the inside.

What Should I Expect from the Counselor?

The role of a biblical counselor is to walk alongside a struggling believer, unpacking what God's Word says about sin, our fallen nature and the solution we have available to us in

Christ. She will pray for and with you, set expectations, and give you Scriptural guidance on how to meet goals. Romans 15:14 lays out the prerequisites for such a ministry: "And concerning you, my brethren, I myself also am convinced that you yourselves are full of goodness, filled with all knowledge and able also to admonish one another." Those counseling other believers must:

- be full of goodness (good-heartedness);
- be filled with all kinds of knowledge; and
- possess a rich understanding of the Word of God.

At this point, let us be very clear: no matter how long you have been bulimic or how out of control this addiction is, no counselor, Christian or secular, is your savior. Only God has that role, and He is the one who will lead you out of the pit. No therapist or support group in the world can do that; nor can another person change your heart (Romans 8:27). She can, however, guide you biblically as you take the necessary steps of repentance.

A typical session with a biblical counselor might begin with the counselor asking you extensive questions about your background, upbringing, faith, and relationships in order to form a frame of reference and see your "whole picture." Although I "counsel" women online, the ideal setting is face-to-face. A counselor is able to pick up on non-verbal cues such as intonation, body language and countenance. Also, you are more likely to commit to change and be kept accountable by a person with whom you will spend actual time.

Is Sin the Culprit?

Helping someone face her own sin, the very root of her current agony, is actually the most loving thing a brother or sister in Christ can do. "[Love]...does not act unbecomingly; it does not seek its own, is not provoked, does not take into account a wrong suffered, does not rejoice in unrighteousness, but rejoices with the truth..." (1 Corinthians 13:5-6). The longer we keep making excuses for ourselves, the longer we stay in the grips of the life-dominating sin; and the longer we stay in misery. God extends grace to us, as we must to each other. The erring brother (or sister) must be restored gently, (Galatians 6:1), but she must be restored. While change can be painful, staying in the pit is ever so much more painful. Shrinking or running from what we must see in order to change will keep us in bondage.

Exposing sin in a firm but loving way is exactly the model Jesus gave us from His own ministry. One of the first recipients of grace (and consequently one of the first missionaries of the Gospel) was the Samaritan woman at the well in chapter 4 of John's Gospel. Jesus did not give her a scathing, angry lecture, but He rather pointedly stated the fact that she had had five husbands and was currently living with a man who was not her husband. He put His finger right on the problem—her immorality. He had already offered the solution: "Everyone who drinks of this water will thirst again; but whoever drinks of the water that I will give him shall never thirst; but the water that I will give him will become in him a well of water springing up to eternal life." (John 4:13-14).

Likewise, in chapter 8 of John's gospel, after forgiving the woman caught in adultery Jesus tells her, "Go; from now on sin no more" (John 8:11). He does not minimize our sin or make excuses for it. He forgives, He redeems, and He has given us everything we need to live a life that pleases Him (2 Peter 1:3). He expects us to let His Word dwell in us richly, where it will transform our hearts (Colossians 3:16). Subsequently, our outward behavior will change.

Isn't this "Works Righteousness"?

Trying to change our behavior without dealing with the underlying motivations is doomed to failure. Superficial change does not acknowledge the lordship of Christ—a deep heart change is not necessary simply to break a habit. True transformation requires us to hate our sin passionately; not just seek to avoid the consequences of it (2 Corinthians 7:10). Simply trying to change our actions means we are still trying to be our own god—thinking that we can change ourselves apart from the Holy Spirit. Rather, Jesus reverses the order: "...first clean the inside of the cup and of the dish, so that the outside of it may become clean also." (Matthew 23:26).

Yet, it is entirely biblical to deliberately make changes in our behavior, while at the same time addressing the spiritual roots. Prayer is important, but don't stop there. Martin Luther's famous saying that "Justification is by faith alone, but not by the faith that is alone" might also be applied to sanctification, in the sense that while God changes our hearts, we are to cooperate with Him by getting our behavior in line. Saving faith and obedience go together: "But someone may well say, "You have faith and I have works; show me your faith without the works, and I will show you my faith by my works" (James 2:18). The Lord Jesus was even more straightforward: "If you love Me, you will keep My commandments" (John 14:15).

If someone is trying to quit smoking, he may pray about the reasons he seeks a chemical instead of God's presence. It would also be appropriate to discuss situations that trigger his desire to smoke with his counselor. But would he not be helping his own cause by throwing away his ashtrays and lighters, as well as consciously avoiding the convenience store where he buys cigarettes? Likewise, a pornography addict needs to repent of his lust and deal with his underlying desires in a God-honoring way. But at the same time, he needs to stop looking at pornography—even if it means installing a filter or accountability software on the computer. This is not "works righteousness" or behavior modification—it is a practical way in which he "make[s] no provision for the flesh in regard to its lusts" (Romans 13:14b).

God's Plan for Transformation—a Trained Mind Leads to Holy Behavior

Everywhere in Scripture, we are reminded of the importance of our thought life. Wrong thinking invariably leads to sinful behavior. Meeting with a counselor weekly helps you train your mind to think as God does, by immersing yourself in His counsel. Homework assignments reinforce the biblical principles you are learning to apply to your situation. However, the real change occurs outside of the counseling room—as you live your life, day to day, with the goal of pleasing Him first and foremost in your mind. The apostle Peter, writing to Christians under intense persecution, outlined the process for consistent holy living:

"Therefore, prepare your minds for action, keep sober in spirit, fix your hope completely on the grace to be brought to you at the revelation of Jesus Christ. As obedient children, do not be conformed to the former lusts which were yours in your ignorance, but like the Holy One who called you, be holy yourselves also in all your behavior; because it is written, 'YOU SHALL BE HOLY, FOR I AM HOLY" (1 Peter 1:13-16).

These four verses contain five explicit commands:

1) Prepare your minds. We do this by studying and meditating on the Scriptures.

2) Keep sober in spirit. The Message renders this command as, "Roll up your sleeves and put your mind in gear." Overcoming a life-dominating sin is serious business, and we must remain singular in purpose.

3) Fix your hope on Christ. Living with an eternal perspective helps root out sin.

4) Do not be conformed to your former lusts. You know better now, daughter of the King!

5) Let your behavior reflect holiness. What's on the inside will show up on the outside.

I can testify that the joy that comes from repentance is far greater than finding a new "coping skill." When I diligently spent time in prayer and deliberately chose to keep key Scriptures at the forefront of my mind, God was faithful to give me strength. The exhilaration I felt at being able to get through a meal; a morning; a whole day; then a whole week without purging is impossible to explain to someone who has never struggled with an addiction. Only someone who has been set free by Christ from such a bondage can understand getting excited about not vomiting all day. "Putting off" the "former lust" ultimately breaks the behavioral habit.

But Isn't My 'Addiction' a Disease'?

Most people now believe that addictions are diseases (or "issues"), catalyzed by some combination of genetics, upbringing, and the environment. Since labeling bulimia (or anorexia) "sin" would cause us to feel guilty, we may be tempted to view it as a "disease" instead. Why would God hold us responsible before Him for a bad gene pool, or a germ we caught? Viewing eating disorders (or other addictions) as something thrust upon us feeds into the "victim mentality" already rampant in our culture. This mindset also evades personal responsibility for our behavior.

The Bible teaches that a Christian can face her own bad choices, realize there are consequences, and rely on the Holy Spirit for strength in turning around: "…in reference to your former manner of life, you lay aside the old self, which is being corrupted in accordance with the lusts of deceit, and that you be renewed in the spirit of your mind, and put on the new self, which in the likeness of God has been created in righteousness and holiness of the truth" (Ephesians 4:22-24). Nowhere in the Bible are we told of a sin that is impossible to overcome—if there were such a sin, how could we be told to repent? God has not demanded anything He has not enabled us to do, but has promised to "supply all your needs according to His riches in glory in Christ Jesus" (Philippians 4:19; emphasis mine).

A Christian view of addiction acknowledges that it is a form of spiritual warfare. Ephesians 6:11-13 informs us that we are doing battle with an invisible foe, called 'the ruler of this world' (John 12:31; 14:30) and 'the father of lies' (John 8:44). Temptation works because we believe a lie. Something that is actually deadly seems good to us. This was Eve's downfall in the Garden of Eden—the fruit was "pleasing to the eye." In our case, we are irresistibly drawn to the food, which we momentarily believe will comfort us if consumed in vast quantities. All the while, deep down we know that we will feel even worse after purging and will return to the same cycle of despair, shame and defeat. But the sin looks good; otherwise there would be no temptation. We believe a counterfeit "god" will satisfy us, rather than the truth that our fullest satisfaction can only be found in Christ.

While psychological therapy methods attempt to lay the blame for one's problems at the feet of another, (a parent or spouse; social conditions; circumstances in one's upbringing); biblical counseling makes no such concessions. Each individual is responsible for his or her own behavior before God. There is not a single case in the Bible where an individual is held guilty for another's sin. Deuteronomy 24:16, 2 Kings 14: 6 and Jeremiah 31:30 drive this principle home emphatically. Confronting one's own sin and dealing with it scripturally is at the core of biblical counseling.

Rather than pointing women towards the Wonderful Counselor, the only One Who can truly set anyone free from the bondages of sin, psychology tells us we are right to be incensed over the great injustice done to us. Ed Welch writes,

> One reason Christians respond positively to a need psychology is that it takes people's pain seriously. However, this perspective can actually make pain worse. It compounds

pain by suggesting that not only did the sins of others hurt deeply, but they also deprived you of something—a right, something you were owed—that is necessary for life. Being deeply hurt by others is hard enough, but when we believe that their sin was a near-lethal blow that damaged the core of our being, the hurt is intensified. 44

When we train ourselves to think with an eternal perspective, it becomes clear that our only true needs are for forgiveness and salvation. When the Lord Jesus Christ warned those who would follow Him to "count the cost" and "take up [his] cross daily," (Luke 14:27-28), it was implied that we would be hurt and sinned against along the way. We must be careful not to use background, environment or the sin of others as a rationale for abusing food.[45]

Don't I Need Medication?

Rather than treating the symptoms of depression, hoping that if we feel better, we'll start to act better, God turns things around. Throughout His Word, we are instructed to deal with our sin first, and as a result, good feelings will follow. Depression is usually a symptom of a spiritual problem—underlying sin. Jay Adams compares drugging sad or guilty feelings to smashing the warning light on a car control panel with a hammer. The light will stop flashing, but the problem will not be solved. Likewise, treating eating disorders with antidepressants ignores the underlying, spiritual problem. In 1990, for the short time in college I was required to see an off-campus psychiatrist. I was given a prescription for Prozac, the "happy pill" of the day (it didn't make me happy; or any less bulimic). Most of the young women I met in off-campus group therapy were also on Prozac. None of them felt any reduction in their compulsion to binge and purge.

Recently, I spoke with a young Christian woman who had been bulimic for years. She was actively seeking a biblical counselor in her area for help. Unable to find one, she was referred to a psychiatrist by her OB-GYN, as she was in the late stages of pregnancy. Within 45 minutes of their first meeting, the psychiatrist had decided that "Lisa" was clinically depressed and gave her a prescription for an anti-depressant. "Of course she is depressed!" I wanted to scream. "She's been bulimic for five years. She needs someone to lead her to the Great Physician—not a prescription for Zoloft!" Evidently, nothing has changed in two decades of treating eating disorders, and this particular addiction entraps more and more young women every year.

In the case of a depressed Christian with an eating disorder, the eating disorder is the cause of the depression and not the result of it. A woman who knows that she is sinning by abusing her body with bulimia, yet continues to do it, will certainly become depressed. In psychology, this unpleasant inner conflict is called "cognitive dissonance." In the Bible, it is called 'hypocrisy' and is always followed by God's discipline. After sinning horribly by committing adultery and then murder, King David came to realize the guilt and subsequent depression he felt was a "wake up call" from God to repent: "For day and night Your hand was heavy upon me; My vitality was drained away as with the fever heat of summer" (Psalm 32:4).

Whereas the guilt of failure leads to depression, the joy following small victories is tremendous. I remember being thrilled when I had made it for a few days at a time without seeking solace in food. Turning around and walking away from what has brought you so low to begin with results in far greater joy and increased energy than any medication could replicate. Obedience is very much its own reward—you will know what it is to feel God's encouraging smile each time you courageously face a meal. Practicing obedience (in this case, deliberately choosing to keep your food down) helps strengthen you against future temptations. One meal at a time, as you learn to "put off" bulimia and "put on" your moderate, self-controlled eating habits, your despair lifts. Experiencing this gradual transformation will enable you to "joyously give thanks to the Father" (Colossians 1:11-12).

But What About My Low Self-Esteem?

The message of self-love, self-acceptance, and self-esteem is one often heard at "addiction support groups." This feel-good 'Gospel' has even infected the Church. If we are to believe many of today's popular Bible teachers and counselors, the only sin worth mentioning is the "sin" of not loving yourself enough, or having shaky self-esteem! In fact, when Christ commanded His followers "…you shall love your neighbor as yourself" (Mark 12:31), He was not instructing us to love ourselves more. Rather, He was exhorting us to direct that same honor and esteem we automatically ascribe to ourselves towards other people instead.

Throughout Scripture, we are emphatically cautioned against self-love: "For men will be lovers of self, lovers of money, boastful, arrogant, revilers, disobedient to parents, ungrateful, unholy, unloving, irreconcilable, malicious gossips, without self-control, brutal, haters of good, treacherous, reckless, conceited, lovers of pleasure rather than lovers of God…" (2 Timothy 3:2-4) and we are commanded to esteem others before ourselves: "Do nothing from selfishness or empty conceit, but with humility of mind regard one another as more important than yourselves; do not merely look out for your own personal interests, but also for the interests of others" (Philippians 2:3-4). Focusing our minds on Christ kindles a heart of gratitude, which in turn produces a sincere desire to serve others. Eating disordered Christians, as all with life-dominating sins, need to foster greater Christ-esteem, and less self-esteem.

Should I Be On Guard for Anything Else?

What if a counseling method claims to be Christian (or "spiritual"), but you're not sure it aligns with what God says? Be forewarned that some of the techniques used to treat eating disorders are dangerously unbiblical. Although my purpose in writing this book is to point you towards lasting freedom found in Christ, it is worthwhile to highlight a few of these methods so that you may be aware and on your guard. While they may seem to have "spiritual" associations, practices such as hypnosis, visualization and "inner healing" actually have roots in the occult and should be avoided. Any counselor who is employing such techniques in her practice needs to seriously evaluate what she is doing in light of Scripture's prohibitions on all occultic or mind-altering activity. While New Age "healing" and alternative health practices such as yoga, reiki, therapeutic touch and transcendental meditation have all become part of the mainstream culture in recent years, here I will focus on the three that I have most often seen being used.

Hypnosis

Over the last 30 or so years, hypnosis (or hypnotic therapy) has become hugely popular in treating behavioral addictions. The word "hypnosis" comes from the Greek word "hypnos," meaning "sleep." During hypnotic therapy, a practitioner puts the client into a state of deep relaxation called a "trance." When in the trance state, a person is presumably very focused, and is also highly receptive to ideas, images, and suggestions. There have been many documented cases of "false memories" being implanted in clients' minds by therapists. The highly-suggestive state that hypnosis induces is contrary to the biblical mandate to be alert, sober and self-controlled (1 Thessalonians 5:6; 1 Corinthians 7:5). Proponents of hypnotic therapy claim it:

...increases your self-control, your self-liking, your self-esteem and therefore, your self-protection. Hypnotherapy provides a safe, healthy way to soothe yourself. With hypnotherapy, you can [supposedly] unlearn messages the family may have implanted about keeping feelings in. You can learn how to safely express emotion, instead of stuffing it down and purging it out."[46]

As we have already seen, God has given us the tools we need to develop self-control and an accurate view of self—that we are redeemed sinners. There are many healthy ways of "soothing ourselves" that do not involve altered states of consciousness. Rather than letting sin control us or yielding power over ourselves to another human being (which is essentially what hypnosis is), the biblical solution is summarized in Romans 6:12-13: "Therefore do not let sin reign in your mortal body so that you obey its lusts, and do not go on presenting the members of your body to sin as instruments of unrighteousness; but present yourselves to God as those alive from the dead, and your members as instruments of righteousness to God." We are to be "Spirit-led," which is another way of saying we let God alone control us.

The Bible outlines how a child of God is to safely express emotion. Whether the issue is dealing with sorrow, disappointment, confrontation or any other difficult situation, we are given clear-cut guidelines. The Psalms, many penned by King David, express the full range of human emotion. As you read through them, you may identify with the man who found solace in pouring his heart out to God during both times of intense trial and victory. Nowhere are we instructed to "stuff down" emotions, but rather the opposite: we are told to pour out our hearts to God (Psalm 62:8) and pray unceasingly (Luke 18:1; Ephesians 6:18).

Lastly, hypnosis emphasizes "refocusing" ourselves and going deep within to find answers. On the contrary, we cannot go any deeper into ourselves than the Word of God can. "For the word of God is living and active. Sharper than any double-edged sword, it penetrates even to dividing soul and spirit, joints and marrow; it judges the thoughts and attitudes of the heart." (Hebrews 4:12). If we count ourselves as disciples of the Lord Jesus, we need to keep our focus on Him, rather than on ourselves (Hebrews 12:2).

Visualization

The practice of visualization involves attempting to create reality with the mind through mental imagery. This idea of achieving mystical union with the divine is inherent in shamanism and tantric yoga. The ancient Egyptians as well as the Native Americans saw a connection between visualization and health, and the spiritual practice has been adopted by many modern metaphysical cults in our time. Unfortunately, many in the Christian church seem to be unaware of its demonic roots. I know several women who have been taught visualization in a Christian counseling context (both eating disorder patients and other clients). Nowhere is this practice encouraged or even hinted at in Scripture. We are told to pray to the God of the Bible, addressing Him as Father. Visualizing scenarios (or opening the occultic "third eye") is a dangerous practice, as it creates a god of our own design.

In *The Seduction of Christianity*, Dave Hunt writes:

> Visualization is as absent from Scripture as it has always been present in the occult. Neither Isaiah, Jeremiah, nor any other biblical prophet created his visualization, but received them by inspiration from God. Jesus didn't teach that His disciples could get Him to appear at will by visualizing Him, or that we should visualize what we are praying for. Yet this is being taught by Christian leaders today who

without intending to lead anyone into occultism, are, nevertheless, pointing them in that direction by some of the methodologies they promote.

Just as in the church today, throughout history shamanistic visualization has been associated with healing, both physical and spiritual. Common threads of belief and practice can be traced from ancient times down to the present. There is no more obvious link between paganism/occultism and modern psychological/religious practices than visualization. Biblical Christianity alone stands outside of and in opposition to these pagan traditions.[47]

Typically, the client is put into a deep state of relaxation and told to clear her mind. Onto the blank canvas of her mind, a past traumatic situation is relived which needs to be more favorably reconciled. The client is guided into visualizing Jesus (often prompted to picture Him any way they would like) appearing on the scene. The client then plays out the scenario by Jesus coming to them and solving the problem. In theory, healing comes through the uprooting of negative memories or "hurts" caused by others in early childhood that are supposedly buried in the "subconscious" from where they dictate our behavior without our knowledge.

Re-creating one's own reality or drawing comfort for future difficulties through this practice appears, at best, a sort of sanctified fantasy-camp. Daydreaming pleasant thoughts with Christ in the picture may seem benign on the surface, but in reality it becomes a form of escapism from the painful realities of life. Instead, we are to face reality with a hope in Christ. The writers of the New Testament assumed that, in this life, we would only see Christ through faith: "… though you have not seen Him, you love Him, and though you do not see Him now, but believe in Him, you greatly rejoice with joy inexpressible and full of glory, obtaining as the outcome of your faith the salvation of your souls" (1 Peter 1:8-9). A few verses later, Peter again reminds the suffering believer to "…set your hope fully on the grace to be given you when Jesus Christ is revealed." (1 Peter 1:13). A man who had been closer to Christ during His earthly ministry than almost anyone else, Peter directs the suffering believer to hope only in the Risen Lord, and seek knowledge of Him in Scripture alone (2 Peter 3:15-17).

Inner healing

Inner healing of memories is built on the premise that our habitual sins, wrong thinking (that which is at odds with God's Word) and emotional problems (depression, anger, etc.) have deep roots in the painful events of our childhood. This supposition is not unlike the various Freudian theories that link antisocial behavior to the "unconscious." In contrast to Freud, however, the pioneer of inner healing technique, David Seamands, is a devout Christian. In his book, *Healing for Damaged Emotions*, he makes many valid points about how self-hatred is not biblical and that because God created and treasures us (Deuteronomy 26:18), we should not despise ourselves or engage in self-destructive behavior. Clearly, his intention is to lead his readers and clients into a healthy realization of their position in Christ, and a faith that God's love is strong enough to overcome the hurt and wounds in their lives. I do not doubt his sincerity, but I question his methodology.

At face value, Seamands' intent seems good. Certainly God cares about every aspect of our lives (Psalm 139:3-4; Matthew 10:29-30), and is aware of everything we've done and all that happens to us. He cares deeply about us and invites us to come to Him with our pain and anxiety (1 Peter 5:7) because of His great personal love for each one of us. Jesus plainly stated that He came for us to have abundant life (John 10:10) and to be filled with joy (John 15:11; Romans 15:13).

However, joy and fulfillment cannot be ours apart from fellowship with Christ. Furthermore, this loving relationship cannot be separated from obedience to God's will (John 14:21; Romans 6:16). God's will for us is to be in joyful communion with Him. God wants us to be able to put the pain of our pasts behind us and walk free, but it was never His intent that we attempt to re-write the past in order to do so. Seeking "emotional healing" outside of His revealed will is therefore doomed to failure.

Theophostic counseling is a variation on inner healing. Christian therapist Ed Smith developed the practice, which purportedly incorporates an experiential encounter with Christ. Neil Anderson is probably the best-known proponent of theophostic techniques. Through contemplative prayer (essentially transcendental meditation with a Christian veneer), Christ is said to remove the negative emotions caused by internalizing lies. Inner healing's guided imagery techniques have also been criticized by biblical counselors and apologists for opening the door to false memories. The power of suggestion makes clients highly susceptible to implanted memories and unbiblical portrayals of Christ.

Let's Get Biblical

Exactly where does the Bible endorse any of this mental role-playing? While it is certainly tempting to comfort ourselves by bringing Christ into in all of the painful events and circumstances of our lives, His Word gives us the assurance that He was already there (Psalm 139:7-8; Matt. 28:20). Just before shouldering the weight of our sins on the Cross, the Lord Jesus tenderly assured His followers, "I will ask the Father, and He will give you another Helper, that He may be with you forever; that is the Spirit of truth, whom the world cannot receive, because it does not see Him or know Him, but you know Him because He abides with you and will be in you. I will not leave you as orphans; I will come to you" (John

14:16-18). He was not referring to mystical experiences, but rather to His abiding presence through the Holy Spirit. As we saw at the beginning of this chapter, the Holy Spirit's role is that of a Counselor and Helper. When we stay in intimate fellowship with Him, He truly does transform our lives.

When we try to re-write the script of events God has allowed in our lives, we call His sovereignty into question. Recasting Him in a fictitious role implies that His empowering presence is insufficient to equip us for trials. Inventing a Savior-role and expecting Him to fill it (even in the imaginations of our minds) in order to heal us is contrary to what Scripture teaches: "These things I have spoken to you, so that in Me you may have peace. In the world you have tribulation, but take courage; I have overcome the world" (John 16:33).

The risen and exalted Lord is not an errand-boy who can be conjured up at will to mystically intervene in the past. He has permitted all unfortunate events in our pasts, although we cannot see the reason. The important thing is how we respond to them, and this is where biblical principles come into play. Are we allowing God to work out the fruit of the Spirit in our lives? Or will we slide into self-pity? The latter is our human nature "default mode." In order to have victory and ultimately peace, Christ expects us to "crucify" our self-centered nature (Matthew 16:24) and rely on Him for grace (Ephesians 2:8-9). In a sense, the hypnotist or inner "healer" attempts to usurp God's authority. Creating a different past, with an imagined "Jesus" participating, is an attempt to manipulate God to meet our own desires. The Lord delights in steadfast love (Micah 7:18), and is not honored when we question the reality of His love by "re-imagining" Him.

"Always in Recovery" or Already a New Creation?

When God promises wholeness and healing of our iniquity, He doesn't stop halfway. There is absolutely no Scriptural support for the oft-held notion that you will "never be recovered; always in recovery." In fact, Paul indicates just the opposite is true in 1 Corinthians 6:9-11. After warning his audience that no idolaters, drunkards or sexually immoral will inherit eternal life, he plainly states, "Such were some of you; but you were washed, but you were sanctified, but you were justified in the name of the Lord Jesus Christ and in the Spirit of our God." (v. 11, emphasis mine).

Once the Christian "puts off" what Paul calls "the former way of life" (the addiction) and "puts on" Christ, it stays in the past." "Therefore if anyone is in Christ, he is a new creature; the old things passed away; behold, new things have come" (2 Corinthians 5:17). A new creature develops new ways—new thoughts; new desires; new patterns of living. A former drunk is no longer a drunk (or an "alcoholic"); likewise, a former bulimic or anorexic has been truly transformed—not perpetually walking in some ambiguous state of "recovery." Seven years after being completely renewed in body, mind and spirit, I can say with the apostle Paul "I can do all things through Him Who strengthens me." (Philippians 4:13). An unhealthy food-related thought has not entered my head since early 2004—despite the many years of non-stop obsession.

The beauty of a transformed mind is that it can be permanent. Once you deliberately begin to "re-program" your mind with biblical truth, it becomes more automatic to think God's thoughts during a trial or temptation. Over time, it becomes "second nature"—or, rather, your "new nature." This is why you should not fear that you will relapse. Relapsing into your eating disorder once God has freed you would be tantamount to jumping back into a slimy pit after being rescued.

God wants us to change and to bear fruit for His glory (John 15:8). The Gospel, not "self-help," is the key to change (Romans 6:11; Isaiah 55:1-2), and we, His redeemed children, are responsible to exert effort in our sanctification (Philippians 2:12). As you come to know God better through

His Word, you will love Him more; as you love Him more; your desire for Him will grow. One biblical counselor describes the whole point of counseling as "getting [addicts] to the place where they recognize Jesus is the one true desire of their heart." As you come to see Jesus Christ as your supreme treasure and more beautiful than all else, idols which currently grip your heart will crumble.

Do not be tempted to think you can never be free of anorexia or bulimia, or that God's Word does not speak to your struggle. He is "able to do far more abundantly beyond all that we ask or think, according to the power that works within us." (Ephesians 3:20). This power over sin He has granted you means that by His grace, you may do far more than simply stop your self-destructive habits. Your whole mind and heart may be completely renewed and transformed, as if you had never had an eating disorder. The energy and passion you now spend obsessing over weight and food can be fully re-directed towards living for God's glory, and joyfully serving His people. Biblical counseling, through His Church, is one means Christ has provided to help you learn to do that.

Chapter 10
The Role of the Church: Help for the Hurting

Not long ago, I received an urgent Facebook message from a seminary student in Edmonton, Canada. He and his wife were on their way to the hospital to visit a young lady, a newcomer to their church, who was severely anorexic and had been placed on suicide watch. He had read my blog "Redeemed from the Pit," and knowing that I have some experience in this area, he was asking my advice on how to minister to their young friend. There are no certified biblical counselors in Edmonton, he said, and the pastor was recommending transfer to a psychiatric ward. Since my own pastor is originally from Canada, I emailed him asking if he knew anyone in Edmonton (he didn't). I also contacted a young woman I had previously counseled from the same city, who had completely overcome her eating disorder. She responded that she didn't know any counseling pastors who knew anything about eating disorders, but that she'd be happy to meet the girl and share her testimony.

I do not know how the young patient fared or how she is doing today, but I do remember thinking, "In an ideal world, that wouldn't have just happened." Of course, in an ideal world, young women would never develop eating disorders, but since we live in a world where sin is a given, let's consider the Church's role in restoring broken lives.

The Local Church's Ministry
In the 1960's, social psychology was a rapidly-growing field. For the first time, the Church embraced this new "science" and the pastoral role of counseling gradually fell by the

wayside. Pastors were actually discouraged from counseling members of their congregations, especially those with more "serious" problems. They were encouraged to "defer and refer"—in other words, stick to preaching and send their members to the "experts" for counseling. Pastor Jay Adams was disturbed by this, as ministers of the Gospel have always been equipped for the business of soul care: "And He gave some as apostles, and some as prophets, and some as evangelists, and some as pastors and teachers, for the equipping of the saints for the work of service, to the building up of the body of Christ…" (Ephesians 4:11-12; Emphasis mine). The Lord used Adams to begin to turn the tide and bring counseling back into the Church.

It was assumed and taught by Paul and other early evangelists that members of the Church would be teaching one another the truths they had learned from the Apostles, confronting sin, encouraging one another, and "consider[ing] how to stimulate one another to love and good deeds" (Hebrews 10:24-25). Christians of the first century depended upon each other for survival, and were very much involved in each others' lives. "Self-help" was a foreign concept. Paul continually confronted and encouraged individuals with the Word of God during his ministry, as is apparent from the many personal names and details in his letters.

Part of the role of a pastor is to be able to open the Scriptures in a deep and personally applicable way to individual members, but as we saw in the last chapter, the counseling role is not limited just to pastors or full-time ministry staff in the same way that preaching is. All Christians are called to spiritual maturity (1 Corinthians 14:20; Ephesians 4:14). Part of that maturation process is to study and apply God's Word and exhort others to do the same. Instructing one another in the Word, encouraging, exhorting and rebuking are responsibilities of all believers as they grow in maturity. Consider the following passages of Scripture:

"But we request of you, brethren, that you appreciate those who diligently labor among you, and have charge over you in the Lord and give you instruction, and that you esteem them very highly in love because of their work. Live in peace with one another" (1 Thessalonians 5:12-13).

"Brethren, even if anyone is caught in any trespass, you who are spiritual, restore such a one in a spirit of gentleness; each one looking to yourself, so that you too will not be tempted." (Galatians 6:1)

Please note that these exhortations were addressed to laymen ("brethren" also includes sisters, as we shall see in a moment). Paul's pastoral letters to Timothy also contain many instructions on rebuking, teaching and exhorting, which are all part and parcel of Christ-honoring counsel. The place for such counsel has, historically, been the local church.

Let's look at another passage, which specifically speaks to the role of women in the Church's role of equipping the saints:

"Older women likewise are to be reverent in their behavior, not malicious gossips nor enslaved to much wine, teaching what is good, so that they may encourage the young women to love their husbands, to love their children, to be sensible, pure, workers at home, kind, being subject to their own husbands, so that the word of God will not be dishonored." (Titus 2:3-5)

This description sounds quite a bit like lay counseling to me! Paul touched on several key topics: personal holiness; teaching of doctrine; marriage roles; parenting; using wisdom; purity; homemaking; kindness; and submission to their husbands—all with the chief end to bring glory to God. Paul covered, in this one verse, nearly all the reasons women seek counseling. And who is to be doing the teaching/counseling? The more mature women.

Paul's broad principle of women ministering to other women takes on even more significance when we consider the sensitive subject of eating disorders. At the risk of stating the obvious, the vast majority of anorexics and bulimics are female. Naturally, there are exceptions; but on the whole it is a women's problem (hence my almost exclusive use of feminine pronouns in this book). While the biblical solution to all life-dominating sin is essentially the same (and the underlying vices of pride, idolatry and self-centered thinking are common to both sexes), empathy is necessary for counsel to be truly compassionate and effective. Women are better able to understand, or empathize, with the particular struggles women face. Additionally, it is simply less intimidating for a woman to speak confidentially with another godly woman about something so personal than it would be with a pastor or elder.[48]

The biblical model, then, is for laymen of both sexes to be equipped to serve as Bible study leaders and counselors—within their local church. When it is known that a church has such a ministry available, Christians would feel less of a need to seek help for their problems outside the Church. When functioning as a normal, everyday ministry of the Church, fewer people would feel anxious or embarrassed seeking counsel (which is really just fear of man). It is far easier for a woman to turn to the Internet than to talk to her pastor about her eating disorder, as my correspondence with countless young women has shown. Unfortunately, the stigma attached to counseling keeps many Christians from being transparent about their shortcomings and need for accountability. This is tragic, given the obvious fact that we are all sinners in need of grace.

Counseling in Context

Very often, young women who read my website contact me requesting help or counsel of some sort for their eating disorders. While I am happy to correspond and talk with anyone seeking assistance, the first thing I always do is direct her to speak with her pastor or pastor's wife about her problem. I also supply contact information for certified biblical counselors in her local area, if there are any. Occasionally, however, a woman tells me that she does not attend church at all. This makes meaningful counsel much more difficult, because it is operating outside of a living, caring community of believers. There is little opportunity for spiritual growth, and therefore little chance of change. Effective, godly counsel does not take place in a vacuum.

Several months ago, I was conducting weekly "counseling sessions" via Skype with a young woman who, at 23, had been in outpatient treatment for anorexia and bulimia. Because of a physical disability, she lived with her parents and was not employed. Although she had been converted as a teen at Bible camp, her parents did not attend church and so neither did she. Other than some Christian books, "Rebecca" had no teaching, no fellowship, and no one to mentor her in her walk with Christ. After just a few weeks, it became apparent to me that Rebecca's real problem had nothing to do with food—it was that she had never been discipled. I encouraged her to join a small group Bible study at a local, Bible-preaching church, but to no avail. Instead, she sought "cyber-fellowship"—by starting an online "support group" for those struggling with eating disorders.

The model we see in the New Testament Church is very different, notwithstanding the fact that the Internet had not yet been invented. In Acts 4, Luke the Evangelist describes a group of believers intimately connected and concerned for one another, a congregation "of one heart and soul" (Acts 4:32). In many of his epistles and pastoral letters to local churches, Paul reminds the believers to "encourage one another" and "admonish the unruly" (1 Thessalonians 5:11,14); help settle disputes (Philippians 4:3), and help lead those caught in sin to repentance (1 Corinthians). Effective counseling grows out of discipleship, the mentoring necessary for a new Christian to grow to maturity. Churches committed to preaching the whole counsel of God produce disciples—who can then, in turn, teach and counsel others. It should never be necessary for a Christian to seek counsel for a spiritual problem outside of the Church. Discipleship and counseling are two closely related ways in which Christ expects the Church to serve its members (Hebrews 10:24-25; 2 Timothy 2:2).

Drawing on the teaching, prayer and fellowship from among God's people is far more profitable than seeking solace in a standard group therapy circle. While para-church counseling ministries are not necessarily wrong, there are obvious advantages to meeting with someone who knows you well, cares about you, and will continue to be involved in your life after you complete "formal" counseling. Your Bible study leader or pastor's wife may be just the "Titus 2 woman" God has placed in your life. In His wisdom, God has provided all the support and encouragement we need by our side as we walk with Him—the members of His own Body.

The Church as Support Network

Reaching out to others for help and encouragement is a God-sanctioned way of overcoming besetting sin. God created us as relational beings, and equipped members of the Church with spiritual gifts in order to build one another up (Ephesians 4:12; 1 Corinthians 12:25). Scripture commands us to carry one another's burdens (Galatians 6:2) and exhorts us that when one falls down, a friend can help [her] up (Ecclesiastes 4:10). A women's Bible study, small discussion group, or prayer circle is a perfectly appropriate venue for sharing one's struggle with gluttony or other food-related sin (although of course, common sense and discretion should be used). Martha Peace encourages a woman with bulimia to get help from the elders in her church, who should instruct an older woman in the church to disciple her and hold her accountable (as well as directing her to a doctor for medical care).[49] I completely agree.

Besides prayer and counsel, the local church provides accountability. This is the mutual responsibility all Christians have to help each other grow and overcome sin. You may have both the comfort of knowing your sisters are praying for you during the week, and the anticipation that they will ask you how your week has gone at the next meeting. This is not a new concept or fad—historically, churches that take personal sanctification seriously have also emphasized mutual accountability. Small groups within a church, sometimes called "cell groups," "care groups" or "home groups," help foster this dynamic.

The purpose of small groups, within a church, is to help participants experience increasing freedom from sin and increasing resemblance to Jesus. Members grow spiritually as they confront their own sin and challenge one another to change. Pastor C.J. Mahaney sees the four clear, Scriptural goals of small groups as progressive sanctification, mutual care, fellowship, and the ministry of the Holy Spirit. "Although one's personal responsibility for sanctification remains paramount, sanctification cannot be accomplished in isolation from the local church," he writes. "Scripture clearly teaches that sanctification is intended to take place in the local church—and small groups contribute invaluably to this process."[50] Relationships with other believers help us achieve sanctification and make changes necessary to please God.

You may be thinking, "How can my Bible study leader or small group better help me than a 'real' therapist?" After all, not every woman can relate to the struggle of anorexia, bulimia, or binge eating. "Don't I need to see someone who's an 'expert' in eating disorders?" Those are fair questions, but no. It is a common misconception that some kind of 'expertise' in eating disorders is necessary in order to offer wise counsel to an anorexic or bulimic. In fact, the specific nature of the addiction is fairly irrelevant. While sin takes many outward forms, 1 Corinthians 10:13 reminds us that there is no temptation that is truly unique; they are all "common to man." God's instruction regarding "putting to death the passions of the flesh" and "crucifying the sinful nature" are general enough to apply to all sinners. That would include every attendee of a Bible study! Furthermore, a Bible study leader is by definition equipped to handle the Word and, even if inexperienced, can offer better counsel about God's will and promises than a secular therapist can.

Besides facilitating personal sanctification, small groups also create an environment where each participant may give and receive encouragement, accountability, and care. One way we do this is by praying for one another. Intercessory or group prayer is an important weapon as you fight daily against this "lust of the flesh." An eating disorder did not develop overnight, and it will not suddenly disappear once it is out in the open. You need the assurance that you are being lifted up daily by women who care. Never underestimate the power of prayer; Scripture frequently reminds us to pray with and for each other unceasingly (Matthew 6,7; 21:22; Mark 11:24; Acts 1:14; 1 Thessalonians 5:17). James reminds us that "The effective prayer of a righteous man can accomplish much." (James 5:16). Sharing your struggle within the context of a small group does not put the focus on you or your addiction. When we collectively approach God on another's behalf, we keep the focus on the answer—grace and restoration from God Himself.

"Elisa" was bulimic for over seven years. As God led her to repentance, she confessed her struggle to her pastor's wife and other members of her Wednesday morning small group. They responded by faithfully praying with and for her, and encouraging her to tell her husband. Once he knew, Elisa opened up about how frequently she bought enormous amounts of food, concealed how much she spent, and how she managed to purge undetected. "I have been meeting with my pastor's wife and she has been helping me see the deception in my heart, and how being open and honest with other people is what God wants from me," she wrote. The ladies in her small group continued not only to pray for Elisa, but also to ask her probing questions motivated by love and concern for her. Now that this dark corner of her soul was brought completely into the light, Elisa's heart and behavior began to change. The women who had so faithfully prayed for and encouraged Elisa rejoiced with her as she walked away from bulimia for good. Elisa's story testifies to the value of strong, Scripturally-based relationships among believers.

Inpatient Centers—What's the Verdict?

It is common for bulimic or anorexic women to view their eating disorder as something that's "too big" for God to handle through His Church alone. Often I am asked for advice about inpatient or residential treatment centers, and whether I think an individual should consider this option. Since there are many factors which must be considered when making such a decision, I can only point out what variables a patient needs to consider about treatment and what the Bible teaches about inward change.

Not long ago, I had coffee with a young woman who had been battling bulimia for most of her life. Although she attends a church where the Gospel is faithfully preached, I could not discern if counsel was unavailable to her or if she was concealing her battle from her leaders. I suspect the latter, as she had received clearance to go on a much-anticipated missions trip overseas. When I asked about her eating, she was clearly proud that she had only eaten a cereal bar and small piece of chicken the previous day. Restriction, in her eyes, was victory. She admitted that most days she still vomits, occasionally abuses laxatives, and had recently begun drinking vodka in the evenings "to relax." We discussed the dangers of what she is doing, and how a right understanding of the Gospel changes things. "I know you don't want to hear this, Mary[51], but you need to repent," I gently told her. "I know…but I'm not ready!" she giggled nervously.

The most amazing thing about this whole encounter, to me, is that this young lady had spent over six months each at two of the best-known Christian residential rehabilitation centers in the country, being taught and counseled daily from the Word of God. What I was telling her was not new to her—she had spent, in total, upwards of 365 days learning about repentance. Moreover, she had been in a controlled environment where she could not freely indulge her addiction without detection. Yet, even as a professing Christian, she went back to her 'drug' of choice (food), and unwisely picked up another habit as well: alcohol abuse.

I share this anecdote not as an indictment against inpatient or residential therapy, but rather to prove a point: the best-equipped, most doctrinally-sound facility in the world will not be able to help someone who does not truly desire to forsake her sin. On the other end of the spectrum, God will grant repentance and a restored life to even the most broken, desperate bulimic or anorexic who calls out to Him with nothing in her hand but a Bible and no one by her side to offer counsel. What determines total victory over an eating disorder is not so much whether you enter a facility, but rather the repentant and humble attitude of your heart. Are you willing to do things God's way? He will lead and enable you: "He leads the humble in justice, and He teaches the humble His way" (Psalm 25:9).

There are a number of Christian residential programs available, both insurance-based and free of charge, to serve candidates with various substance and behavioral addictions. Typically, these facilities accept teens and young adults with eating disorders, unplanned pregnancies, alcohol and drug addiction, sexual abuse histories, homosexual tendencies, and other self-destructive habits such as "cutting." There are residential biblical counseling centers which are rooted in Scripture and uphold a high view of God. Vision of Hope (located on the Faith Baptist Church campus in Indiana) is one such facility (see addendum for more information). Sound, reliable Christian help is available, and can be found outside the church walls for addicts who are truly ready to repent.

Be forewarned, however, that many eating disorder clinics, while claiming to implement a Christian worldview, subscribe more to the behavioral models of the psych fields than to Scripture. Some well-known inpatient facilities boast an implausibly high success rate among anorexics and bulimics who complete their programs, although many of their patients seem to return to the programs after release. "Success" is a subjective and ill-defined concept for the staff of these counseling centers, who steadfastly cling to the theories that external factors are largely at fault for their clients' eating disorders. The high rate of attrition among patients would seem to indicate that deeper, spiritual needs are going unmet.

Residential Programs vs. Medical Facilities

Inpatient centers vary in what needs they are equipped to meet. The medical severity of the eating disorder, as well as the patient's overall condition, are two important criteria to consider when looking at whether residential treatment is an appropriate option. Is the patient medically unstable? Is she severely underweight? Does she have electrolyte imbalances? If so, hospitalization or a medically staffed inpatient center might be a better option (at least initially) than a long-term Christian residential program. There is a definite medical rationale for severely malnourished eating disordered patients to be admitted to facilities. The critical care and 24-hour monitoring of their vital signs cannot be guaranteed in outpatient settings, and in this sense, inpatient centers fill a legitimate need. A physician can best determine what type of medical intervention is necessary (if any), based on blood profile, kidney function tests, weight loss, frequency of purging, and other factors. Anorexia and bulimia have frighteningly high mortality rates, and 20% of people suffering from anorexia die prematurely from complications related to their eating disorder. When your life is at stake, hospitalization is the best option.

Long-term residential programs, on the other hand, are aimed at helping the participants identify deep-seated patterns of sin in their hearts which have led to the eating disordered behavior. The focus is on changing their behavior through renewing their minds and hearts. Inward, lasting, spiritual change is the goal– not medical intervention. As part of ongoing individual counseling, a young anorexic or bulimic might spend several weeks just coming to understand her purpose in life (to glorify and enjoy God). Basic discipleship then gives way to identifying the progression of idolatry in her heart (Deuteronomy 4:1-24; 5:8; Romans 1:18-25). Finally, the counselee is ready to see how sinful actions become sinful habits; subsequently, how these habits become life dominating (Romans 7:14-25). A big part of counseling long-term residents, especially in the beginning of counseling, consists of helping them to be truth tellers, to be authentic, and to be transparent.

Group Therapy vs. Building Up the Body

Group therapy started in the 1960's, and has taken on many forms since. At the time, Adams wrote: "I now have come to the conclusion that such group activity is unscriptural and therefore harmful."[52] Quoting atheist psychiatrist Mowrer, Adams concludes that group therapy symbolically offers a "personal atonement for sin" which degenerates into "story swapping."[53]

If we are talking about what is commonly known as group

therapy, I would offer a qualified assent. The standard model of "chairs-in-a-circle, everyone-share-your-feelings-and-validate-one-another's-experiences" does nothing more than give a bulimic a social network of sympathetic peers with whom to commiserate. Sometimes group therapy helps the girl to hold onto a label such as "cutter" or "bulimic," etc. instead of prompting her to give it up in order to embrace a better one: "Christ follower" and "God lover." At worst, she picks up new tips on effective purging and tricks on fooling the doctor at the weigh-ins. In my experience, group therapy (even when led by an "eating disorder expert") is a subtle way for women with eating disorders to encourage one another in their thinking and behavior, while creating an "us versus them" victim mindset. This is especially true on the college campus, where many of the young women have been mandated to attend such meetings against their will.

Notwithstanding these drawbacks, in the context of a Scripturally sound environment, education and growth can occur in a small-group context. Identifying common patterns of sin and temptation and learning how to please God is one way in which the Body "grows and builds itself up in love" (Ephesians 4:16). Jocelyn Wallace, Executive Director at Vision of Hope, affirms that while a group dynamic is not ideal for counseling, being taught as a group is often helpful and encouraging. "There is a lot to be said for someone struggling with a similar issue being able to get encouragement from each other. In general we steer away from group therapy because counseling life–dominating sins is such a personal thing. Drug abusers generally use for a multitude of reasons and it is easier to make the counseling applicable if they're only dealing with their "stuff." On top of that there's just issues like gossip, slander, etc. that become so much easier if counseling is done in front of other people."

Given these caveats, she continues: "Now, just because group therapy may not work for counseling I don't think you should discount that group education would be helpful. There is probably going to be a lot of encouragement from realizing other people with the same temptations are using certain principles and truths to deal with problems that are common to that group. There is a lot to be said for someone struggling with a similar issue being able to get encouragement from each other." This type of interaction, when done in a spirit of repentance and a desire to obey God, is exactly the sort of "building up" Paul encouraged: "Therefore encourage one another and build each other up, just as in fact you are doing" (1 Thessalonians 5:11). When members of the Body come alongside one another, that is the most effective form of "group therapy" there is.

When "Support" Goes Wrong

Talking about our feelings and swapping testimonies has no therapeutic or restorative value. Some meetings tend to be very man-centered, rather than Christ-centered—even the so-called "Christian" support groups. The 12-step programs, which have been overwhelmingly popular among addicts of all stripes, focus more on the steps themselves than on God. Even when the ambiguous term "Higher Power" is conceded to be the God of the Bible, He is delegated to a backseat role in the patient's "recovery." This low view of God portrays Him more as cheerleader than omnipotent Redeemer. The Bible is displaced by the humanistic Little Black Book, and the sufficiency of Scripture is augmented by Alcoholics Anonymous'[54] works-based dogma.

John Lanagan, a freelance writer who has researched the spiritual roots of AA in great depth, writes:

Unfortunately, it is the Christians who are being "evangelized" as they are exposed to AA's inherent universalism. Christians both in AA and in groups such as 'Celebrate Recovery' are greatly influenced by 12 Step theology. According to the Alcoholics Anonymous Big Book (the AA "bible"),

"We found that God does not make too hard terms with those who seek Him. To us, the Realm of the Spirit is broad, roomy, all-inclusive; never exclusive or forbidding to those who earnestly seek. It is open, we believe, to all men. When, therefore, we speak to you of God, we mean your own conception of God."

Well, that sounds very loving and reasonable. Yet Christ Himself warns us against such a thing. Jesus said to him, I am the way, and the truth, and the life; no man comes to the Father but through me. (John 14:6). The Lord, in fact, specifically warns against the broad way. "Enter through the narrow gate; for the gate is wide and the way is BROAD that leads to destruction, and there are many who enter through it." (Matthew 7:13). Nor is there any reference in the 12 Steps to sin or repentance. There are terms that are close, allowing Christians to believe this is what they are dealing with, just as many believe the "God as we understood Him" in Step 3 was originally Christ. AA's 12 Steps suggest the alcoholic deal with "shortcomings," "moral inventory," "defects of character," "wrongs," and "making amends." Millions of unsaved people have come to believe they are right with God and man because of the Steps.[55]

There is no mention of Christ, no definition of sin, no emphasis placed on biblical repentance, and no offer of salvation inherent in the 12-Step creed. The program's spirituality may appear to mimic Christianity on the surface, but its advocates often are "holding to a form of godliness, although they have denied its power; Avoid such men as these" (2 Timothy 3:5). Because of the unbiblical answer offered to sin, I believe that Christians should avoid 12-step groups.

Countless former addicts (although they will never refer to themselves as 'former' addicts, conceding only that they are "in recovery') credit the 12-step programs for helping them get their lives back on track. I maintain that any program may help an addict change her behavior, if she wants to badly enough, but not every program is going to lead them into greater intimacy with God, teach them to renew their minds according to His revealed truth, or develop the fruit of the Spirit. As we saw in the last chapter, learning to modify your behavior is not the same thing as total victory over a life-dominating sin. The two main principles of restoration I laid out in Chapters 5 and 6, spending time in the Bible and seeking God in the prayer closet, are not emphasized (if they are mentioned at all) in a typical eating disorder support group. In a Bible-believing church, these spiritual disciplines are taught as foundational to true transformation.

Dr. Mark Shaw, founder of Truth in Love Ministries and author of *The Heart of Addiction* writes:

> In a group setting, "self-help" meetings, which are often devoid of the Word of God and the leading of the Holy Spirit, are like the blind leading the blind. Eventually, you are going to fall into a ditch or walk off a cliff. Turn to your pastor, elders, biblical counselors, and trusted Christian friends for support, help, accountability and counseling. God ordained the Church to do His work, and helping you to overcome addiction is included. Matthew 16:18b quotes Jesus Who says that He is the foundational rock for God's church: "I will build my church, and the gates of hell shall not prevail against it." Addiction feels like hell on earth. You must utilize God's church in overcoming addiction because it is an integral part of His plan.[56]

"So what should I do?"

As you repent from your eating disorder and "put on" new ways of living, the first place you should turn for support and counsel is your local church. Many Bible-believing churches either counsel as part of their overall ministry, or may refer you to another local church that does. If you cannot connect with an appropriate, trained biblical counselor through your local church, check NANC's website for a full listing of all their certified counselors. (See addendum for more information). If, after speaking with your pastor (and parents, if you are a minor) you feel that you would best be able to overcome your eating disorder in a controlled, residential facility, you might choose to look into Vision of Hope or a similar program.

If you are severely underweight or otherwise medically at risk, referral to a medical inpatient facility may save your life. Even after your weight and physical health stabilize, however, you will still need to confront the idolatry in your heart that has lead to this addiction. God's transforming work in your life will be an ongoing process. Fortunately, He has provided all the help, support, and counsel you need through both His Word and members of His Body, the Church. While it may be an appropriate option for you to seek admittance at a residential biblical counseling center, it is by no means the only option. Those who deepen their relationships with God and repent in a residential facility are also free to find Him at home—God promises that all who truly seek will find Him (Matthew 7:8; Luke 11:10). Seek counsel at your local church first; discern whether or not you can be counseled in your home environment. Living out the biblical principles you learn, whether from a local biblical counselor or one at a center, is something that must take place wherever you are. Your regular, home environment presents the "real life" situation in which you must learn to grow, change, and glorify God.

Do not be afraid to reveal your "dark secret" to an appropriate individual at church (someone in a position to mentor you). Without fail, women I have counseled tell me of the great relief they experienced when their revelations were met with love and compassion, rather than the disgust and judgment they feared from "church people." God uses the members of His Church to help one another deal with temptations, trials and even life-dominating sins in His way. Small groups are one specific way in which our relationships with other believers help us pursue holiness. One-on-one counsel with a trained biblical counselor, ministering through her local church or a biblical counseling center, is another. Like Elisa, you, too, may know the joy of freedom as the Lord uses members of His own Body to help you overcome your eating disorder. As you grow in fellowship with those keeping you accountable, you will mature in your relationship with God and He promises your life will be genuinely transformed. As His power is thus perfected in your weakness, (2 Corinthians 12:9), God will be glorified.

Danger Lurking Online

With the Internet age, women with eating disorders are increasingly reaching out into cyber-space for "support" and counsel. I have personally seen the danger of this: "Christian" online programs designed to overcome food-related sins are rarely, if ever, doctrinally-sound. Bulletin board forums become the cyber-equivalent of "group therapy"—a group of strangers "sharing" and promising to pray to each other, with no Scriptural exhortation or commitment to change. An even more sinister version of "support" has developed: pro-eating disorder forums. In these so-called "Ana and Mia" chat rooms and forums, young women buoy and applaud each other's dangerous behavior and post "thinspiration" photos of emaciated models. The trend has alarmed many parents and even been reported by the media, who pressure webmasters to remove the sites. Still, the micro-culture grows. Applauding and justifying a self-destructive lifestyle under the guise of "support" is tantamount to enabling sinful rebellion, and is categorically unwise. The book of Proverbs warns us against such self-styled counsel:

"The way of a fool is right in his own eyes, But a wise man is he who listens to counsel" (Proverbs 12:15).

"He who trusts in his own heart is a fool, But he who walks wisely will be delivered" (Proverbs 28:26).

Chapter 11
A Biblical Approach to Dealing with Abuse

We have already seen in our discussion of biblical counseling how Jesus, while sympathetic to human weaknesses, (Hebrews 4:15), does not allow us to use our past or current circumstances to justify sin. We are not to rationalize continuing on in a dangerous or self-destructive lifestyle because of what others have done to us. The biblical approach to sin is always "stop it"! Whatever it takes, the sin must be "cut off" in order for us to enjoy fellowship with God. Resist the devil, flee temptation, put on the full armor of God to withstand the enemy, be aware of the devil's schemes and pray unceasingly; but don't let your past abuse keep you enslaved to sin.

Now that we know not to use old wounds or abuse as an excuse for our behavior, how are we to view our pasts? What is God's answer to abuse, and is there anything good that can come out of it? Do we just need to "forgive and forget"? Is God unsympathetic? Let's consider these questions next.

When Sin Begets Sin
Let's consider the biblical figure of a young woman—a true victim of sexual abuse—to see if we can find a biblical precedent for "sin loopholes." In 2 Samuel 13, we meet Tamar, King David's daughter. Because he had at least eight wives, King David's children had different mothers. One of his sons, Amnon, lusted after his half-sister Tamar and raped her. This violent action was completely non-consensual and it devastated Tamar, who had been a virgin. Her prospects

for marriage were destroyed. Verse 20 tells us that she lived in her brother Absalom's house (presumably until the end of her life), "a desolate woman." She had committed no sin. The Bible gives no indication that she developed an eating disorder or any other addiction as a result of being violated, only that she was "disgraced" through no fault of her own and lived in despair. However, given what the Bible says elsewhere about the "lusts of the flesh," (excessive drinking and other vices), it seems doubtful that Tamar would have been excused if she had sought solace in such addictive behavior.

In fact, even given the heinous circumstances of the crime, her brother Absalom clearly sinned by taking vengeance into his own hands and murdering Amnon. For his part, King David sinned by not exacting judicial authority—his own daughter was raped by one of his sons, and the king does nothing? After Absalom killed his brother, he fled to Geshur (v. 38) and King David fell into a deep depression because he missed his son and desperately wanted to see him. After they were finally reunited, in Chapter 15, Absalom conspired to overthrow his own father and procure the loyalty of the populace. His treachery necessitated David's fleeing Jerusalem for his own safety.

King David truly had one of the most "dysfunctional" families in the Bible, but many of his problems could have been prevented if he had confronted sin (his own or someone else's) in time. After Tamar is raped, we see "sin giving birth to death" in a literal fashion. Absalom commits vigilante justice, thinking Amnon's heinous abuse of Tamar excused it. In God's economy, however, circumstances never justify more sin. This includes cases of abuse—verbal, physical, or sexual.

Sexual Abuse

It is not uncommon for women with eating disorders to have been victims of abuse in their early lives, sexual abuse in particular. Studies on the supposed connection between abuse and food addiction have produced conflicting data, and cannot be considered conclusive. Still, the percentage of eating disorder patients in the United States who have reported physical or sexual abuse is twice as high as among the general population. Since there appears to be a correlation between childhood sexual abuse and later eating disordered behavior, bulimia in particular, it makes sense to examine the connection as best we can in the light of Scripture.

A victim of abuse develops intense shame and a feeling of irreversible "dirtiness," although she had no blame in whatever happened. These painful memories are carried around, festering within, with no resolution. As we saw back in chapter 2, shame can stem either from our own sin, or being sinned against. CCEF counselor Winston Smith writes:

> We trod through a fallen world. We tramp through the mess of our own sin and we've been smeared by the sinful deeds of others. We are rebellious. We are wounded. We are proud. We are ashamed. We need all of it washed away. Jesus insists that we accept him as God who kneels before us in love and humility to cleanse, forgive, and restore us.[57]

While the shame and anger provoked by a history of sexual abuse may be a contributing factor, the abuse *per se* does not cause anyone to develop an eating disorder. The answer to the shame generated by any kind of abuse is found in the Person of Christ. As I noted in the introduction to this book, Jesus Christ began His earthly Messianic ministry by quoting the promise made about Himself in Isaiah 61: "He has sent me to bind up the brokenhearted, to proclaim liberty to captives And freedom to prisoners...to comfort all who mourn...giving them a garland instead of ashes, the oil of gladness instead of mourning, the mantle of praise instead of a spirit of fainting…" (Isaiah 61:1-3)

Dr. Laura Hendrickson, a biblical counselor who is herself an abuse survivor, points out that the Lord's covenant promise to His shamed children may be found a few verses later: "Instead of your shame you will have a double portion, And instead of humiliation they will shout for joy over their portion. Therefore they will possess a double portion in their land, Everlasting joy will be theirs" (Isaiah 61:7). Laura says, "The Lord reminded me through this passage that He's with me, to comfort and heal me, and that the day will come when I'll never struggle with shame again, but instead will rejoice. He calls me to wait in faith for that day (Psalm 27:14)."

Being excessively controlled by those who are supposed to be protectors will evoke intensely angry and even vengeful emotions in a person. An attitude of mistrust towards authority develops, and abuse victims sometimes develop a skewed, inaccurate view of God. Rather than cry out to Him, a common human response is to rely on one's own resources to deal with pain. Bulimics "anesthetize" or comfort themselves with food, much as a drinker seeks solace in the bottle and a cocaine addict in freebasing. If these illicit means of obtaining relief and sinful thoughts of revenge are not taken captive and redirected biblically, they will fester and intensify. While anger that the abuse happened is certainly justified, developing an addiction is never a godly response.

The Great Physician's Healing

While God's holiness prohibits us from using painful memories to rationalize our sin, His love gives us the courage to heal. Why does this take courage? Because by allowing Him to restore us, we are trusting that His love is really enough to sustain us. We can drop the familiar "security blanket" of an addiction (which never provided any lasting comfort, anyway) and rest securely in His love. In the depths of our pain, no matter how bad or humiliating those memories may be, it is enormously helpful to know that God understands.

Psalm 94 assures us that He sees abuse. For reasons we cannot now understand, He sovereignly permitted it to happen in order to make us more and more like His Son. Obedience to the precepts laid out in His Word is His loving answer to our pain and our only source of lasting joy. God has never promised to protect us from suffering in this life, but He has promised to be with us through earthly trials and to be our Comforter (Psalm 71:21; Psalm 119:50-52; Isaiah 12:1, 49:13; Matt. 5:4; 2 Cor. 1:3-6, 7:6).

The Man of Sorrows

By taking on human flesh in His incarnation, the Lord Jesus chose to fully identify with us. He has lived through the entire range of emotions and experience that are common to all humans. He is certainly no stranger to verbal or physical abuse. We will never experience the depths of His humiliation on Calvary, which He endured in order to remove both the full weight of our sins and the shame associated with them. Any Christian may take great comfort in knowing that Jesus truly does understand what it feels like to be treated unjustly, because He's been there. Even today, the mocking continues. Many more revile and despise the King of Kings in His physical absence from this earth than worship and submit to Him as Lord and Savior.

Even long before His suffering and death, Jesus bore what seemed to be an unceasing tirade of verbal abuse and harassment from other people. It started with His own family. The gospels record that Mary and Joseph had four sons after Jesus was born (named James, Joses, Simon and Jude; see Matt. 15:35) and at least two sisters. Scripture doesn't record how His sisters reacted at the onset of Jesus' public preaching, but it clearly states His own brothers didn't believe in Him (John 7:5). His family tried to terminate His ministry, thinking Jesus had gone crazy (Mark 3:20-21). At one point, His brothers became sarcastic, trying to bait Jesus into showing off with a few miracles up in Judea during a major holiday: "Now the feast of the Jews, the Feast of Booths, was near. Therefore His brothers said to Him, 'Leave here and go into Judea, so that Your disciples also may see Your works which You are doing. For no one does anything in secret when he himself seeks to be known publicly. If You do these things, show Yourself to the world.' For not even His brothers were believing in Him" (John 7:2-5).

Somehow, the barbs and undeserved taunts from our families seem to cut the deepest. Jesus knows all too well what it is to be rejected by one's own family. When I became a Christian in 1990, both of my parents mocked my faith—my father more openly; my mother in a more covert, passive-aggressive way. As a new Christian, my mother told me that I was a "deep disappointment" to her for "leaving the religion in which [I] was raised." It was a surreal choice—obedience to the Lord Jesus Christ's command to be born again (John 3:3; 1 Peter 1:23) brought yet more scorn from my family. I am thankful that my Savior is well acquainted with every type of mocking, and He has promised to reward those who endure such derision for His sake. He Himself not only endured, but the patience, humility and gentleness He demonstrated while still confronting His brothers' sin (John 7:7) ultimately bore fruit. Immediately after His resurrection, we find those same brothers and Jesus' mother gathered with His disciples "continually devoting themselves to prayer" (Acts 1:14). James and Jude even went on to write books of the New Testament.

The Lord also had to deal with the constant barrage of slander from the religious establishment. The two predominant Jewish religious parties of the day seemed to tag-team harassing the Galilean Preacher. The Sadducees were the liberal, upper-class sect who controlled the balance of power in the Sanhedrin. The Pharisees were the uber-conservative traditionalists who hated Jesus' grace-filled message. Both groups considered His claims of deity to be blasphemous, and are recorded as repeatedly "testing" Jesus. Much of John's gospel reflects a verbal back-and-forth in which they try to provoke Jesus into an argument. Our Lord is no stranger to verbal abuse, and He can best counsel us on how to respond to it in a God-honoring way. The writer of Hebrews exhorts believers persecuted for their faith, "For consider Him who has endured such hostility by sinners against Himself, so that you will not grow weary and lose heart." (Hebrews 12:3). Knowing that the King Himself is acquainted personally with every type of abuse should bring great comfort to us, His servants.

How, then, are we to respond to abuse; and what does this have to do with overcoming eating disorders?

Christ warned us to anticipate abuse for being His disciples (Matthew 5:11, 24:9; Luke 21:12; John 15:20) and it is reasonable to expect we will be mistreated unfairly for lesser reasons (or no reason at all). Everyone suffers mistreatment at the hands of another at one time or another, and it is unrealistic to think that we will somehow be exempt. But too often, those of us who have developed addictions use the past abuse as a "crutch" to somehow rationalize our anger and self-destructive habit. Or, we buy into the lie that 'since it's not my fault, my eating disorder must be a by-product of the abuse I suffered." The Bible teaches that anger can sometimes be an appropriate, even righteous response to injustice (Matthew 18:34; Mark 3:5) when God's glory is being debased, but that it can more often be a snare and we are never to use it as an excuse to sin (Psalm 4:4; Ephesians 4:26-27; James 1:20). There are several general principles which we see running all throughout Scripture:

1. We are not to pay back or take revenge. This is probably fairly obvious to most Christians, although in our "flesh" revenge is the most automatic response. Someone slaps us; we

instinctively slap back. Our Father has a much higher standard of behavior for His children:

"You shall not take vengeance, nor bear any grudge against the sons of your people, but you shall love your neighbor as yourself; I am the LORD." (Leviticus 19:18)

"Never take your own revenge, beloved, but leave room for the wrath of God, for it is written, "VENGEANCE IS MINE, I WILL REPAY," says the Lord." (Romans 12:19)

"You have heard that it was said, 'AN EYE FOR AN EYE, AND A TOOTH FOR A TOOTH.' But I say to you, do not resist an evil person; but whoever slaps you on your right cheek, turn the other to him also. If anyone wants to sue you and take your shirt, let him have your coat also." (Matthew 5:38-40)[58]

For we know Him who said, "VENGEANCE IS MINE, I WILL REPAY" And again, "THE LORD WILL JUDGE HIS PEOPLE." (Hebrews 10:30)

God makes it clear repeatedly throughout Scripture, both Old Testament and New, that He will deal with unrepentant sinners—in His own way and timing. It is not for us to preemptively strike. While it seems to defy justice that He delays so long in exacting vengeance, 2 Peter 3:9 explains that it is only because of His great mercy and desire to give sinners ample opportunity to repent that He restrains judgment. If He, Who is infinitely holy, is so enduringly patient with sinners (including us, lest we forget that apart from Christ, we have the same standing as the unregenerate), we should likewise exercise patience and resist the opportunity to "slap back."

Since most offenses we deal with are of the personal variety, it is important to realize that God gives us no justification for repaying such affronts in kind. The "eye for an eye" Levitical command was given to prevent civic justice from becoming excessive; it was never intended to be perverted into a rule in cases of personal vengeance. It was this misapplication that

Jesus was addressing in Matthew 5:38 when He laid down the Law of love. Rest assured, God will right every wrong.

An Eternal Perspective

Thinking about where our unsaved abusers are headed if their hearts remain stubborn should make us tremble. An eternity of torment, separated from God, is a fate I would not wish on my worst enemy—no matter how vilely he or she had behaved on earth. The greatest obstacle in the unrepentant sinner's heart is pride. No one wants to see his own sinfulness from God's vantage point, and mankind desperately wants to believe he can be good on his own merits. Many people believe, in the deceitfulness of their own lying and manipulative hearts, that they are "good people" and good works (combined with ecclesiastic rituals) will earn their way into heaven—despite the Bible's clear teaching to the contrary. It is under this deception that many people live until God supernaturally opens their eyes.

The beautiful paradox of the Gospel is that while no one can have a change of heart and turn to God unless the Holy Spirit draws Him (John 6:44), repentance is a gift extended freely to all (John 3:16; 6:37). God has chosen and predestined those whom He will save (Romans 8:30; Ephesians 1:11), but calls all to a saving faith in Him to have eternal life (John 3:15; Acts 13:26; Romans 10:11-13). We cannot know when or if our abusers will repent. Whether they confess their wrongdoing and repent of it or not, God has promised to deal with them—either in mercy, or in judgment. We are simply to stay out of it and trust Him.

2. We are to pray for our abusers. It may seem relatively simple not to attempt revenge—if not out of the fear of God, at least fear of governing authorities might be enough to keep us from doing any real damage! But pray for those who have wronged us? Everything in our human nature screams against it. But Christ, the ultimate example of an intercessor

for the undeserving, was crystal clear:

"But I say to you, love your enemies and pray for those who persecute you" (Matthew 5:44).

"But I say to you who hear, love your enemies, do good to those who hate you, bless those who curse you, pray for those who mistreat you" (Luke 6:27-28).

But Jesus was saying, "Father, forgive them; for they do not know what they are doing." And they cast lots, dividing up His garments among themselves" (Luke 23:34).

Even Stephen, while being stoned to death, prayed for his murderers:

"Then falling on his knees, he cried out with a loud voice, 'Lord, do not hold this sin against them!' Having said this, he fell asleep" (Acts 7:60).

Since God's forgiveness is conditional upon repentance, both Stephen's prayer and that of Christ on the Cross were implicit pleas for the Holy Spirit to open spiritually blind eyes. They were pleading with God to grant their murderers repentance unto salvation. Fifteen hundred years later, another martyr made a similar petition. As William Tyndale was burned at the stake for translating and circulating the Bible, his last prayer was, "Lord, open the king of England's eyes." Three years later, God did indeed honor Tyndale's intercession when King Henry VIII required every English church to make a copy of the English Bible available to parishioners.

Jesus instructs us to "bless" those who curse us. Since we're already praying for them anyway, we may as well pray for good things to come upon them—that is a way of "blessing" them. When our "enemies" or abusers do not know the Lord, the only meaningful blessing we can pray over them is that God would lead them to repentance. Persisting in prayer on behalf of others pleases God, and often He grants salvation to people after years of someone else's fervent intercession.

The Power of Intercession

James 5:16 exhorts us, "Therefore, confess your sins to one another, and pray for one another so that you may be healed. The effective prayer of a righteous man can accomplish much." In context, James is acknowledging that physical illness may be connected to underlying sin, and he encourages examining one's conscience to see if there is a connection. Confessing it to the elders who intercede for him effects healing, which comes from God. The Greek word used for 'healed', also rendered 'restored' in some translations, is *sozo,* which deals with spiritual healing as well as physical (as does its Hebrew equivalent, "raphe"). The word can also mean 'save'. Clearly James is not talking about simply organic illness here. We're also to pray for one another's healing from our common 'spiritual disease'—sin.

The Bible is clear that without repentance before God, there can be no redemption. That is why when we are praying for a non-Christian, first and foremost we are asking God to lead the person to repentance unto salvation (2 Corinthians 7:10). He or she must first see his need for a Savior. Until our "enemy" sees the utterly lost state of his or her depraved, sin-sick soul, he or she will remain blind and utterly incapable of repenting. When we are the injured party, often all we can focus on is the wrong that was done to us. We lose sight of the fact that in any sin, the far greater crime is actually against God. Anything that has been done to us pales in comparison to sin's magnitude against a holy and just God. Whether an individual regrets (or even recognizes) an offense against us is inconsequential in the eternal picture. What matters is that our enemies come to see their hopeless, sin-infested estate through God's eyes, and bow the knee to Him before it is too late. Apart from Christ, temporal blessings are meaningless.

We cannot coerce anyone to come to faith. We cannot force that "godly sorrow" for wronging us or wronging God, but we can pray that the Holy Spirit will soften their hearts. This Spirit-led conviction is especially needed in the case of unsaved "religious" people. As my pastor often says, "Sometimes you need to get folks 'unsaved' before you can get them saved!" As of this writing, my husband and I are still the only Christians from either side of our family. Although we have shared the Gospel repeatedly with our parents and continue to pray that God will draw them to salvation, it is not realistic to expect them to react as disciples of Christ would in a conflict. Also, remember that many people have depended on a works-based righteousness for so long that they literally cannot grasp what Isaiah meant when he penned, "...For all of us have become like one who is unclean, and all our righteous deeds are like a filthy garment; and all of us wither like a leaf, and our iniquities, like the wind, take us away." (Isaiah 64:6; emphasis mine). This offended the self-righteous religious devotees of Jesus' day, and it still does in ours.

3.) We are to confront our abuser(s). While bitterness and revenge are not biblical ways of handling our abusers, confrontation is. Christ and Paul both laid out some very specific guidelines on how to confront wrongdoing biblically and repair personal relationships:

"If your brother sins, go and show him his fault in private; if he listens to you, you have won your brother. But if he does not listen to you, take one or two more with you, so that BY THE MOUTH OF TWO OR THREE WITNESSES EVERY FACT MAY BE CONFIRMED. If he refuses to listen to them, tell it to the church; and if he refuses to listen even to the church, let him be to you as a Gentile and a tax collector." (Matthew 18:15-17)

"If anyone does not obey our instruction in this letter, take special note of that person and do not associate with him, so that he will be put to shame. Yet do not regard him as an enemy, but admonish him as a brother." (2 Thessalonians 3:14-15)

"Reject a factious man after a first and second warning, knowing that such a man is perverted and is sinning, being self-condemned." (Titus 3:10-11)

To be sure, these passages (especially the Pauline exhortations) are most commonly used to prevent divisiveness in a local Body of believers. Congregations which practice church discipline refer to the practice of escalating confrontation as "the Matthew 18 process." Church discipline is the application of biblical practice to maintain order (and prevent scandal) within the Body of Christ, and therefore only applies to believers. A Christian submits to the authority of his local church when he becomes a member, and understands that God has prescribed the process in order to keep His Church's witness pure and make reconciliation possible. However, it is equally clear that the principle of righteous confrontation can be applied to personal relationships among Christians. When there is disharmony, God does not want us to stew in silence—which very often breeds bitterness. Jesus' command in Matthew 5:23-24 makes this clear: "Therefore if you are presenting your offering at the altar, and there remember that your brother has something against you, leave your offering there before the altar and go; first be reconciled to your brother, and then come and present your offering."

The guiding principle in our relationships with others is to be love. Love for one another is what should mark us as Christians (John 13:35; Romans 12:10; 1 Peter 1:22). When we need to confront, or are confronted for an offense against another (real or perceived), our attitude should be of concern for the relationship and a desire for reconciliation. Generally, we shrink from going to another and rectifying the situation because we are conditioned to think that confrontation is nasty, mean, or unchristian. It can be, if we are not submitted to the Holy Spirit's guidance and only care about our "rights" being violated. However, using Christ's guidelines for clearing the air is the best way to restore damaged relationships within the Church, and can also be applied, to some extent, to our relationships with non-Christians.

What if our "enemy" or "brother" refuses to listen to us (i.e., repent of his wrongdoing against us)? We already know from Scripture that we are not to retaliate in anger or vengeance. (Retaliation would include gossip, even if our grievance is justified. Gossip that is true is still gossip). If the offending party we confront remains hard-hearted, there can never be true reconciliation. The goal of confrontation is always resolution and ultimately restored fellowship, but when the offending party refuses to change his or her ways, this is not possible.

What does this look like in real life? We get an idea by taking the Bible as a whole—Jesus and Paul instruct a break in relationship with the offender, but not mistreatment. Jesus says to "treat them like a tax collector or a pagan." In the context of Church discipline, reaching this final step in attempted resolution would mean removing the unrepentant party from the Church. In family situations where the offender is not saved anyway, appealing to ecclesiastical authority is pointless. However, unless estrangement is absolutely necessary (such as in cases of violence, threats of violence or danger of physical abuse), it is not God's will. You cannot evangelize someone if you refuse to speak to him or her. Proverbs 25 instructs: "If your enemy is hungry, give him food to eat; and if he is thirsty, give him water to drink; for you will heap burning coals on his head, and the LORD will reward you." (v. 21-22). While He alone knows when and how He will grant repentance, He expects His children to be willing vessels of His grace.

Charles Spurgeon once preached,

> Brother, the most splendid vengeance you can ever have is to do good to them who do you evil, and to speak well of them who speak ill of you. They will be ashamed to look

at you; they will never hurt you again if they see that you cannot be provoked except to greater love and larger kindness.[59]

How did Jesus relate to tax collectors and pagans? He didn't shun them, but He didn't seek them out for fellowship, either, unless it was for the purpose of converting them. Of course, some were drawn by His witness and repented (like Matthew, the tax collector who became an apostle and later a Gospel writer). There is no record of Jesus mistreating anyone in the Gospels, and since His followers are repeatedly told to treat the wicked with kindness, it is safe to assume that rule applies here, too.

The Gospels record Jesus as accepting dinner invitations from His antagonists—the Pharisees. It is unknown whether His host in Luke 7, Simon, was a believer or not, but the context implies there were many there who wished to trap Him and hang Him on His own words. What a tense meal that must have been! Nevertheless, Jesus had no interest in self-protection. He actually used the dinners as teaching opportunities—"lifestyle evangelism" at its finest. (See Luke 7:36-50, 11:37-54). Even though they opposed Him, Jesus continued to witness and offer them reconciliation right up until Wednesday of Passion Week. The fact that they rejected the Gospel (the ultimate message of repentance and reconciliation) grieved Him greatly.

Selective Confrontation

Often, there is simply no point in bringing up many personal slights and old wounds. The Bible makes it clear that it is better to suffer abuse than to defend ourselves. Furthermore, very often we remember old grievances with remarkable clarity long after the offender has forgotten it. In most cases, where the wrong was against only ourselves, Scripture tells us it is better to "cover" the sin by simply not bringing it up

(Proverbs 10:12, 17:9; 1 Peter 4:8). We are not to keep a record of wrongs suffered (1 Corinthians 13:5). Abusive rhetoric? Passive-aggressive comments? The Christ-like reaction is to "let it go."

Christians should be prepared to suffer wrong rather than cause reproach. When I think of a gracious response and the ultimate "covering" (as opposed to confrontation), I recall Christ's first post-resurrection words to the disciples in the Upper Room, after they had all abandoned Him in Gethsemane: "Peace be with you." (If someone pulled a stunt like that on me, you'd better believe they'd be hearing about it!) Although the disciples were certainly repentant, we have no reason to believe Jesus brought up their cowardice to shame or confront them. He graciously forgave and instantly restored. That is to be our model, insofar as it depends on us (Romans 12:18).

However, there are times when you need to confront someone who has sinned against you, either because of the seriousness or duration of the abuse. In his book, *The Freedom and Power of Forgiveness,* John Macarthur sets forth the following guidelines for when confrontation is necessary, and the situation must be set right for forgiveness to be extended:

> If you observe a serious offense that is a sin against someone other than you, confront the offender. Justice does not permit a Christian to cover a sin against someone else. I can unilaterally and unconditionally forgive a personal offense when I am the victim, because it is I who then bears the wrong. But when I see that someone else has been sinned against, it is my duty to seek justice. (Exodus 23:6; Deut. 16:20; Isaiah 1:17; Isaiah 59:15-16; Jeremiah 22:3; Lam. 3:35-36.)

> When ignoring an offense might hurt the offender, con-

frontation is required. (Gal. 6:1-2).

When a sin is scandalous or otherwise potentially damaging to the Body of Christ, confrontation is essential. (Hebrews 12:15).

When there is a broken relationship between Christians, both parties have a responsibility to seek reconciliation (Luke 17:3; Matt. 5:23-24). [60]

Additionally, if a crime has been committed, the police may need to be involved. Romans 13:1 states: "Every person is to be in subjection to the governing authorities, for there is no authority except from God, and those which exist are established by God." In the case of a felony or misdemeanor, it is not necessarily our right to simply "overlook" an offense.

The other person's response is not for you to worry about; just trust God to be in control of the whole situation. As long as you are being obedient, that is all He asks of you. Praying first and rehearsing what you will say to the other person is the best way to proceed. Treat "abusers" in your life with kindness. Pray daily for their salvation. If you have done your part in attempting biblical reconciliation, the rest is up to them.

When you have an addiction, there are often many people whom you have hurt in one way or another, and you should try and make amends as best you can. Let the other party(ies) know that you have repented of whatever bondage held you, but seeking forgiveness should be as specific as possible. Confession should not go beyond those directly affected by the sin, and third party discussions of your eating disorder are inappropriate. A pastor once said, "General repentance brings general forgiveness." If another sister is holding a grudge against you over something you said, let her know that you repent of whatever it was that hurt her

(if she continues to nurse the grudge, she is herself now sinning; that is between her and God). The freedom that comes
with "getting it off our chest" and being forgiven by others is
exhilarating, and goes a long way in our restoration. One of
the keys in recovery from eating disorders, as in other addictions, is forgiveness—both receiving it and extending it.

4.) We must be willing to forgive our abusers. This is probably the hardest command we've been given in dealing with
those who have mistreated us, because it's purely a heart issue. The other three principles—not retaliating, praying for
the abuser, and biblically confronting are actions we can
train ourselves to do, even against our wills, strictly out of
obedience to God. Forgiving our brother "from the heart" is
a tool of grace no one can fake. Even if we say we've forgiven
someone but secretly still harbor a grudge, God knows.

It is extremely important to understand exactly what forgiveness is and is not, especially when talking about continual, habitual abuse. (By "abuse," I include not only physical abuse, but all forms of manipulation, passive-aggressive
behavior; verbal mistreatment such as lying, slander and
gossip; sarcasm; and interfering/intruding in the personal
life of another). Forgiving does not mean saying that these
behaviors are okay (they aren't) or don't matter (they do).
Dealing with the problem biblically often requires going to
the person and confronting in love, as we have seen. How the
other person will respond is beyond our control. Being willing to forgive means we are doing everything that depends
on us—we agree to bury the offense and be reconciled to the
offender as if nothing had happened.

Often, a Christian's offer of forgiveness itself will be enough
to soften the offender's heart. Nevertheless, when dealing
with non-Christians, our expectation of any type of meaningful repentance (or even a superficial apology) should be
very low. Keep in mind that the Holy Spirit has not enlight-
ened their consciences, and be careful not to offer forgiveness

unless the offending party acknowledges his or her wrong and asks your pardon. Following an unfruitful confrontation over the matter, how are we to proceed if the Matthew 18 process does not even apply to unbelievers? Again, the answer lies in how the Lord would have us treat "tax collectors and pagans." Evangelize them—with words and deeds. There can be no meaningful reconciliation in the relationship, but our kindness may be the very thing God uses to draw our abuser to repentance. I have searched for scriptural loopholes to justify repayment in kind, and there are none! As we have seen from His response to friends and enemies alike, Jesus gives us the model for how we are to relate to the unrepentant. We are to love and pray for them (Matthew 5:44); act charitably towards them (Luke 6:27); and seek to live at peace with them (Romans 12:18; Hebrews 12:14). (Forgiveness will be more fully discussed in chapter 12).

Pity, Not Contempt

In 1949, a year after the Communists took power in Bulgaria, thirteen evangelical pastors were rounded up and dragged from their homes in the middle of the night. They were tried as spies and each spent between eight and thirteen years being beaten, starved, and indoctrinated in concentration camps. A contemporary of Romanian minister Richard Wurmbrand, (who later founded "The Voice of the Martyrs"), Pastor Haralan Popov described the torment he and the other men endured at the hands of their interrogators in his autobiography, *Tortured For His Faith*. One of the most amazing things about Popov's ordeal is that during his imprisonment, God enabled him to lead not only other prisoners to Christ; but to be a powerful witness to the hardened Communist agents, as well. Every chance he was given, this physically broken man countered Marxist ideology with the message of new life in Christ. Rather than despising his abusers, he prayed for them. Popov wrote, "When a man is without God, there is no limit to his depravity or to the depths to which he will sink."[61] He never lost sight of the fact that without Christ's work in his own heart, he would have been as vile as his abusers. Rather than despise the Communists, he pitied them.

Although most of us may never expect to be imprisoned, starved, or beaten, we can learn a great deal from Popov's example. A godly response to an unrepentant abuser simply means that regardless of his or her response, we agree to forfeit our "rights" to be angry; to expect recompense; to justify our grudge. We decide to suspend judgment, and overlook the offense in order to let God deal with the other person's heart. God's call on us to repay the offender only with kindness and agape love (an unconditional commitment to another's well-being, with no expectation of reciprocation) is a call to Christ-centered living, and is the path to true freedom from the anger that grips us. We have assurance from His Word that God will ultimately right every wrong, but we must also do all we can to keep our own hearts right before Him. This includes ridding ourselves of hatred, bitterness and slander (discussing the offender with others).

Allowing ourselves to grow bitter over the hurt and abuse done to us—even by a parent—will only poison our relationship with God and other people. While it was given in the context of relationships within the Body, the author of Hebrews issued a warning against letting a "root of bitterness" spring up and defile many (Hebrews 12:15). Even in relationships with non-Christians, becoming bitter hurts no one but yourself and will be a hindrance in overcoming other sin in your life, including your eating disorder.

The only way to guard against this "bitter root" is prayer. Keep bringing the matter before God, and ask Him to guard your heart against grudges and anger. Pray for your tormentor, regardless of her spiritual state. Ask God to grant her the gift of repentance, that she may see the error of her ways and turn from them. Don't allow yourself to be embittered by the lingering memories of abuse. "Watch over your heart with all diligence, for from it flow the springs of life." (Proverbs 4:23).

In no way does God's requirement that we forgive (at least attitudinally) minimize the seriousness of the abuse, or diminish the pain we suffer. God fully understands, and feels deeply every sorrow we have experienced. He Himself promises to wipe our every tear away (Revelation 7:17; 21:4). We have the comfort of knowing Jesus Himself has gone through everything we could possible have been handed, and then some. His response was always to seek the others' well being, as is evidenced by His continual invitations to His tormentors to repent. Unlike us, though, only He has a perfectly holy and just heart and can therefore judge sinners' spiritual state.

The tragic reality about those who do not know Christ and abuse His children is that they do not even realize the gravity of their own situation. The unsaved are, by definition, "blind" (Matthew 15:14) and are unable to see their own sin. We were all in the same blind, unregenerate and unrepentant state once—before Christ called us. Justification is completely a work of God, and not of our own initiative (Ephesians 2:8-9), so we have nothing to boast about. In fact, Paul reminds Christians of where they themselves had been before God saved them: "Do not be deceived; neither fornicators, nor idolaters, nor adulterers, nor effeminate, nor homosexuals, nor thieves, nor the covetous, nor drunkards, nor revilers, nor swindlers, will inherit the kingdom of God" (1 Corinthians 6:9b-11).

Look up and meditate on the verses in the next chapter that deal with forgiveness, asking God how to apply them to your situation.

Chapter 12

Forgiveness:

What is it and Why is it Important?

An amazing example of the power of forgiveness happened a few years ago on national television, during the taping of the hit show *American Idol.* Cynical judge Simon Cowell made a snide remark about overweight contestant Mandisa Hundley, not realizing that the microphone was on. His hurtful remark was broadcast nationwide, and although her singing talent got her to the finals, understandably Mandisa was terribly hurt. She publicly admitted to having struggled with food addiction for most of her life, and such a thoughtless remark must have cut her to the quick. However, what Simon didn't realize was that Mandisa didn't just sing gospel songs; the Gospel was the driving force behind every aspect of her life.

Despite her feelings and the judge's smugness, this beautiful young woman decided to glorify God. She confidently walked into a room full of spectators and informed Cowell: "What I want to say to you is that, yes; you hurt me and I cried and it was painful; it really was. But I want you to know that I've forgiven you and that you don't need someone to apologize in order to forgive somebody. I figure that if Jesus could die so that all of my wrongs could be forgiven, I can certainly extend that same grace to you." Cowell told Mandisa that he was "humbled" and embraced her. Such decisions that go against our carnal desire to get even do far more to show unbelievers the power of the Cross than putting a fish on our bumper ever will.

But What About Luke 17:3?

In Luke chapter 17, Jesus warns His disciples about the seriousness of sin and, in particular, leading someone else into immoral behavior. All sin is ultimately against God, because it violates His perfectly holy rule, and has been referred to as "cosmic treason." However, we know from numerous passages that God is consistently faithful to forgive all who earnestly seek Him in repentance, no matter how many times. His mercy is never-ending and His patience is limitless.

Since man is made in the image of God, and the goal of the Christian life is to be ever more closely conformed to the image of Christ, He expects us to extend the same mercy we have received. In verse three, Jesus instructs: "If your brother sins, rebuke him, and if he repents, forgive him." It is tempting to take this one verse out of context and interpret it to mean that unless an offending party comes to us with a heartfelt apology, we're "off the hook" and don't need to have an attitude of goodwill (forgive "attitudinally," if not judicially). However, the intention of the lesson was not that our forgiveness to a fellow sinner is to hinge on his or her contrite attitude. Taken with all of the other verses that deal with doing good to enemies and showing kindness impartially, we can assume that the type of forgiveness Christ refers to means a full restoration of fellowship—as if nothing had ever happened. Complete reconciliation is generally only possible when wrongdoing is admitted and repented among believers, but we are to extend mercy, gentleness and love even to our enemies.

Forgive as You Have Been Forgiven

Sin is an attack on the moral government of God; not just a personal affront. Yet Christ Himself, the only One who truly had a claim to justice, was willing to lay aside His right to vengeance on Calvary. Although He never relinquished His deity, He deferred judgment in order to glorify God—

through some of His tormenters' later repentance (Acts 2). His long-suffering throughout His ministry and death is the perfect model for us. Sometimes, believers rationalize their unforgiving spirit over relatively minor offenses by reasoning that God (who hates injustice) would never want them to suffer injury and forgive the offender with no sign of remorse. We somehow assume we have immunity to suffering, or a right to respect. But Christ had another point of view for His followers: "If the world hates you, you know that it has hated Me before it hated you....Remember the word that I said to you, 'A slave is not greater than his master.' If they persecuted Me, they will also persecute you..." (John 15:18, 20).

John Macarthur writes, "As Christians, we should be obsessed with forgiveness, not vengeance."[62] Why? Because it is a reflection of the very heart of Christ, Who is One with the Father. In the parable of the unmerciful servant (Matthew 18:23-27), we see the infinite size of our sin-debt to God, how the "debt" that our fellow sinners "owe" us pales in comparison, and how we are to reflect the King's gracious character out of sheer gratitude. Since God's judicial forgiveness is not conditional upon a sinner's subsequent behavior (He does not "withdraw" salvation), the severity of the king's punishment here actually illustrates how God will discipline unforgiving believers. Scripture upholds that God does, indeed, discipline as sons those He loves (Hebrews 12:6).

The King's indulgent grace to the servant is the very picture of what God does on behalf of every sinner who repents. When we realize the enormity of our debt and the hopelessness of our true estate before the King, the only appropriate response is to do as the servant did and fall prostrate before Him in a desperate plea for mercy. Neither the debt-ridden servant, nor we, deserve the King's pardon. Yet the King elevates His servant to a position of unmerited favor, which is the very definition of grace.

Unforgiveness toward others represents a lack of appreciation or awareness of what we've truly been forgiven. We underestimate our own sin-debt to God, freely and compassionately forgiven, by "choking and demanding" that our fellow sinners repay us. By the world's standards, we do have a legitimate and rightful claim on what is "owed" us. Forgiveness makes no sense. But when we really see ourselves in the first servant, guilty of an infinitely more grave debt to the King, debts against us pale in comparison. It's when we move away from the feet of the King—or the foot of the Cross—that the unforgiving, carnal spirit that demands its "rights" to restitution sneaks in. Scripture makes clear that God takes this seriously. We need to extend forgiveness, not based on our own flawed sense of justice, but because God demanded it. If we truly see ourselves as the first servant, we will rejoice to offer that same grace.[63]

It is non-negotiable that a sinner needs to repent to receive God's judicial forgiveness. No one gets into heaven without turning from his or her sins and being born again. Still, we see God's patience and continual offer of salvation to even the basest of sinners. Bill Fields writes, "God does not forgive where there is no repentance, but God does show common grace and mercy as He invites sinners to Him through Godly repentance." He does not allow us to act as judge and jury (James 4:12).

Jay Adams clarifies divine pardon:

> Forgiveness by God rests on clear, unmistakable conditions. The apostles did not merely announce that God had forgiven men, who should acknowledge and rejoice in the fact but, rather, they were sent forth to preach "repentance and the forgiveness of sins" (Luke 24:47; Acts 17:30). The sins of those who repented and trusted in the Savior as the One Who shed His blood for them were forgiven on the conditions of repentance and faith. Paul and the apostles

turned away from those who refused to meet the conditions, just as John and Jesus did earlier when the scribes and the Pharisees would not repent.[64]

Now we come to perhaps the toughest issue, and the one that presented the biggest obstacle to me: Biblically, do we need to forgive when the offender does not repent? Scripture makes it clear that it is better to suffer a wrong patiently for the sake of righteousness than to exact re-payment. However, among believers, the biblical model is to confront one another in love and intentionally seek forgiveness for causing offense. When a fellow Christian does so, forgiveness is complete and instantaneous: the wrongdoing is buried, and by pardoning the offender, we agree never to bring it up again.

Even when no repentance is forthcoming, however, our attitude must be merciful. Technically, the sin is still "on the table" and has not been resolved. Nevertheless, we are exhorted to deal in kindness with the one who has hurt us, ever ready to extend grace. We do not have the same claim to justice that God does. When He requires us to extend grace to a fellow sinner, we are essentially agreeing to relinquish our "rights" to compensation. The point of the command to "forgive as you have been forgiven" (as well as similar exhortations throughout the entirety of Scripture) is to be lavish and abundant in our forgiving, as our Father is, and thus glorify God. Macarthur writes,

> For a Christian to be willfully unforgiving is unthinkable. We who have been forgiven by God Himself have no right to withhold forgiveness from our fellow sinners... Whereas Abel's blood (and the blood of other martyrs) screams for vengeance, Christ's blood pleads for mercy.[65]

But what about the unrepentant? In a word, God will deal with them. We often dwell on the fact that others have not been conscience-stricken over their behavior towards us, but we forget that Christ died for us while we were yet sinners (Romans 5:8). We were powerless; ungodly; enemies of God; in slavery to the world (Romans 5:6; 5:10; Galatians 4:3). When we consider the plight and behavior of an unbeliever, we can truly and literally say, "There but for the grace of God go I." The correct response is one of humble gratitude that God has opened our eyes and allowed us to receive His grace; there is truly no other difference in our respective standing before the Righteous Judge. Since only Jesus is perfect, He alone has the right to call the "snakes and vipers" out on their behavior. He alone must mete judgment on the unrepentant and unbelieving; it's not our job. He simply calls us to be salt and light in the world by sharing His message, and to show love impartially. We are incapable of judging sin and convicting the world; that's the Holy Spirit's responsibility, and He does it in His way and His timing. Therefore, we are to "attitudinally" pardon them, as unbelievers are unable to truly repent.

Paul asks the rhetorical question, "But you, why do you judge your brother? Or you again, why do you regard your brother with contempt? For we will all stand before the judgment seat of God" (Romans 14:10). The term "brother" indicates other believers—who are already indwelt by the Holy Spirit and will be convicted by Him. Yet the warning also serves against judging unbelievers prematurely—they are without the truth and unable to respond to God until He opens their eyes. Many hardened cynics have been led to the Lord by the witness of Christians who showed unconditional love and mercy, as Rev. Popov's testimony in the last chapter illustrates. If you are holding a grudge against someone, it will show. Decide today that you will allow Christ to change your heart towards your abusers, and treat them with kindness. In God's sovereign plan, your witness may be what He uses to soften the person's heart. Whether the offender repents or not, it is in God's hand and He will deal with it as He sees fit. Do we really want to be running the universe? Many of us have trouble enough just balancing our checkbooks!

Let's consider again the discourse in Luke 17: "And if he sins against you seven times a day, and returns to you seven times, saying, 'I repent,' forgive him." (v. 4). I can't tell you how many times this verse blessed me while I was struggling with bulimia! We know that Christ never asks us to do anything He Himself doesn't fulfill. The implication here is that those who have a relationship with God, through faith in His Son, can be forgiven as often as they sin and come to Him in repentance. What a promise of hope to the Christian addict! This one verse saved me from despair many times when I fell daily, and helped me realize that as God's daughter, I could not exhaust my allotment of grace because of my failings. (I am not saying we should presume on His grace and fail to take sin seriously. But when we do fall, we should get up immediately). Clearly, God expects His children to extend the same grace to one another. The standard for God's blood-bought, born-again disciples is of a different caliber than that of the world.

Obedience is its Own Reward

There is a modern philosophy often quoted in evangelical circles today: "Forgiveness is a gift you give yourself." While it may be true that forgiveness makes us feel better, unfortunately, that rationale has more in common with humanism than with Christianity. Forgiveness is a demand made of a holy God to His undeserving and redeemed creation. Christ is clear in the gospels: if we expect to be forgiven by our Father in heaven, we must be willing to forgive anyone who hurts us.

This is a difficult fact to accept, and forgiveness does not come naturally. In fact, probably the last thing in the world you "feel" like doing right now is forgiving your abusers! After all, no one has ever come to you to make amends. However, don't be discouraged that your emotions are not in line with God's instruction—just make the decision to obey. Ask God to make you willing to extend forgiveness. If you obey, and continue to lay down your perceived "rights" to be angry and hold a grudge day by day, in time He will begin to change your feelings. God is faithful, and He never asks us to do something He doesn't equip us to do. I believe that one reason Jesus instructed us to pray for those who persecute us is that it becomes virtually impossible to hate someone for whom you are praying.

Much of the anger women with eating disorders carry around is rooted in unforgiveness and bitterness. We resent those who, with their cutting remarks and cruel actions, "made" us this way. While this is a familiar and comfortable hole to crawl into, ultimately the "blame game" becomes a prison, as Christ poignantly warned in the parable of the unforgiving servant: "And his lord, moved with anger, handed him over to the torturers until he should repay all that was owed him. My heavenly Father will also do the same to you, if each of you does not forgive his brother from your heart." (Matthew 18:34-35)

Harboring grudges will get you nowhere, and the more resentment and bitterness you accumulate, the more likely you are to continue bingeing and purging. There are two reasons for this:

1) The sin of unforgiveness is rebellion against God. Without a willingness to humble yourself and repent of unforgiveness, you are blocking your own fellowship with Christ. You desperately need His grace to overcome this addiction; unforgiveness will distance you from Him.

2) Unforgiveness and the anger it churns up in you is an intensely negative feeling. Since you have long been using food to numb and "purge" these poisonous feelings, holding onto bitterness will only aggravate bulimic behavior.

Nowhere will we find a better example of forgiveness towards the undeserving than in Jesus Christ. Fortunately, we need look no further than to Him. If we look to ourselves for a sense of justice, we will most assuredly fail. A crucial step in your restoration from any eating disorder is that you release others from the "debt" you feel they owe you and learn to forgive. We cannot conjure up the wherewithal to do this on our own, but need His supernatural strength to obey in this area. Do not be discouraged if you find the old feelings of anger and resentment resurfacing—just take the thoughts captive as soon as they come into your mind. Forgiveness is rarely a one-time deal—you will probably find yourself having to forgive, as a simple act of the will, over and over—even every day. Remembering that Christ continuously does the very same for us should help us keep it in perspective!

Verses that discuss forgiveness and right relationship with others

Exodus 25:21-22	Ephesians 4:1-3	Galatians 5:15
Matthew 5:7	Proverbs 16:32	Ephesians 4:32
Matthew 5:44, 45a, 48	Matthew 5:23-24	Colossians 3:12-13
Matthew 6:14-15	Matthew 6:12	Hebrews 12:14
Matthew 18:34-35	Matthew 18:21-22	James 5:9
Luke 6:37	Mark 11:25-26	1 John 3:14-15
Romans 12:9-10	John 13:34-35	1 John 4:20-21
Romans 14:10-13	Romans 13:10	

An Ongoing Choice

Taking the time to consider what the above verses teach us about God's will for relating to others, and meditating on them (thinking deeply and continually as you seek their personal application) will help you counter that carnal, human response to "get even" with those who have hurt you. When you have nursed grudges and harbored unforgiveness for any length of time, even after you have made the deliberate decision to forgive the offender (or at least to relinquish any bitterness in your heart and desire for revenge, if the other person remains unrepentant), you will find that the old, angry emotions tend to sneak back in at times. Very often, you will have to remind yourself of your commitment not to rehearse the wrong done. Don't allow yourself to become angry all over again. Unlike the anorexia or bulimia itself, which you are unlikely to resume once you have "put on" new habits and attitudes about food, unforgiveness can sneak back into your thinking before you're even aware of it. You may find yourself talking about (and even exaggerating) things said or done; a painful memory may be triggered by a television show; even seeing the person may bring an unexpected sense of annoyance. Forgiveness is a conscious choice you will have to make, in obedience to God, over and over again—even long after your eating disorder is in the past.

"Sandra" is a young woman in counseling for self-destructive behaviors, including anorexic tendencies, bingeing and purging, and "cutting." Her father molested her as a child, and although he now claims saving faith in Christ, Sandra finds his profession of faith hard to believe. Her pastor's wife explained to her that if her father is truly a Christian, there will be evidence of fruit in his life but she must assume, for the moment, that he is sincere. Sandra comes to understand the Matthew 18 process of godly confrontation, and goes to her father about his sin. He admits what he did was wrong, and, seeming relieved, finally asks Sandra's forgiveness. Sandra says she forgives her father, and really tries to—she is careful never to bring the matter up again, although it still enters her mind and causes her pain. As she continues "putting off" her old habits of slinking into self-pity and rage and "putting on" her new practice of rehearsing the promises of God, praying, and deliberately choosing to forgive her father, she stops turning her rage inward and seeking relief through self-destructive means. Whereas festering anger and bitterness never helped her feel better (and indeed aggravated the problem), the joy she slowly begins to experience in obeying God's command to forgive helps her overcome her besetting sin.

"Jennifer" is a 16-year-old student who is clearly angry. Her heavy mascara, black clothing and hair covering her eyes are outward symbols of the deep melancholy she carries inside. Although she trusted Christ at Bible camp last summer, lack of discipleship and unresolved anger have stunted her spiritual growth. Although she loves God deep down inside, Jennifer is angry at Him. She has been a ward of the state since she was taken away from her parents at age three. Embittered by their absence in her life, Jennifer began self-medicating her feelings of abandonment and betrayal as an adolescent. Vomiting and drinking made her feel good for a while, and seemed like something she could take or leave. Now she can't stop. She admits that when she thinks about her absentee parents and foster parents who didn't want her, she is most inclined to binge and purge. When her youth pastor explains that she must repent of her unforgiveness towards her parents and others, Jennifer is horrified and becomes even more angry. "Forgive them? After what I've been through?" she responds. "My life is a mess, and it's all their fault!" As Jennifer's anger and rebellion increases, she pulls away from her Christian friends. Her bulimia worsens to the point where she must be hospitalized.

"Mary" is a 30-something mom who has struggled with bulimia for years, but recently has repented and seems well on the way to overcoming her eating disorder. As she immerses herself in God's Word, she feels conviction for attitudes she has long considered "righteous anger." She believes strongly that the many caustic and insensitive remarks made by adults during her childhood, especially her mother, caused (at least in part) her eating disorder. Although her mother has not been born again, (she is convinced she will

go to heaven because she is a "good person"), Mary feels confident that if she confronts her mother honestly over specific
incidents, her mother will at least apologize and ask Mary's
pardon. Mary is eager to grant forgiveness.

Her efforts are frustrated; met only with distorted facts,
rationalizations, and "conditional apologies" such as "Well,
I'm sorry if anything I said was 'misinterpreted'....anything I
ever said was motivated by love!" Mary leaves, heartbroken
and more frustrated than before. However, God has worked
in her heart, and no matter how her mother continues to
deceive herself, Mary is determined to "walk in a manner
worthy of the calling she has received" (Ephesians 4:1). She
refuses to use her mother's unrepentance as an excuse to
relapse into her eating disorder; reminding herself that her
mother's sin is primarily against God, and not her. As she
prays daily for strength and wisdom in her interaction with
her mother, she is comforted by a theologian's words: "Those
whom God blesses and favors have reason enough to forgive
those who hate them, since the worst enemy they have cannot do them any real hurt." Although she realizes that no
"transaction" of forgiveness can take place until her mother
becomes a Christian and repents of her sin, Mary determines
to keep bitterness out of her heart. She knows that to become
a bitter person or entertain evil thoughts against her mother
would be a grave offense against the Lord Jesus Christ; not
just make her repentance from bulimia more difficult. When
her mother is hospitalized with cancer, Mary quickly visits
her and brings a pot of beef stew to her father—recalling
how Christ washed even the feet of Judas, His betrayer. She
seeks to bless, and stands ready to forgive.

What can you see about the importance of forgiveness
(and the toxic effects of an unforgiving heart) in these three
examples? Whereas the decision to forgive is a deliberate
act of obedience, as we see in Sandra's case, feelings do not
change overnight. Even when you choose to forgive someone

who has freely repented, especially if the hurt occurred over a long period of time, you may constantly have to remind yourself that the past has been buried—as your sin also has been by God. When you have been wronged by a non-Christian or a fellow believer who refuses to repent, you cannot offer forgiveness—but you can (and must, biblically) treat him or her with kindness and mercy. Letting go of malice in your heart and standing ready to forgive, with reconciliation the goal, is what God expects of His children under all circumstances. As Jennifer's case shows, the way of the transgressor is hard (Proverbs 13:15).

Remember that the motivation behind forgiveness is ultimately to please God. In his letter to the Colossians, Paul prayed that the believers would be "...filled with the knowledge of His will in all spiritual wisdom and understanding, so that you will walk in a manner worthy of the Lord, to please Him in all respects, bearing fruit in every good work and increasing in the knowledge of God..." (Colossians 1:9-10). We may gain knowledge of His will of how we are to relate to those who have hurt us in His Word. Forgiving, forbearing in love, serving and seeking to bless those who have wronged us in the past pleases God, because it shows that the fruit of the Spirit (love, joy, peace, patience, kindness, goodness, faithfulness, gentleness, and self-control) is being produced in us. No one showed greater kindness to antagonists than Christ, and it is in imitation of Him that we seek to forgive.

As you obey God in this way, you will grow closer to Him. The joy of being in close communion with God, as you continue to renew your mind with His Word, helps you to reject habitual sin (such as an eating disorder). With your anger cooled and bitterness defused, there is less temptation to "stuff" and "purge" those emotions through bulimia. Just as one sin very often leads to another, disciplined training in righteousness (learning to forgive, even though it goes against our wills) can likewise lead to changed behavior and "putting on" of self-control in another (overcoming food addiction).

Suppose you have already taken a good hard look at the past, forgiven those whom you need to, and sought forgiveness yourself. You keep unrighteous anger at bay by stopping those bitter thoughts the moment they come into your mind and confessing them to God...but you still have trouble around food. How do you deal with that? Are there any "survival tips" when you are climbing the walls? And what about weight gain? Let's consider these questions next.

Chapter 13
Practical Considerations

Thus far, I have discussed the spiritual roots of an eating disorder and the importance of repentance in overcoming this behavior. We have looked at the principle outlined by the apostle Paul (and elaborated on by biblical counselors) of "putting off" and "putting on," and how it relates to anorexia and bulimia. Since all sin starts in the mind, we have considered the need to "take every thought captive" and renew our minds with the truth of God's Word. As we grow progressively stronger and develop these disciplines, we find ourselves walking in victory and our obsessive thoughts of food diminishing greatly. We learn to forgive our abusers and those who have hurt us. God is restoring us—mind, body and spirit.

In this chapter, I would like to lay out some specific, practical advice that hopefully will help you as you put this eating disorder behind you permanently. This is not intended to be medical advice, nor is it to be considered exhaustive nutritional counseling. I strongly recommend that you visit your primary care physician, who will probably refer you to both a cardiologist and a nephrologist. As I have stated from the beginning of this book, anorexia and bulimia are spiritual bondages and must be treated as such. Nothing will replace the importance of regular prayer and Bible study in your restoration, but there are certainly habits and physical practices you can implement which will help you overcome the behavior more easily.

Some of the "advice" to bulimics I have seen online is unbelievable. It ranges from the silly ("Use a good concealer to hide under-eye circles." "Pack a few cubes of ice in a hand towel and hold them over your eyes for ten minutes for a quick fix for puffiness.") to the dangerous ("Keep in mind that you have three hours to vomit after a meal. Throwing up every hour is unnecessary.....you can alleviate heartburn symptoms by taking Tums or Rolaids regularly.") Popping antacids is actually dangerous for bulimics, who may already have compromised renal function from chronic electrolyte imbalances. Antacids contain calcium, which in accumulated doses can lead to painful kidney stones. Doctors strongly advise patients with impaired kidney function against taking antacids which contain magnesium, like Mylanta. There simply are no "tricks" that will make you healthier. Bulimia will wreak havoc on your body. You are probably aware of the physical side effects of this behavior, which include:

- Esophageal problems
- Vocal chord damage
- Stomach ulcers
- Osteoporosis
- Hair loss
- Digestive problems
- Decreased body temperature
- Irregular heart beat
- Elimination problems
- Dental Damage
- Organ damage
- Vitamin and mineral deficiencies
- Enlarged salivary glands
- Dry skin
- Decreased bone density
- Menstrual dysfunction
- Hormone irregularities
- Insomnia
- Low red blood cell levels

- Weak muscles
- Immune system damage[66]

Laxatives and Diuretics

If you are using laxatives and/or diuretics to control your weight, stop immediately. Diuretics (water pills) unnaturally flush fluid out of the body, and in so doing put extra strain on the kidneys. Kidney damage is serious and irreversible. If you are vomiting, you are already risking damage both to your heart and your kidneys because of electrolyte imbalances. Each time you purge, you lose potassium (K+) and fluids. Over time, low potassium levels will lead to renal insufficiency and cardiac failure. You are increasing the damage with diuretics.

Laxative abuse is also serious. Although an occasional laxative to combat constipation is not harmful, chronically abusing them to purge food from the body and lose weight unnaturally can lead to dependency. Ironically, this is an ineffective method of purging calories from your body, since most of the food eaten is absorbed by the small intestine soon after eating. Bulimics who have used laxatives for any length of time usually notice that they need to continually increase the dose they take to achieve the same results. The over-stimulation of the nerves in the bowel can eventually cause it to become non-responsive. The National Eating Disorders Association web page, www.NationalEatingDisorders.org, lists the following health consequences of laxative abuse:

Upset of electrolyte and mineral balances. Sodium, potassium, magnesium, and phosphorus are electrolytes and minerals that are present in very specific amounts necessary for proper functioning of the nerves and muscles, including those of the colon and heart. Upsetting this delicate balance can cause improper functioning of these vital organs.

Severe dehydration may cause tremors, weakness, blurry vision, fainting, kidney damage, and, in extreme cases, death.

Dehydration often requires medical treatment.

Laxative dependency occurs when the colon stops reacting to usual doses of laxatives so that larger and larger amounts of laxatives may be needed to produce bowel movements.

Internal organ damage may result, including stretched or "lazy" colon, colon infection, Irritable Bowel Syndrome, and, rarely, liver damage. Chronic laxative abuse may contribute to risk of colon cancer.

It's simply not worth it. Decide today you will quit; throw them in the trash and rely on God to guide your eating as your body re-adjusts.

What to Expect (and What to Do About It)

As you stop purging or starving and start digesting food again, it is reasonable to expect some bloating and even discomfort (as much mental as physical—most anorexics and bulimics have come to truly dislike the feeling of food in their stomachs). The first few days of this are the hardest. When you wake up in the morning, you may notice your stomach is a bit less concave than it was when you routinely purged dinner. Again, this is normal. Bulimics typically experience edema around the abdomen while they are actively purging anyway, and once their bodies have re-adjusted to digesting normal amounts of food and fluids it tends to go away.

During what nutritionists call the "re-feeding process," your tissues are absorbing more fluid (which they were previously deprived) and your weight will increase slightly as your metabolism gets back up to speed. There is no need to panic! You may put on a few pounds the first week, and a couple more the following. Remember that this is mostly water weight. This weight gain will not continue indefinitely; as you continue taking in adequate fluids, the initial bloating should subside. As your digestive system accommodates meals, (especially if you have been abusing laxatives), you may suffer from constipation. A natural fiber supplement (with additional water) should help. Better yet, a high-fiber, low sugar cereal such as All-Bran™ or Fiber One™ is an excellent choice for breakfast, and is less likely to trigger a binge than higher-sugar breakfast foods.

In cases of extreme or prolonged starvation, there is a risk of "re-feeding syndrome," which can be fatal. The sudden shifting of electrolytes and fluid balance increases the heart's work. (Acute heart failure, the cause of Karen Carpenter's death, was thought to be caused by sudden re-feeding). You have probably heard of the many concentration camp survivors who then died after gulping down bowls of the Allies' soup—they were killed by a metabolic reaction in their own bodies. Oxygen consumption is increased, which strains the respiratory system. Significant risks arising from re-feeding syndrome include confusion, coma, convulsions, and death. Because of these risks, more severely malnourished women are kept on feeding tubes and monitored around the clock in inpatient treatment centers. One reason it is so important for you to see a doctor is so that a complete blood profile may be done. Low levels of potassium, phosphate or magnesium may indicate a risk for re-feeding syndrome, and may be treated with supplements.

The average bulimic is still digesting enough food that the mortality risk of re-feeding syndrome is not major. However, as you learn to trust your body with food and your stomach becomes less concave, the biggest battle you will have to wage is against your own pride. Even insecurity over the weight you gain can be submitted to the authority of Christ, if you are renewing your mind daily. Think of eating and digesting the food as an act of trust. You are, in a very literal sense, "honoring God with your body" (1 Corinthians 6:20) each time you digest a meal. Allow me to share an incident from my own experience during this time.

By the spring of 2004, I had not purged a meal in months. Over the course of time, as I learned to surrender fear of weight gain to God's will, I relaxed and had a new-found sense of joy in my freedom. The fact that I had gained around 10 lbs. didn't bother me—I was staying close to God, in regular prayer and fellowship, and was beginning to get through meals without thinking too much. For the first time in my Christian life, I knew what it was to be Spirit-led, and it changed my thoughts, behavior, and emotions. The knowledge that I was slightly heavier than I had been a few months earlier didn't disturb me in the least. Christ had redeemed my life from the pit, and nearly all I thought about was living for Him.

One warm day in May, I needed to stop by the Occupational Health office at Boston Children's Hospital, where I work as an interpreter, to pick up some paperwork. I was wearing a lightweight rayon and polyester dress, which, while not tight, clings to the contours of my body. My ID badge rested just above my navel, which was eye-level to the nurse seated near the filing cabinet. "Oh, are you pregnant, Marie?" she inquired, gently poking my belly. Whoa! "Uh, no," I replied. "Just getting fat, I guess!" I said it so nonchalantly that there was no way the nurse could have been embarrassed, but as I left the office, my mind started to spin. "Father…did You see that? She thought I was pregnant!" I silently prayed. Realizing God was there and had witnessed the whole thing, I didn't replay it for Him. I dismissed the idea of fasting for several days, and called to mind the lesson He had been teaching me so tenderly over the last few months. I was His daughter. Nothing could take that wonderful knowledge away from me. Any anorexic or bulimic knows the potentially devastating effect a comment like that could have had, but the habit of "screening" thoughts biblically was already becoming a habit. Realizing that whether my abdomen was concave or convex held no eternal significance, I simply let it roll off. I was able to successfully "take that thought captive" and move on victoriously.

Developing Healthy Eating Habits

As you walk away from this behavior and rebuke the obsessive thoughts as they pop up, you will find that you need to learn how to eat all over again. An anorexic or bulimic has typically lost all perception of what "normal" eating habits are, and feels as if she is standing on the edge of a cliff each time she must face food choices. The anorexic sees all food as the enemy; she is convinced that even a bite will lead to obesity. The bulimic, on the other hand, often has convinced herself that she can have "just one" or take a small amount of a "binge food," only to lose control and keep going. Once the frenzied binge has begun, she rationalizes, "I've already blown it now; I might as well keep going!" It never occurs to her to plan ahead or pray through the "food encounter." (Not all choices with food are made at mealtimes—we are constantly confronting food all day. Few office meetings are conducted without bagels, and supermarkets routinely offer free samples. The list of potential "food encounters" is endless).

I have found that certain types of food tended to be "binge triggers"—I was much less likely to avoid an all-out binge once I'd had a taste. As a drunkard's resolve weakens after the first sip, a repenting bulimic is setting herself up for failure if she starts eating junk food too soon. Some things that are typically "binge foods" include sugary and fatty things like doughnuts and pastry; salty snack food like chips; fried food; pizza; pasta; fast food and sugary cereal. High-carbohydrate items tend to trigger binges and are harder for bulimics to resist. There is, in fact, a physical component involved in the addiction—the brain chemistry has become altered due to food being used repeatedly as a "reward." It has to do with endorphins providing a "rush" in the pleasure centers of the brain, and this is why the behavior is habit-forming. However, just as the brain has been conditioned to respond in a certain way, so it can be "de-conditioned" by no longer giving it the "drug" to which it has grown accustomed.

This does not, of course, mean you are not going to eat! Starving yourself (or taking appetite suppressants, which force the adrenal glands to release hormones affecting the central nervous system) will only make the problem worse. (Trust me; I tried it. Many times.) Allowing yourself to get too hungry will also set you up for a binge. You must get used to eating as often as you are hungry, but you will learn to pray and plan ahead what you are going to eat, knowing you will be keeping it down. In the beginning, this process will be deliberate and methodical. As time goes by, you will find the cravings decrease and you will grow more and more relaxed about food. Within a few months, eating normally should be so routine that it will no longer be necessary to plan ahead. Right now, however, you must be on your guard. As author and biblical counselor Mark Shaw teaches, wisdom dictates that if you struggled with something in the past, you must be careful with it in the future. Habitual sin has a clinging effect (see James 1:14-15; Hebrews 12:1-2), and someone waging war against bulimia must be vigilant against temptation.

The Abstinence Phase

In the very first weeks of "re-feeding," you must be diligent in avoiding "binge triggers." You know best what your own triggers are, but most likely simple carbohydrates are up near the top of the list. Avoid them, plain and simple. In fact, there were times when even relatively healthy foods, like Raisin Bran, would trigger me to binge first thing in the morning. Because Raisin Bran has a lot of added sugar, I recommend a plain bran cereal or a similar low-sugar cereal with complex carbohydrates. Other meals require similar diligence. I do not recommend giving up carbohydrates entirely, but to be more selective in the types you consume. Nutritionists agree that complex carbohydrates are healthier, and they seem to pose less of a problem for binge-eaters. Bread can also be a trigger, but I found that eating sprouted whole-wheat bread to be a good solution. Sources of complex carbohydrates include potatoes and other root vegetables, brown rice, oatmeal (not the instant kind, which is loaded with sugar and sodium), whole-wheat pasta, beans and lentils. All of these are good choices for someone overcoming an eating disorder.

A friend of mine, who has struggled with weight and emotional eating her whole adult life, recently told me that she has temporarily cut out all simple carbohydrates from her diet. While she needs to lose weight for health reasons, her over-eating has been an addiction for so long that she feels the need to abstain entirely from certain types of food. "Once I get started with bread or any starches, I just eat and eat…. I'm like a bulimic, only without the purging," she told me. After prayerfully seeking God and talking to her doctor, she decided that abstinence would be the best route for her—for now. As she develops healthier eating habits and renews her mind, she plans to put rice and baked potatoes back into her diet. In the meantime, she is getting the carbohydrates her body needs for energy from vegetables alone. I told her that her initial "abstinence game plan" is exactly what I followed when God was delivering me from bulimia, and what I encourage other sisters with eating disorders to do.

Of course, as soon as you set out with all your resolve, fortified with prayer, you will run into big, fluffy white bagels and cream cheese in the break room; sheet cake at the mid-afternoon baby shower (when cravings are at their highest); and a table of complimentary jelly doughnuts at the bank for Customer Appreciation Day. What are you to do in these situations?

Abstain, at all costs. You know very well what will happen if you manage to convince yourself you can "handle it." You can't. Not yet. You are still in the process of "putting off" gluttony and learning to "put on" self-control, which takes time. One day you will eat dessert without giving it a second thought—but not yet. You do, however, have the power at your disposal to resist the temptation (remember our discussion of taking those binge-thoughts captive back in Chapter 8?) Now is the time to rehearse those Scriptures you've committed to memory. You are not a slave to sin, and no matter how strong the urge may feel, you are not being compelled by a force outside of you to take a piece of that cake. Which will lead to another. And another, and then a clandestine raid of the vending machine and anything else you can get your hands on. There is no reason why you, as a redeemed child of God, should have to go down that road. Is your brain still functioning? Use it to talk to God. He can hear your thoughts from heaven as easily as your shouts, so mental prayer is one weapon in your momentary battle against the flesh.

As we have seen, there are no "good foods" and "bad foods." Food is created by God for a life-giving purpose, but you know the effect certain types currently have on you. Common sense plays a big part in renewing your mind in regards to food. Another tactic to consider in the "unexpected food encounter" scenario is this: leave. Flee temptation. Just leave the premises. If the doughnuts are not right there, staring you in the face, their allure will be much easier to resist. Just as a porn addict would be wise to avoid certain internet sites and streets that feature "adult film" cinemas, you must learn not to put yourself in harm's way. Do not walk into Dunkin Donuts, telling yourself you will order just a coffee. Steer clear of the fast food drive-thru windows, and avoid going to the supermarket stressed, depressed or hungry. These tips should be so obvious as to be common sense, but they bear mentioning. We bulimics are masters at deceit—especially at deceiving ourselves.

Of course, there are many work and social situations which you simply cannot leave; in those cases, keep praying through it and know that for every temptation you face, God has provided a way out and fortified you with His Spirit to be able to resist. Do not stand next to a food-laden table. At parties, involve yourself in a conversation and ask the other person about herself. Another hint to stave off office cravings: eat breakfast at home. You will be less tempted to binge on a full stomach of All Bran™ or oatmeal.

When temptation hits at home, you cannot exactly leave but at least get away from the kitchen. It was at these times that I eventually disciplined myself to go into the bedroom and lose myself in a Bible study. I grew much closer to God through this time of desperate clinging to His hand. In the Bible, God is described as a fortress or a stronghold to His people. A stronghold is an impenetrable fortress where the people took refuge (1Samuel 22:4-5; Psalm18:45). This metaphor is used for God (especially throughout the Psalms), because He is the safe and mighty fortress to Whom sinners flee. I found this imagery to be extremely accurate on a personal level when I was on my way out of bondage. Like the Psalmist, in all moments of temptation, I learned to say, "The LORD is my rock and my fortress and my deliverer, My God, my rock, in whom I take refuge; My shield and the horn of my salvation, my stronghold" (Psalm 18:2).

Withdrawal and Re-learning to Eat

As you break off the addictive habit that has gripped your waking hours for so long, you can expect the bulimic's equivalent of "withdrawal symptoms." No, you will not hallucinate, have tremors or night sweats; but you can expect some difficulty. Much like a smoker who craves her nicotine fix, you may start to get agitated and irritable when escaping into the familiar comfort of the binge is no longer an option. Cravings are real, and they can be intense. The worst thing you can do in such situations is sit there and entertain the thoughts about food, or focus on how much you want to binge. Bring it to God in prayer. Put on some praise music and worship Him for His amazing love and patience. Go for a walk or call a friend or accountability partner (more on the importance of accountability in the next chapter). Whatever you decide to do, have a plan. These cravings are temporary and they do subside within a few short weeks. On the positive side, as you begin to eat normally and regularly, you will notice a vast improvement in your energy level. Your concentration will be much better, and you will be able to stay focused for much longer periods of time. The exhaustion that generally follows purging will be replaced by a steady, even keel throughout the day. Now that your blood sugar is no longer peaking and plummeting, your emotions as well as your energy will stabilize.

How much should you eat, and of what? Well, we've already established that there are no "bad foods," although you must learn to steer clear of obvious triggers during the first few weeks. What we are going to use as a rule of thumb is, again, good old-fashioned common sense. Get out of the habit of counting calories. Stop counting fat grams. Stop looking at every food's glycemic index, and forget about Weight Watchers "points." These are all arbitrary man-made "rules" or systematically grading how worthwhile a certain food is, and we are going to throw them all out. A calorie is a metric unit of energy. It has absolutely no bearing on your real life, and every time you catch yourself mentally tabulating a meal's caloric content, I want you to take that thought captive and discard it.

These habits are hard to break, but they are enslaving you. While some former bulimics counsel women to stick to health food (go organic; macrobiotic; raw only; or whatever the current "health trend" is), my philosophy when it comes to food is "use common sense." Obviously, the closer a food is to its natural state, the healthier it is. We should avoid processed foods as much as possible, but let's be realistic. We live in a world where the demands of career and children take us far away from the organic farm and the kitchen. Most of what we buy at the supermarket is at least minimally processed in one way or the other.

A few years ago, Jordan Rubin wrote a popular book titled, *The Maker's Diet*, in which he extolled the health benefits of free-range, hormone-free, organic and pro-biotic enriched everything. His premise was that in order to eat food as God originally created it, we would have to decline nearly everything in the modern Western diet. To have optimal health, he claimed, we must go back to an Edenic state of purity in our food choices. While he made many good points in the book, I do not think that such an extreme approach to eating is practical or realistic for most people. Additionally, I do not believe it is healthy for someone overcoming food addictions to spend so much time and energy obsessing about food. It defies common sense.

Portion Control

An anorexic or bulimic woman tends to have a sliding scale in her mind, upon which she rates individual foods as "safe," "good," "bad," or "binge." In college, I once drew a diagram of concentric circles with the foods I considered "safe" in the very center. This included vegetables, fruit, diet soda and oatmeal. In the next circle, I wrote items that represented a "danger zone" to me—most forms of carbohydrates, protein, and dairy products. In the outermost circle, I listed my "binge foods"—items that once consumed, would lead inevitably and irreversibly to an all-out binge. This category included everything from sausages to éclairs. As you ask God to renew your mind and learn to restore food to its proper place, you are going to reject all such self-imposed spectrums and methods of categorization. While you must use wisdom and avoid obvious binge triggers in the abstinence phase (roughly the first six or eight weeks of your journey), no food is inherently "dangerous" or "off-limits."

Depending on your age and current season of life, you may

be the one responsible for preparing your family's meals. A family sitting down to dinner together is more than a mere consumption of food—it is a time of intimate fellowship (or, ideally, should be). Eat whatever you're preparing for your family—just in "manageable" amounts. For example, in the early days of my re-learning to eat, I remember making a lasagna and actually feeling trapped. Lasagna definitely fits the description of "binge trigger" to a bulimic! However, I recognized that I was no longer a bulimic, because I was no longer a slave to sin. I had a choice, and my choice was non-negotiable—I had decided to honor God with my body (1 Corinthians 6:20). I made a point of confessing my anxiety to God well before mealtime, asking Him to be with me and guide me through dinner. I ended up cutting myself a half-portion of lasagna, eating it slowly, and being very well-fed (without being overly-full). This is a process you need to go through with each meal—view it as a challenge, which must be approached with prudence and in God's strength.

Sitting down to a meal, keep God at the forefront of your mind, thanking Him for His provision of food and grace abounding to you as you repent of your unhealthy bingeing. I can honestly say that I never verbalized these "arrow prayers" (quick ones that I shot up), but as long as your mind is stayed on Him it is not necessary to tell others what you are doing. As with the first weeks of abstaining with alcohol, I would remind myself that Jesus was always present and remember that He was with me. Showing love to God and choosing to abide in Him, in those moments, meant a commitment to self-control. Turning my focus away from the food and my relationship with it and onto Him made mealtimes easier.

Nutrition

Do not eliminate entire food groups. Many eating disordered women decide to become vegans, rationalizing their Spartan diet as being for "health reasons." This is another form of restriction. Recently, a study published in the Journal of the American Dietetic Association established a link between young people who become vegetarians and eating disorders. Dr. David L. Katz, director of the Prevention Research Center at Yale University School of Medicine, was quoted as saying "Adolescent vegetarians were more prone to disordered eating and outright eating disorders. This is not due to vegetarianism but the other way around: adolescents struggling to control their diets and weight might opt for vegetarianism among other, less-healthful efforts."67 The study indicated that 21 percent of teens who choose to become vegetarians practice some form of disordered eating, compared to about 10 percent in the general population. Many times, young people will go vegetarian in order to mask their unhealthy eating habits or in an attempt to regain control. Because their bodies are not getting adequate nutrition, (vegetarian diets lack iron, amino acids and B-12 vitamins), these youngsters are more prone than ever to episodes of binge-eating. Likewise, replacing food with a liquid diet is not the answer. You need to get used to eating normal food, and disciplining your mind to overcome your aversions and fear (of gaining weight, or of feeling compelled to purge).

The best diet is a well-balanced one, eating everything in moderation. Taking a multivitamin or calcium supplement is fine, as long as the bulk of the nutrients you consume come from food. Many therapists recommend keeping a food journal in which you write down everything consumed, but I do not think such a practice is either necessary or helpful. Again, where is the focus? On the food. The food is not the issue; the sinful obsession is. Writing down in detail what is consumed in the course of the day will not improve an unhealthy view of food. Actually getting used to eating it in the way and amounts that God intended will. As you get adequate nutrition, your body's intense cravings will subside—along with any dizzy spells you may have been experiencing due to electrolyte imbalances.

If you are able to do so, I highly recommend meeting with a nutritionist. When I was in college, for a semester I met weekly with a nutritionist at the Student Health Center. I actually found her counsel far more helpful than anything that came out of the many psych consults and group therapy meetings that were forced on me. A nutritionist can greatly facilitate "getting comfortable" with digesting food, by explaining exactly what nutrients are present and how your body utilizes them. For example, I learned that consuming beans or other vegetable sources of protein without carbohydrates yields an incomplete protein—because several amino acids are lacking in the molecular structure. Nowadays, I could care less about the amino acids in navy beans, but at the time it gave me confidence that eating meat was not somehow being morally lax. She helped me to get comfortable with the changes in my body during the "re-feeding process"—I was far from delivered from bulimia, but I achieved a normal weight.

Many women with eating disorders know an impressive amount about nutrition science, but it is theoretical—as if drinking Diet Coke and subsisting on iceberg lettuce is actually healthy for them. While a nutritionist's role is not to address the underlying spiritual issue of your anorexia or bulimia (that is between you and your Lord), she can be very helpful in helping you navigate the day-to-day practicalities of "what should I eat and how much?" Nutritional counseling may be seen as a helpful (although secondary) supplement to spiritual counseling. In addition to some form of discipleship and your own commitment to spending time with the Lord, a nutritionist can give you practical counsel as you walk away from your eating disorder.

"What about Fasting to Break the Bondage?"

It is with hesitation that I approach this question, as there are conflicting opinions among Christians who have repented of eating disorders about the appropriateness of fasting. Additionally, I am not a physician and cannot predict the effect of a fast on an individual's body. While it is true that fasting, combined with prayer, is a biblically-mandated spiritual discipline, my personal opinion is that fasting from food completely can be counter-productive and even dangerous to an anorexic, bulimic or binge eater. If you are severely undernourished and have electrolyte imbalances to begin with, the dangers of eliminating all food (even for a short period of time) should be obvious. Even in less extreme cases, you are still setting yourself up for failure. When are you most likely to binge? When you are hungry.

A much better and God-honoring plan, in my experience, is to practice abstinence (as defined above; deliberately avoiding all "trigger" foods for an initial period of time) and prayerfully planning ahead of time what you will eat and how much. We have already established how important it is to "flee temptation" no matter how spiritual your intentions may be. The temptation to binge on food is inarguably much greater when you are hungry. While God always provides a way out in the temptation, it is better to avoid it in the first place. Trying to overcome bulimia by a total food fast is like a drunk holding a prayer meeting in a bar. It is better to continue to seek God and pray for His sustaining power in a "safe" place.

At the same time, it should be noted that the purpose of a fast is to draw closer to God while drawing away from the world. When we realize this, it becomes apparent that fasting doesn't necessarily have to be food, although that is, in fact, the model presented in the Bible. I have known people to "fast" from TV and read the Bible during that time instead. Sometimes, Christians "fast" from audio-visual distractions for a while, and deliberately keep the radio off in their cars in order to pray. I even knew one woman who greatly enjoyed

Christian fiction, and spent evenings reading the latest novels. While there is nothing wrong with reading fiction per se, she realized this was a distraction and was filling her mind with trivial information. For about a month, she "fasted" from fiction in order to spend that time with God instead. Her spiritual life benefited, and she had read much more of the Bible by the end of her fast. I would encourage you to look at the different areas of your life and ways you spend your time to see where you might be "distracted" from God. His goal is to make you holy, and the only way to greater holiness is to focus completely on Him. Fasting food for the sake of merit was never the goal.

Those Pesky Emotions Again

As God is transforming your mind and soul, and you are growing accustomed to eating normally, there are times when it will seem particularly difficult to stay the course. When something upsetting happens (like an argument with your husband, or a bad day at work), the temptation to start abusing food may flare up suddenly and without warning. Although you may no longer be thinking like a slave, your "default" setting has been to turn to food for comfort and control for so long that the temptation is bound to be stronger when you are upset. Ex-smokers will testify to similar, occasional cravings for a cigarette in times of unusual stress.

During the exact time God was granting me repentance from bulimia, my husband was laid off from his job. The months of unemployment that followed caused him enormous stress and anxiety. For me, it was easier to trust God with our finances than with the emotional strain his unemployment caused. Under immense pressure and fearing for the future, Ivo was uncharacteristically short-tempered and caustic towards me. He would often answer me sarcastically and lose his temper with the children over trivial matters. Unbeknownst to him,[68] my own emotional state was tenuous because I was repenting of a long-standing addiction. For the first time, I was learning to deal with my anger, doubts and fears by bringing them to God rather than numbing them with food and alcohol. Already insecure and needy, his callousness hurt me further. I remember irrationally thinking that I didn't deserve to have food in my stomach when he seemed annoyed (I always assumed his irritation was directed at me).

Several times, hurt by an impatient remark, I drove to an empty parking lot and wept uncontrollably to God. "Please fix this situation, Father," I remember crying. "I know You're with me, but I don't think I can hold on much longer." Amazingly, I held on without going back to the destructive cycle. I groped for His hand, and God held me tightly. Not once did I give in to the emotionally driven urge to purge. Without a rock-steady, vital relationship with Christ, it would have been impossible for me to maintain abstinence. God was literally my only support during this time—and He proved to be wholly sufficient.

Of course, in this life you will always have to deal with conflicts and undesirable circumstances. The only antidote is to talk yourself down from the ledge using biblical truth as the plumb line. The urge to purge supper if my husband is in a bad mood defies logic. Even if I had sinned in some way, the biblical solution is to repent of that sin and receive forgiveness—not expel food from my stomach. I reminded myself that regardless of circumstances, God loved me unconditionally and was for me; not against me. "Punishing" myself for some vague infraction (real or imagined) was diametrically opposed to His will. At these times, I would pull out my Bible, talk to Him about the rawness of my hurt feelings, and digest supper. Gradually, I stopped making the irrational connection between food and my feelings, and it would now never occur to me to "get rid of" food if my husband were annoyed with me (which rarely happens, anyway).

Looking to the Future

Believe it or not, there will come a time when you will enjoy fish and chips without a thought of saturated fat. As I now do, you will relish chocolate cheesecake on holidays, eat too many Christmas cookies in December, and never give it a second thought. Birthday cake will not call to you like a siren, luring you to a clandestine midnight binge; it will simply be birthday cake (getting stale on your kitchen counter). You will order pizza without tabulating calories. You will be transformed; if you continue to walk in repentance, this obsession will be behind you.

Like most women, your weight may fluctuate by a few pounds in the course of a month, but it will not torment you (if, indeed, you even notice). Not only will the scale not dominate your life, you will simply not think about it anymore. Food will truly be restored to its appropriate place—that of God's means of sustaining life and giving us variety (It's okay to enjoy it). Your mind will be restored.

One of the unintended and somewhat ironic "side effects" of my victory over bulimia is that I have lost nearly all interest in cooking. Like most food addicts, I used to subscribe to cooking magazines and pour over illustrated cookbooks. As a new bride, my feelings were terribly hurt if my husband did not care for a particular recipe I had prepared, and I took tremendous pride in being a good cook instead of focusing on serving God by being a good and submissive wife.

Since God has healed my mind and soul of "food fixation," I have inadvertently gone the other way (although thankfully my husband has been too gracious to mention it!). Of course I still cook for my family, but food does not occupy my thoughts when I am not actually hungry, and I rarely think ahead to what I will cook. Going grocery shopping bores me, and I can never decide what to buy once I'm there. I remember once being so distracted pondering the doctrine of Limited Atonement that I was unable to concentrate on what meat and produce we would need for the week. Staring blankly at the canned corn, I weighed the relative merits of monergism vs. synergism. On our anniversary last year, I was working so intensely on a pharmaceutical translation that Ivo had to interrupt me and insist we leave for a restaurant. Throughout the meal, all I could think about was the translation and what remained to be done.

In a similar vein, it is not unusual for me to wait until 5:00 pm to start thinking about what to fix for dinner—especially when I am preparing a Bible study lesson. More than once, my husband's late-afternoon question of "What are we having for supper?" has been met with a blank look, as I lift my head from my Bible concordance or laptop. I am not proud of this, but if anything, it shows how completely my mind has been transformed. (At least it is on "loftier things"!)

Still, while cooking may now be as enjoyable as cleaning or ironing, it is no less important and I would be remiss before God if I neglect this important responsibility. As a wife and mother, I have found that in order to keep my household duties in order, I must be organized and give at least some thought ahead of time to what I will cook and when. Since I work outside the home, planning meals in advance relieves the burden of extra stress. You will find that simple, methodical planning and organization is much easier after being restored from an eating disorder—your thoughts are no longer scattered, frantic, or interrupted by overwhelming cravings to binge. At the same time, your physical energy will be so improved that you will be able to complete the tasks God requires of you with much less effort.

Eight years ago, all I thought about was food. I could not keep up my end of a conversation without images of food intruding into my mind. Without realizing it, my cognitive function was continually divided between the task at hand and planning my next binge. (This is one reason your concentration and productivity will so dramatically increase once you are fully restored from the anorexia or bulimia). At the same time this "love affair" with food was going on, my greatest source of pride came from usually being the thinnest person in a room. If I saw a woman who was thinner than me, my purging increased with a new intensity. Yet my compulsion to eat everything in sight and inability to resist "trigger" foods was my ugly, life-dominating secret. In 1982, when I vomited that first bowl of ice cream, I had no idea of the addictive power of bulimia. I had no clue what it meant to be a "slave to sin." Only when one has been as deeply in bondage as I have been can one fully appreciate what it means to be a "new creation." If you are willing to truly lay it all down, Christ can and will make all things new—including your current destructive relationship with food. Put on the armor of God and stand your ground.

Chapter 14
Telling Someone

I have purposely left this chapter until the end because the prospect of telling her "secret" to another person is often a terrifying prospect to a bulimic. If I had mentioned in chapter one, "Oh, by the way, you should find an appropriate person and confess your sin to her if you really want to walk free," you probably would have put this book down in a hurry and dived back into your pit, more hopeless than before.

Quoting verses such as "Therefore, confess your sins to one another, and pray for one another so that you may be healed" (James 5:16a) and citing David's penitential Psalms may not have convinced you of the power of confession, (or what it has to do with you being delivered from your eating disorder), but it is an important part of the full repentance and restoration process and thus needs to be addressed. There is no need to be anxious about repercussions; relax and hear me out. I would like to be able to convince you of three things:

First, telling someone about your bulimia is not nearly as scary as you may think. You will feel more relieved than ashamed once someone else knows.[69] **Second,** someone else knowing will greatly facilitate your repentance from the eating disorder. And, **third**, confessing the sin to another is God's will, and He will give you the supernatural strength to do so.

Before getting into a detailed explanation of these three principles, I will publicly confess that I erred in this area, and it greatly delayed and complicated my ultimate victory over bulimia. I did not tell my husband until five years after God had already restored me, and that was wrong. My shame and fear (of how Ivo would react) kept me in bondage, which was never God's intention. In essence, the longer we keep the secret, the longer we stay stuck in the destructive cycle of addiction. Once a secret is brought out into the light, it starts to lose its power over a person. A pastor once remarked that when someone confesses some secret sin to him and says, "You're the first person I've ever told that," he actually starts getting excited for the person! Why? Because he knew that now the person was going to have victory over it. I have found this principle to be absolutely true in the realm of eating disorders (particularly bulimia, as it is easier to keep hidden).

In corresponding with dozens of women over the past five years, two variables seem to indicate whether one will completely overcome bulimia: 1) seeking out local biblical counseling, and 2) revealing her secret vice to her husband. Several women who sought their husbands' support testified to God using the added accountability to help them stay on track. One woman wrote me, "We prayed together, and then I talked to my small group leader about finding a counselor." She had initially been afraid to tell anyone, but with her husband's support and the help of her local church small group, "Shana" walked away from her ten-year addiction to bulimia and is now living for God.

Not Walking the Talk...

Knowing all this, and realizing that the biblical injunction to confess our sins to one another is for our own good, it is a testimony to God's bottomless mercy that He granted me repentance from my bondage to bulimia. The fact that I was able to repent of a seventeen-year addiction without help from a human counselor is evidence that God poured out unbelievable amounts of grace on me. That He did it without my confessing to my husband is evidence of His infinite patience. Keeping my bulimia a secret from Ivo displayed lack of wisdom on my part. God, being sovereign, saw the end from the beginning and knew that one day (albeit belatedly) I would reveal the past. When I finally did, He was there to help me deal with the consequences of my deceit.

Deliberately withholding information is the same as lying. In the courtroom, a witness under oath commits perjury if he omits information from his testimony. Very often, we Christians will rationalize keeping some sin from our pasts under wraps, telling ourselves "what he doesn't know won't hurt him (or her)." In fact, some "Christian" counselors have even advised their clients not to reveal past affairs to their spouses, reasoning that it would cause unnecessary pain and damage to the relationship. This is wrong, and the logic behind it is faulty. If a past sin has no bearing on a current relationship (for example, the rolls of Lifesavers I stole as a child), there is no need to bring it up. However, in the case of an eating disorder, we are talking about a serious and potentially life-threatening behavior that continued almost daily for eight years into my marriage. Ironically, I feared my husband finding out far more than I feared dying of a ruptured esophagus over a toilet bowl.

In early 2004, after I had visited a prayer room several times for intercession, I began attending a weekly women's fellowship at the same church. I was euphoric—God was finally changing me (although I was stumbling clumsily along). At last I had found a group of like-minded Christian ladies who loved God passionately. I "clicked" with them immediately. We were doing a small group study of Martha Peace's *The Excellent Wife*, and as I eagerly sought to obey Christ, He taught me about submission to my husband through His Word. I felt as if I were making up for lost time in my walk with God; after all, I had spent over a decade unable to rid myself of this life-dominating sin! Fellowship with God and

His people more than compensated for the alcohol He had convicted me to give up. After the first few weeks of abstinence, I no longer craved a Friday night cocktail. My husband never asked why I had stopped drinking abruptly, but he must have observed God making changes in my life. I was actually joyful for a change.

My speech became more edifying, as the Holy Spirit was never far from my mind. He would convict me before I opened my mouth, and most of the time, I would listen. When I sinned, by quarreling with friends or becoming frustrated with the kids, I felt remorse more intensely than before and repented more quickly. I made a conscious effort to become a more submissive wife and to focus more attention on my husband and children. Every day I read the Bible, and devoured Christian books as much as time permitted. Suddenly convicted about the sexual immorality glorified by a certain medical drama, I stopped watching it and spent time doing a Bible study instead. Most of all, I spent as much time as I could at my newfound haven, the charismatic church. Besides going there every Wednesday for teaching and fellowship, I often snuck in for intercessory prayer on Saturday mornings between running errands. I also faithfully listened to Sunday's sermons on CD each week.

The Lure of Neo-Gnosticism: From One "High" to Another
It was here that I had anonymously confessed my bulimia (and drinking problem), been prayed over, and ultimately overcame the addictions. Subsequently, I was unable to evaluate my ongoing repentance and diligent Bible study apart from the subjective experience in that church. Much emphasis was placed on receiving "rhemas" and prophetic words; presumably personal messages from the Holy Spirit. I never had any of the mystical, esoteric experiences many of my friends claimed. In a sense, I was beginning to replace one addiction with another: freed of the eating disorder and eu-

phoric "buzz" from drinking, I now pursued a highly experiential faith that promised mystical encounters with God.

I am not an emotional person by nature. Initially, I felt uncomfortable with the spontaneous shouts and displays of devotion; in fact, I do not even raise my arms while worshipping. As time went on, however, I let my guard down and came to see the joy and ecstatic experience as an inside track to intimacy with God. Like the Gnostics and Montanists of ancient times, I craved the "secret" knowledge of God promised to a select few rather than the straightforward way He has revealed Himself to His followers. Whereas His speaking to me through His Word had been sufficient in overcoming addictions, now I became dissatisfied. I wanted "personal revelation" to bolster my faith. I forgot that true relationship with God is based on knowledge of Him and obedience to Him, which He had been teaching me as I sought Him in the prayer closet. Even after putting this life-dominating sin behind me, I was nearly seduced by the siren of the New Age in the guise of Christianity.

After three years of chasing a counterfeit, God opened my eyes to the many doctrinal errors of the charismatic movement and I walked away. My spirit was scarred, but still alive. While 1 Corinthians 12-14 discusses the sign gifts (tongues, predictive prophecy and healing through human agency) in depth, Paul indicates that those miraculous occurrences were signs to unbelievers and would not be permanent. He reminds believers in chapter 13 that their emphasis must be on loving God and one another; not on "sensational" manifestations of the Spirit. Both the biblical and historical record show that the miraculous gifts had ceased entirely by the end of the first century, when John received the final revelations on Patmos and the Canon of Scripture was closed. The means God has chosen to reveal Himself to His children is through His Word, and He is not honored when we seek extra-biblical "experiences" or private revelation.[70]

In time, God led our family to a sound, Gospel-preaching church where we continued to grow spiritually. I tried to forget the past—how God had granted me victory over bulimia (a changed life is clear evidence of the supernatural work of the Holy Spirit), and how I had sought Him in all the wrong places. I never doubted God's sovereignty, but I began to wonder if His personal involvement in my healing had been a figment of my imagination. I was well aware that many psychologists would say the power of suggestion is so strong that if I believed God was involved, it would be sufficient for my "recovery" (the placebo effect). I could never, even in my most cynical moment, buy into this reasoning. To claim I had "healed" myself would have been tantamount to denying Christ, something I could never do.

As I distanced myself both from the charismatic movement and my bulimic past, my faith became purely intellectual. Determined to avoid further deception, an analytic approach to theology became a source of pride to me. Constantly, I felt insecure and alienated from God, as I could never "feel" His presence. All the while, God had greatly strengthened our marriage and family. All four of our children love God, attend church with us, and participate in the AWANA program. Christ had definitely taken up residence in our home, and our family was ordered around Him. How could I deny His hand in our lives? And yet, the years of seeking a feeling or experience had left an indelible mark. If I could not "sense His presence," I reasoned, God must be angry with me. Perhaps I had not achieved enough for Him. I needed to earn His favor back; somehow repay Him for restoring me from the pit of bulimia.

"And I will tell of what He has done for my soul..." (Psalm 66:16)

Throughout this time, I had been corresponding with eating disordered women whom I had met on Christian Internet forums. In 2005, pregnant with my fourth child, I had started posting on an online bulletin board community for young moms. One day I discovered a forum called "Eating Disorders During Pregnancy" and anonymously shared my testimony. I candidly talked about how Jesus Christ had set me free from the chains of bulimia and how they could know the same freedom. Since this particular forum was not "religious," it didn't take long for someone to complain and get the thread locked. Immediately, over a dozen Christian women from the forum started emailing me, confessing that they had the same ugly secret and begging for some word of encouragement. I began to realize that God truly could use my testimony, if I were willing to encourage His other daughters. I did the best I could, but found myself repeating the same things over and over again via e-mail, hoping the young women would take what I was saying to heart and seek God to truly transform them. (Because counseling is far more effective face-to-face, in a formal setting with homework completed and accountability in place, I now encourage these ladies to see a biblical counselor in their local area in addition to writing to me for support).

Time went on and I still didn't tell Ivo the whole story. When we were dating, I had explained that I had been anorexic in high school, and that in college I had been forced to see psychiatrists and gained weight. (Before our Sofia wedding, my mother included several very unflattering photographs of me from the period of my lowest weight in an album, so it was fortunate that I had prepared Ivo.) This was a true account, insofar as it went—I had just left out rather important details, such as the fact the anorexia had given way to bulimia, and was still going on. I was terrified he would leave me if he had known. Now, I felt trapped. As of 2008, I had been freed from these "demons" for five years, and was very happy to leave the past in the past. I wanted to bury the memory of that awful sin under concrete—after all, I reasoned, hadn't God forgiven me?—and never have to go through the humiliation of revealing it to Ivo. Yet I knew that someday, it would come out. Maybe when we're old on a cruise ship somewhere. Or in a retirement home. But definitely not now.

The old feeling of conviction began to grow again. I knew that I owed it to him to be honest about this—as I had about every other detail of my life, both the shameful and the mundane. Besides, we have two daughters, and I have always known that even if they don't struggle with weight or body image problems, my history is something I would tell them for their own good. Ivo and I had discussed the importance of brutal honesty with our children, not covering up our own misdeeds when teaching them the way they should go (Proverbs 22:6). The same principle applied to my "ugly secret," and it confirmed the need to reveal it. Some day. But not today.

"But encourage one another day after day, as long as it is still called "Today," so that none of you will be hardened by the deceitfulness of sin." (Hebrews 3:13)

"Today" finally came, on November 14th, 2008. I had gone to meet privately with my sixth grade daughter's health teacher, in order to discuss some minor concerns I had with the curriculum's ideological bent. During the course of conversation, I asked her if addictions were taught in the curriculum as being "diseases." "Yes," she replied. "Oh no," I countered. "I have a huge problem with that, and I speak as a former addict." Without launching into my full testimony, I succinctly explained to her that addictions are not diseases, but rather learned behaviors and that as such, they can be unlearned. I told her that I had been bulimic for over a decade, but had changed completely—not on my own strength, but it had been Jesus Christ Who had forgiven and restored me. I admitted that it had not been easy, but if I had believed I suffered from a disease I would probably still be in the pit. The teacher clearly recognized my strong convictions in this area, and respectfully told me that I would simply have to talk to my daughter about our family's "belief system" before it was inadvertently contradicted in class.

As I drove home, I realized the time had come. I was prepared to witness to a public school teacher about my repentance from addiction, but I was still afraid to tell my husband. After praying for courage, I resolved to tell the whole story, regardless of the consequences. Relaying my exchange with the teacher, I asked my husband over dinner if he had ever suspected in the earlier years of our marriage that I was bulimic. "What's that?" he asked. "Throwing up on purpose," I said. "What?" He had no idea what I was talking about, nor the fact that it had consumed me for half my life. I backed up, and told Ivo the whole story from childhood—pausing only for breath, and occasional sips of Ginger Ale to alleviate my dry mouth. I concluded my epic with my testimony of God's work in my life five years prior, and waited for the fallout.

He was incredulous; absolutely shocked. "How did you finally stop?" he asked. "God freed me," I repeated. "I can't explain it….He was just there. It wasn't like something magical or spontaneous happened, when I went to the prayer room, but that's where it started. It was just a lot of prayer and repentance on my part. He met me there, and He just somehow worked in my heart and carried me." Ivo was amazed that living in the same house with me for so long, he had never suspected what was going on. Trying to explain the uncontrollable urge to eat, only to induce vomiting a short while afterward is like describing the color blue to a blind man. Understanding (much less empathizing) with such a compulsion is harder still.

As my husband tried to process the information I had just delivered, both of us began to wonder about the "what ifs." What if I had revealed my ugly secret, back in 1994, when we began dating? What would he have done? "I was just wondering about that," he said. "I probably wouldn't have thought it was that big of a deal—as I understand it is now. I definitely would have been more concerned about the alcohol," he admitted. "I probably would have assumed that it [the bulimia] would have gone away after awhile, after you'd have been with me for some time. Maybe I could have helped you. But I probably would have just thought it was 'girl stuff', and not that serious."

I began to consider how differently life might have turned out. It was now clear that he wouldn't have abandoned me, my haunting fear during our engagement. He had stood by me through my failed attempts to "moderate" my drinking, forgiving me each time I failed and never bringing up my past drunkenness as ammunition against me. If I had told him about my other secret vice, and determined to leave it behind, my road to restoration might have been much shorter. The fact that there were no biblical counselors in Bulgaria at that point (and that eating disorders were unheard of) is irrelevant—God transformed me without the help of an outside counselor in the United States; He certainly could have worked in my heart in the same way in Bulgaria. There were good churches, pastor's wives, and small groups available there as well. The fact is, however, that God was my only Counselor—and He is not limited by geography. He was only limited by my delay in responding to His call to repentance. It took far too long for my heart to become broken, but telling the secret (especially to my husband) surely would have made the situation seem less overwhelming. In any event, he would have provided consistent accountability.

"Whatever a man sows, this he will also reap…" (Galatians 6:7b)

What "might have been" was now futile speculation. Initially, Ivo was not visibly angry. Naturally, he felt more betrayed by the fact I had concealed my addiction for so long than he was by the actual bulimia itself. He could not grasp how food could become an addiction, but having lived in the United States for thirteen years he had heard about compulsive overeating, morbid obesity and eating disorders. He tried hard to wrap his mind around it. However, two days later, an unrelated incident at church pushed his anger towards me over the edge. Later in the week, he confronted me and insisted I didn't respect him and he wondered what else I was hiding. This time, it was I who was completely taken aback and couldn't understand where this 'delayed reaction' was coming from.

The most painful part of his confrontation was the part that was true: "When you were telling me all that, by the way, you never apologized," he chastised me. "Not once did you ask for my forgiveness." I was horrified—he was absolutely right. I was truly sorry, but I was so nervous at the time I was telling him the whole story I just concentrated on telling it thoroughly, without leaving out any important details. I had forgotten the most important part—to ask for his forgiveness. I crumpled. All of my fears of his rejection; my shame and horror at my past nightmare; my frustration at my own striving to be perfect so he (and God) would love me came pouring out. "I can't change any faster!" I screamed at him. I wanted to just walk away and never come back—to escape the reality of the situation. I was reaping the consequences of what I had sown.

Ivo forgave me once we "had it out" and never brought it up again, but I was devastated. Not by him (his reaction was understandable), but by my own failure. I had messed up many times in the past and somehow always seemed to put it behind me and get back on the right track, but this time was different. After my tears dried, I became numb. For weeks, I walked around in a spiritual fog so dense I couldn't see my way out. I wasn't exactly depressed, because I refused to let myself feel the emotions that threatened to drown me. I held them at bay—and felt nothing but emptiness. For the first time in over five years, I was completely unable to pray.

I couldn't cry. I was unmotivated to open my Bible. I felt as if God had abandoned me, even though I had tried to obey. Although I had known confessing the sin to my husband was the right thing to do, He didn't have my back. Why had He withdrawn His favor?

A New Pit…and New Mercies

In late November, I wrote in my prayer journal: "Hope there will not be more consequences to this sin….want God to keep healing; keep using. Need assurance from God I did the right thing and didn't just make everything worse. I never "sense" God's presence anymore. I just need Him to be my friend right now, but don't know how to approach that w/o being irreverent or emoting like a charismatic." As the weeks went on, a heavy sadness settled on my soul, and as I replayed Ivo's angry confrontation over and over in my mind, I started to regret telling him. When I allowed myself to feel anything at all, I felt deep shame. This shame kept me from turning to God, and my feelings of isolation increased. Although I would tentatively try to approach God, knowing that He was still my Rock and stronghold, I remained totally prayer-less. I simply didn't know what to say or how to approach God, even realizing He knew all the details anyway. For weeks my attempts at prayer sounded something like this: "Lord. Um, yeah. So……..yeah. Ah, that's where we're at. [Long pause] Are You mad at me, too? Well, anyway." Then I would go and fold the laundry or vacuum.

The Christmas season came, and I simply wished it were over. I cannot remember a single detail about Christmas of 2008, other than a devastating ice storm that hit northern New England about two weeks beforehand. For four days, we holed up in a hotel room, where I mechanically banged out an article for Christianity Today. I used my Bible only to double-check references.

Just before the New Year, I was asked to cover an extra

shift in the church nursery so that the scheduled worker could participate in a "cardboard testimony" demonstration at the end of service. (The Australian mega-church Hillsong popularized the practice on YouTube—each participant writes something that Christ freed him or her from on a piece of cardboard, walks across the stage, and turns it over—revealing the new creation He has made of them). It is a powerful witness of God's transforming power, but I had nothing to celebrate. Acutely ashamed and isolated, I skipped Communion and fought back tears in the solitude of the pre-service nursery. In January, I wrote: "Last week Pastor Eric said the more you get to know Jesus, the more you come to trust Him. I thought I knew Him so well, but I stopped trusting...what if He really is angry? Struggling and doubting His love for me this week. Feel like I never knew Him. In Ephesians 1:17, Paul's prayer was for the Father to give the Spirit of wisdom and revelation, so I may know Him better. That's what I want, but He seems so far away. Feel like giving up."

Although I had counseled others to reveal their struggle with bulimia, and above all, to stay close to God, I was utterly incapable for some time to take my own advice. Finally, after several months, the "fog" started to lift and I got back into the Word. The antidote to my spiritual quagmire was the same as the answer to my original problem, the eating disorder: prayer and repentance. I knew there was still much work God wanted to do in me, but there was no use in living in shame and regret. The sin had been confessed; both God and my husband had forgiven me; and I needed to accept that and move on. There are always consequences to our disobedience, and the longer we let it go on, the harder repentance may be (see Psalm 51 for David's agonizing experience of concealing sin). If Christ could deliver me from bulimia, He could heal my wounds from the aftershock, as well.

In his book, *When People are Big and God is Small*, Ed

Welch asks the rhetorical question, "What do I do when I don't "feel" God's presence? The answer is so simple that it would seem to be common sense: pray by faith. Since we are very often influenced more strongly by our experience or what we "feel" than by what we know to be biblical truth, there are times when we simply need to continue on in the means of grace (reading and studying the Bible; praying; serving; attending church and worshiping) despite how we feel. It is a common error, when things are going well in our life, to take it for granted that God is with us…but when we hit trials and relationships are strained, to believe He has departed. If Bible-believing Christians were to sit down and think about that statement, we would all likely emphatically deny it (and rightfully so). Perhaps we could even quote from memory some of the verses that promise God's abiding presence to His children:

"But this is the covenant which I will make with the house of Israel after those days," declares the LORD, "I will put My law within them and on their heart I will write it; and I will be their God, and they shall be My people." (Jeremiah 31:33)

"…I am with you always, even to the end of the age." (Matthew 28:20)

"…the Spirit of truth, whom the world cannot receive, because it does not see Him or know Him, but you know Him because He abides with you and will be in you. "I will not leave you as orphans; I will come to you." (John 14:17-18)

"If you abide in Me, and My words abide in you, ask whatever you wish, and it will be done for you." (John 15:7)

"…for He Himself has said, I WILL NEVER DESERT YOU, NOR WILL I EVER FORSAKE YOU,' so that we confidently say,'THE LORD IS MY HELPER, I WILL NOT BE AFRAID. WHAT WILL MAN DO TO ME?" (Hebrews 13:5b-6)

Despite how I felt, God had not turned His back on me or withdrawn His presence. When we are dealing with the consequences of our sin, we may be tempted to think that God is punishing us and has left us to struggle alone. Nothing could be further from the truth: the Bible confirms repeatedly that we may have assurance He is with us by faith. How we feel does not change His promise to us. Our feelings change daily and new doubts surge in when we are at our lowest, but Scripture reminds us that God never changes and His Word remains true (1 Samuel 15:29; Hebrews 13:8). When going through a "dry" season of doubt, sometimes we have to force ourselves to open our Bibles. When it would be easier to stay under the covers, that's exactly when we need to get up and go to church to hear the Word preached.

"So What's Your Point?"

My purpose in telling you this, my dear sisters, is to encourage you not to make the same mistake I did. Do not conceal your bulimia (or other food addiction) from your husbands. I can very nearly guarantee you that his reaction will not be anywhere near as bad as what you now fear. God has given you to him and him to you to be "one flesh" (Mark 10:8) and any secrets kept will affect the marriage relationship. You are actually sinning against him by not being forthright, although I completely sympathize with your feeling ashamed. It will cause you far less shame in the long run to get this sin out in the light where it can be "put to death" biblically than to keep it hidden. Even if you do repent before God and rely on Him for victory, as I did, it is a far more solitary and steep climb alone than it will be with your spouse by your side.

If you are not married, please consider carefully who at church will be able to provide you with compassionate and godly counsel. Speak confidentially to an older woman who has discipled Christians before, or confide in a small group leader. She may be able to help you find a biblical counselor if she feels ill equipped to help, or speak with your pastor's wife. The important thing is not to try and deal with a life-dominating sin, such as an eating disorder, alone. God never meant for the Christian life to be lived in isolation, yet that is exactly what many of us try to do when we struggle with sin.

Why Tell?

Besides the biblical principle of confessing our sin to one another (which has the moral weight of a command in Scripture), the battle simply becomes easier. I actually felt as if a physical weight was being lifted off my shoulders when I finally came clean with Ivo, notwithstanding the repercussions I later had to face. You will very often be relieved at the other person's reaction—we expect disgust, yet often receive compassion and concern. People are simply not as shocked at our shortcomings as we expect them to be—perhaps because they have enough problems of their own. Ours are not all that big of a deal to them! However, the very fact that someone else knows your "ugly secret" automatically makes the burden lighter.

"So if the Son makes you free, you will be free indeed" (John 8:36) indicates you may even be free from fear. In nearly every book of the Bible, the command to "fear not" is given. God never intended for you to live in constant fear of man. Worrying excessively about how others will react is actually a manifestation of pride. From an eternal perspective, all that matters is what your Father thinks of you. He wants you to be free of this sin burden, once and for all. Confessing it makes freedom a closer reality. He will provide all you need to get through the process (2 Corinthians 12:9).

We have discussed at length how the first step in repentance is to humble ourselves before God. When we do this, we are essentially throwing ourselves on His mercy; admitting our great need and lack of ability to change our own hearts. This command, however, comes with a promise: the assurance that God cares for His children and invites us to come to Him with our anxiety. "Therefore humble yourselves under the mighty hand of God, that He may exalt you at the proper time, casting all your anxiety on Him, because He cares for you," (1 Peter 5:6-7). Paul, likewise, exhorts believers to "be anxious for nothing, but in everything by prayer and supplication with thanksgiving let your requests be made known to God" (Philippians 4:6). If you have great anxiety about revealing this "secret sin," be comforted by the fact that you are obeying God. He does not want you to bear the additional burden of fear or anxiety; He commands that you trust Him with the outcome. He will bring good out of your testimony in due time.

Intercessory prayer

I am a huge believer in the power of intercessory prayer (approaching God on another's behalf), and feel it is a helpful practice for anyone battling an eating disorder. Christ affirmed the importance of intercessory prayer in Mark 9:29, and He Himself interceded for His disciples, knowing that their faith was about to be tried: "Satan has demanded permission to sift you like wheat; but I have prayed for you, that your faith may not fail…"(Luke 22:31-32). Throughout their epistles, Peter, Paul and John encourage the believers to pray continuously in a spirit of gratitude, and James assures us, "The effective prayer of a righteous man can accomplish much" (James 5:16).

The message is clear: prayer works. Being members of the same Body is both a privilege and a responsibility—a privilege because all of the benefits God has graciously given us as His children; a responsibility because we are accountable to one another and need to bear one another's burdens. Intercessory prayer is one of the highest acts of love that we can do for another, because it mirrors what Christ Himself does for us (Romans 8:34).

When we are praying for another, there is no thought of "self." There is no expectation of reciprocation, and our prayer is bolstered by the agreement of others interceding alongside us. In a sense, we approach the throne of God along with our sisters. Jesus Himself is right there with us, and we may be sure He hears and answers our pleas for help. Having others pray with and for you as you are turning daily from this bondage is another weapon in your arsenal against the darts of the enemy. I strongly encourage you to seek out your church's prayer team, small group or a group of trusted women to come alongside you in intercession. God will give you His supernatural strength to break those chains of besetting sin.

A Word of Caution About "Deliverance Ministries"

There is a current wave of teaching popular in the evangelical Church today which focuses on "deliverance" from supposed demonic oppression. While the forces of hell can certainly conspire to tempt and influence Christians, demons have no power to "possess" or reside within the born-again believer. The Holy Spirit occupies the soul of the Christian, and theories of demons "attaching" themselves to the soul are completely unfounded. In fact, much of what is currently being taught about spiritual warfare is not found in the Bible.

Paul wrote: "For our struggle is not against flesh and blood, but against the rulers, against the powers, against the world forces of this darkness, against the spiritual forces of wickedness in the heavenly places" (Ephesians 6:12). We are plainly engaged in a spiritual battle, and previously we have examined what Paul meant by "the armor of God." Disciplines such as prayer, worship, reading and studying the Bible and accountability to other mature believers are all necessary practices to overcoming besetting sin, but we are not called upon to engage in "cosmic assault" with the powers of darkness. These techniques originated in the imaginations of man. A recent article in the Los Angeles Times reported,

Fascinated with the notion that Satan commands a hierarchy of territorial demons, some mission agencies and big-church pastors are devising strategies for "breaking the strongholds" of those evil spirits alleged to be controlling cities and countries.[71]

This is esoteric mythology that has no basis in the teachings of Christ or the apostles. Deliverance "ministries" are steeped in the aberrational theology of the charismatic Word of Faith movement, and I would caution you to avoid them. Faith healer and intercessors' claims of "binding" and "loosing" specific "spirits" are based on a faulty exegesis of Matthew 16:19 and 18:18, which refer to church discipline. Practices such as "rebuking" the devil, "claiming" spiritual blessings, and "breaking off" of "curses" may sound sensational, but they are not biblical doctrines and will not help you grow in holiness.

Accountability

Throughout this book, I have already touched on the importance of accountability in walking away from an eating disorder. Asking another sister to 'hold you accountable' (follow up with you and see how you're doing) is Scriptural—it is a natural and caring outgrowth of confessing our sin to one another. What is the point in confessing to another an ongoing sin, unless she will help you walk away? Having someone you can call, meet with regularly and just ask for prayer can be a powerful assistance in overcoming the urges to binge and purge as they hit. All help and comfort ultimately comes from God's gracious hand, but very often He uses another person to aid and strengthen the struggling sinner.

Solomon wrote about the benefits of two coming together in Ecclesiastes 4:11-12: "Furthermore, if two lie down together they keep warm, but how can one be warm alone? And if one can overpower him who is alone, two can resist him. A cord of three strands is not quickly torn apart." Certainly, this wisdom is not limited to the bondage of addictive sin, but we can clearly see how the principle applies. Repent-ing bulimics who have some sort of accountability partner generally do better, if for no other reason than the fact that they will have to admit to a binge if it occurs. Needless to say, confessing our fleshly weakness as a present tense struggle is humiliating! We tend to do better with sin that is far back in the past, but it is more humbling to admit to what we did yesterday in our most unlovely moments.

When Others React Negatively

Suppose you share your struggle with a fellow Christian or your husband, and he or she reacts with shock, anger, or even questions your salvation. (I have personally experienced all three reactions at various times). This is hurtful and there is no sense in pretending otherwise. An eating disorder is besetting sin just like any other, and is no more or less re-pugnant in God's eyes. The very fact that you are baring your soul enough to confess it to another is a cry for help, which deserves to be met with dignity and compassion (if empathy is too difficult for the other person). Many in the Church may be more inclined to look disparagingly upon those with addictions, which they see as greater moral failings than their own "respectable" sins. If this is the case, rest assured that God fully forgives and accepts you, even if some of His children do not.

Charles Spurgeon once delivered a touching sermon on the Prodigal Son. In his discussion of the elder brother's scorn-ful reaction to the wayward son, he drew a parallel to how a repentant sinner may take comfort and solace in the Father's love when other sinners reject him:

> Finally, the father's kisses mean SECURITY BEFORE THE CRITICISMS OF MEN. All this was given before the prod-igal son's meeting with the elder brother. If you get your Father's many kisses, you will not mind your elder brother

being a little hard on you. Suppose that you have honestly repented and come to the Father, but your brother does not accept your return, withholds his love, and does not welcome you; go and get a kiss from your Father and never mind your brother. Someone may remind you how you have squandered your living, painting the picture even blacker than it ought to be; but your Father's kisses will make you forget your brother's frowns. If you think that in the household of faith you will find everybody friendly, and everyone willing to help you, you will be greatly mistaken. But your Father's kisses will make up for it.[72]

In Conclusion...

It is tempting for someone repenting of an addiction to think, "Once I overcome this sin, I will have no more problems! I will always live a victorious, Christian life for the Lord!" The truth is that while God forgives and restores you completely, there will always be something impeding your intimacy with Him until you are home in Heaven. Satan will not let up on you; if anything, you are more of a threat to him once you have overcome a particularly besetting sin in your life. God is glorified by your redeemed life, but you will always have your sinful nature to put to death daily. Do not be discouraged in your pursuit of sanctification, and don't ever give up. Stay involved in a Bible study or personal growth cell group, and attend a church where the Word of God is preached. Most importantly, stay in the Word daily and invite Christ into every area of your life. As you spend more time with Him, God will transform you more and more into the image of Christ.

"Now the Lord is the Spirit, and where the Spirit of the Lord is, there is liberty. But we all, with unveiled face, beholding as in a mirror the glory of the Lord, are being transformed into the same image from glory to glory, just as from the Lord, the Spirit" (2 Corinthians 3:17-18).

Appendix

What is a Christian,
and How Can I be Sure I am One?

As you reach the end of this book, it is my hope that if you have gleaned nothing else from it, you have begun to understand the importance of a right relationship with God. Everyone, Christian or not, who believes in a "higher power" or some sort of god associates Him with great, unfathomable love. We think a lot about God's love, and rightfully so. But to know the true God of Scripture, we must understand Who He is and who we are in relation to Him. God is infinitely loving, but He is also infinitely just and holy. Entire books have been written on His many attributes, and none of His qualities contradict each other. In order to worship Him in spirit and in truth, we must know Him. Having a proper concept of God is crucial to entering into a saving relationship with Him.

Most people are familiar with the assertion "God is love" (1 John 4:8) and try to follow Him. When asked what the greatest law was, Jesus said: "You shall love the Lord your God with all your heart, and with all your soul, and with all your mind." (Matthew 22:37). However, everyone has sinned (acted, thought or spoken in rebellion) against God. "For all have sinned, and fall short of the glory of God." (Romans 3:23) Because God is perfectly holy and good, He must punish sin—hatred, lust, lying, and breaking the commandments. "The soul who sins will die." (Ezekiel 18:4) The death of your soul means eternal separation from God in what the Bible calls hell. God's impeccable nature means He cannot love good without hating evil. Anyone who has sinned even once deserves hell justly: "For whoever keeps the whole law and yet stumbles in one point, he has become guilty of all." (James 2:10)

Even though we have sinned, the amazing truth is that God still loves sinners: "The Lord is not slow about His promise, as some count slowness, but is patient toward you, not wishing for any to perish but for all to come to repentance" (2 Peter 3:9); "But God demonstrates His own love toward us, in that while we were yet sinners, Christ died for us" (Romans 5:8). God gave His only begotten Son, Jesus Christ, who was born of the virgin Mary, and lived a perfect and sinless life, to be a sin offering for His children: "He made Him who knew no sin to be sin on our behalf, so that we might become the righteousness of God in Him." (2 Corinthians 5:21)

In an unfathomable demonstration of lavish love, God displayed His glory through the death and resurrection of Christ on our behalf. Isaiah predicted this hundreds of years in advance: "But He was pierced through for our transgressions, He was crushed for our iniquities; the chastening for our well-being fell upon Him; and by His scourging we are healed. All of us like sheep have gone astray, each of us has turned to his own way; but the LORD has caused the iniquity of us all to fall on Him." (Isaiah 53:5-6)

Eternal Life—God's Greatest Gift

Jesus Christ was born to suffer and die for all the sins of His people. He was buried, and rose again in victory. His sacrifice was the payment for all sins of those who would trust in Him, and is the only way a person can make it into heaven. It is a free gift of Jesus Christ: "For by grace you have been saved through faith; and that not of yourselves, it is the gift of God; not as a result of works, so that no one may boast," (Ephesians 2:8-9). You can't earn heaven—no one is good enough. Only Jesus, Who is fully God and fully man, has ever lived a perfect life. When the Holy Spirit opens our "spiritual eyes," enabling us to trust in Christ alone for eternal life, He imputes His righteousness to us. In an incredible, divine transaction, He becomes our Savior from death and the Lord of our life. "For the wages of sin is death, but the free gift of God is eternal life in Christ Jesus our Lord" (Romans 6:23).

To become a Christian, turn from your self-directed life to Christ to save you from your sins, and accept His forgiveness: "…Believe in the Lord Jesus, and you will be saved…" (Acts 16:31). This belief is more than an intellectual assent to the claims of Christ. It is more than accepting that the historical Person of Christ existed, and is eternally in heaven. Conversion is a supernatural act of the Holy Spirit, Who is God. He orchestrates a heart change that is deeper than simple agreement—only He gives the sinner the desire to know God. The ability to repent and put one's faith in Christ for salvation is generated by God Himself. In the Bible He repeatedly provides assurance of His love and that He is a sinner's only hope.

Jesus Christ gave his life for you. There is no other way to Heaven: "Jesus said to him, 'I am the way, and the truth, and the life; no one comes to the Father but through Me.'" (John 14:6). Being a member of a church will not save you. No institution has the power to save a single soul. Likewise, the "good works" and religious rituals, rules, and activities have no power to save—although many people cling to them in the hope God will be impressed. In fact, God leaves no room for doubt in Scripture: in relation to His holiness, our self-generated "holiness" is like filthy rags (Isaiah 64:6)! Thinking we can be "good enough" to be accepted by God or approach Him on our terms is the highest form of pride. Trusting in man-made rites or traditions is exactly what the Pharisees of Jesus' time did—and it damned them. They were too blind to see the Messiah (Christ)—their only hope of salvation because they were stuck in their self-made religious bondage.

Jesus also said, "…unless you repent, you will all likewise

perish" (Luke 13:3). This means you must humble yourself before God: "But he gives a greater grace. Therefore it [Scripture] says: "God is opposed to the proud, but gives grace to the humble" (James 4:6; 1 Pet. 5:5). If you will repent toward God and have faith toward the Lord Jesus Christ, you will be saved and spend eternity with Him (Acts 20:21). God will give you a new heart, with new desires: "I will give you a new heart and put a new spirit within you; and I will remove the heart of stone from your flesh and give you a heart of flesh" (Ezekiel 36:26). By placing your trust in Christ, you will be born again, into the family of God: "Jesus…said to him, 'Truly, truly, I say to you, unless one is born again he cannot see the kingdom of God" (John 3:3). God draws all those who will trust in Christ as Lord and Savior (John 6:37, 15:16); giving them the right to become His children: "But as many as received Him, to them He gave the right to become children of God, even to those who believe in His name" (John 1:12). This relationship is eternal: "I will never desert you; nor will I ever forsake you" (Heb. 13:5).

This new life in Christ is the greatest gift anyone could give you, and is the "good news," or Gospel. Will you receive God's free gift of eternal life? Repent—turn to God —and believe on the Lord Jesus Christ before it is too late: "Seek the LORD while He may be found; call upon Him while He is near," (Isa. 55:6), "for, 'Whoever will call on the name of the Lord will be saved.'" (Rom. 10:13). God is the Father of Luke 15, waiting with open arms for His children, whom He has known from the foundation of the world, to come home. You can pray to God, and He will forgive you because of what Christ has done on your behalf. Jesus has already paid an enormous price to present sinners, now cleansed and spotless to God. He is the only One qualified to do so—the only Redeemer there is.

Finally, if you've trusted Christ, it's important to read the Bible and pray to grow in your relationship with God. Find a

Gospel-preaching church and be baptized. Baptism has been described as a symbol of a new covenant with God, and as an outward sign of an inward change. Going under the water symbolizes death of the self, or "old man," and rising back up represents our new life in Christ. When we identify with Christ's death and resurrection in baptism, we are publicly proclaiming that we are now one with Him—"putting off" the old nature day by day, and "putting on" the new, spirit-filled nature. Although baptism is not what saves us—only faith in Christ will do that—Jesus Himself commanded His disciples to be baptized in the Name of the Father, the Son, and the Holy Spirit. If you have been born again, you are His disciple. It's time to celebrate your new life!

Your desires, motivations, activities and actions that used to be self-serving will gradually begin to change—simply out of gratitude for all God is and all He has done for you in Christ. You cannot have a truly regenerated spirit and not have a changed heart although "producing fruit in keeping with repentance" (Matthew 3:8) may seem slow at times. Do not let this discourage you—stay close to Christ, and ask Him to reveal His will to you. Once you have known His love, you cannot help but be changed by it, and your obedience will be motivated by His great love.

Addendum

More Information on Biblical Counseling

NANC and CCEF

The two major associations which are devoted to training and certifying biblical counselors are the National Association of Nouthetic Counselors (NANC) and the Christian Counseling and Educational Foundation (CCEF). Both organizations were founded by Jay Adams with the goal of training pastors and laymen to effectively handle the Word of God in counseling situations. NANC's headquarters is in Indianapolis, Indiana and CCEF's School of Biblical Counseling is based in Glenside, Pennsylvania.

NANC training centers at churches throughout the United States offer the basic, 30-hour training course for those interested in this ministry. Applicants then take exams in both theology and counseling practice, after which they are supervised and mentored through their first 50 hours of counseling. They are then fully-certified counselors who serve in their local churches. NANC is a valuable resource to the Church at large, as the organization ensures a certain standard of doctrine and practice across the board. Counselors who complete the process are now much better equipped to counsel and become a real blessing to their respective churches.

CCEF provides both onsite and distance education, but for three different certificate levels. Counseling services are provided from their Glenside facility, but CCEF also has affiliate offices in Montana and Vermont. Their counselors typically do not serve part-time in their local churches, but rather full-time in CCEF counseling centers at one of these locations. The Institute for Biblical Counseling and Discipleship (IBCD) in San Diego County is another good training and counseling ministry. Seeking a local counselor through any of these organizations is an excellent option if your own church is not prepared to help you.

> National Association of Nouthetic Counselors
> (NANC)
> 3600 W. 96th Street
> Indianapolis, IN 46268
> (317) 337-9100
> email: info@NANC.org
> http://www.nance.org (has directory of NANC certi-
> fied counselors by state)

> Christian Counseling & Educational Foundation
> (CCEF)
> 1803 East Willow Grove Avenue
> Glenside, PA 19038
> (215) 884-7676 (for counseling appointments)
> http://www.ccef.org

> The Institute for Biblical Counseling and Discipleship
> (IBCD)
> 655 West Eleventh Avenue
> Escondido, CA 92025
> (760) 747-9252
> email: info@ibcd.org
> http://www.ibcd.org/

Faith Baptist Church Ministries and Vision of Hope

For the last thirty years, Faith Baptist Church Ministries has provided free biblical counseling to its local community. Senior Pastor Dr. Steve Viars is a NANC Fellow (an experienced, supervisory-level counselor) and is on the Executive Board of NANC. FBCM offers an eleven-week training program to help pastors and lay leaders develop counseling ministries in their own churches. There has been such a demand for biblically-sound counsel, as well as the equipping of pastors to provide it to their own congregations, that Faith Ministries has grown exponentially over the last few decades. Vision of Hope, a residential facility serving young women with various life-dominating sins, is one of the ministries that has grown out of FBCM's commitment to counsel through the church.

Vision of Hope accepts young women between fourteen and twenty eight, but occasionally bends the age requirements to help those who truly want assistance. The structured time includes Bible study, school work for teen-aged residents, and one-on-one counseling sessions. Resident mentors are also on staff, and the girls are taught life skills (such as managing a budget in order to be able to practice good stewardship) as well as theology. All of Vision of Hope's staff are NANC certified counselors.

"Our focus is to help these young ladies get their lives back on track so that they can glorify God," stated one VOH counselor in the ministry's informational video. This high view of God (and humanity's purpose—to serve and glorify Him) sets Vision of Hope apart from most other rehab centers. Their philosophy of treatment is best summed up by Executive Director Jocelyn Wallace: "Scripture makes it clear that God's Word has answers for real problems, and our staff loves working with girls who have gotten stuck in some part of their life they can't figure out the answer to… we love taking God's Word and showing them how to have answers for that." One resident added, "My goal is to live, today, for the glory of God." Vision of Hope is the only Christian residential facility I would endorse, without any hesitation or disclaimers, for eating disordered young women.

What sets Vision of Hope apart from other Christian residential homes? Jocelyn discussed the program's biblical counseling model in detail.

Besides the NANC affiliation, are there any other distinctives about Vision of Hope that set it apart?

Jocelyn Wallace: I think there are several. First, our number one belief is that the Bible is sufficient and authoritative. So many people, counselors, parents, and families believe that eventually but not first. So the Bible's truths are filtered through their other Greater Truths. Secondly, we believe that choices have consequences and frequently that's how God deals with his people, so that's how we deal with our people. Thirdly, scripture makes it clear that we're habitual beings. If you do the same thing long enough it will become what characterizes you. That's good when what you're doing is good, and that's bad when what you're doing is sin. Fourthly, Ephesians 4:22 clarifies that everything about the old man is characterized by lies and deceit. Ephesians 4:24 clarifies that everything about the new man is characterized by the truth. We spend a ton of time helping girls pick apart the lies that they've been believing and acting upon that are now such an intricate part of who they are they don't even see them anymore. There's probably more, but that's a good start.

Do you have medical personnel on staff? If (for example), an anorexic girl were to go into cardiac arrest, would the home be able to react?

JW: We have a volunteer nurse on staff. She is trained in NANC as well and is very active in our organization. If she weren't here we'd probably have to hire a nurse. However, we frequently refer to the fact that we are not a medical facility and will not help a girl restore her weight. We will only help her with treatment after weight is restored and she is medically stable. If anyone went into cardiac arrest, anorexic or not, all of the staff is trained to respond and we would immediately seek medical help from the hospital that is less than five minutes away.

The girls in the VOH testimonial video looked quite healthy, to be honest. Do you accept young women well below their ideal body weights, and/or on feeding tubes?

JW: No we do not. As I stated, we will not accept girls who are medically fragile. The biggest reasons that we've found are that girls who are anorexic have so much work necessary just to gain one pound. We have one girl who we've worked with that had to consume 4,500 calories just to gain a single pound. Financially we can't afford the kind of high calorie, high fat supplements needed to consume that many calories. Additionally, when the body is going through that much stress medically most young women's brains are not functioning very adeptly. A lot of the thinking and processing required to fight sin and build new lifestyles are beyond what an anorexic is capable of doing. We need girls to be functioning at peak capacity to do the hard work of Biblical change. We require that anorexic girls come in at least at 90% of their recommended weight. We currently have a girl on our waiting list right now that is working on gaining weight so she can be admitted.

Jay Adams and Donn Arms (Institute of Nouthetic Studies) cite the whole concept of sending folks away to a separate facility as being unbiblical. Is the better option for them to receive counsel in the local church?

JW: I also agree that sending girls away to a separate facility is generally not as good an idea as counseling in the local church. The closer to home you can keep the situation, the better, because then change is happening in a real context. One of the downsides is that girls come here from far away and then make changes in the "VOH Bubble"; thinking that it's the same as making changes back home. That's pretty hard when they realize the changes they make at home are actually the ones that "stick" better, because the context is more real. On the flip side, sometimes getting out of your context and away from bad influence is good for you.

The girls receive one-on-one biblical counsel from certi-fied counselors, which seems to be the first thing that sets VOH apart from other facilities. Secondly, they attend Bible studies, and the girls mention their goal as being to live for the glory of God.

JW: Exactly! Gen 1:26 is the cornerstone for everything about my life and everything about what I teach the girls here. We are made in God's likeness and image and as a re-sult everything about us is giving the world around us a view of God. I don't keep myself from sin to have a high view of myself, I keep myself from sin because that gives others a high view of God.

Vision of Hope combines one-on-one biblical counseling with Bible study, worship, and community. The residents are not allowed to discuss with each other the particulars of why they are at VOH. This rule keeps the focus on the solution (Christ's finished work on the Cross) rather than on the indi-vidual and her particular sin. It also thwarts residents' well-meaning attempts to "fix" one another—each must remem-ber that she is there for her own spiritual benefit.

Vision of Hope Ministries, Inc.
5652 Mercy Way
Lafayette, IN 47905
(765)447-5900
(765)447-5900
www.vohlafayette.org
willbesetfree.blogspot.com

Recommended Resources

Information about Eating Disorders and Nutrition:

National Institute of Mental Health (NIMH)
6001 Executive Boulevard
Rockville, MD 20852
(866) 615 6464
email: nimhinfo@nih.gov.
http://www.nimh.nih.gov/
American Dietetic Association
http://www.eatright.org/
(Provides nutrition links and resources for finding a nutritionist)

Renovation: Genuine Freedom from Eating Disorders
http://www.livrite.com/renovation/

Creed Counseling Cottage Online Biblical Counseling
Christian Resources Embracing and Edifying Disciples
http://creedcounselingcottage.com
counsel@creedcounselingcottage.com

Books:

Addictions: A Banquet in the Grave: Finding Hope in the Power of the Gospel
Edward T. Welch
P&R Publishing, Phillipsburg NJ

Eating Disorders: The Quest for Thinness
Edward T. Welch
New Growth Press
Love to Eat; Hate to Eat: Breaking the bondage of Destructive Eating Habits

Elyse Fitzpatrick
Harvest House Publishers, Eugene, OR

Thin Within: A Grace-Oriented Approach to Lasting Weight Loss
Judy Halliday, R.N., Arthur Halliday, M.D.
W Publishing Group, Nashville, TN
(Despite the title, this book really addresses the spiritual issues
behind any emotional eating and helps formulate a plan for God-
honoring eating. Restoring food to its proper place is the primary
goal, not weight loss, per se.)

The Pursuit of Holiness
Jerry Bridges
NavPress Publishing Group

The Ultimate Priority: On Worship
Dr. John Macarthur, Jr.
Moody Press, Chicago IL

The Freedom and Power of Forgiveness
Dr. John Macarthur, Jr.
Crossway Books, Wheaton IL

From Forgiven to Forgiving:
Learning to Forgive One Another God's Way
Dr. Jay Adams
Calvary Press, Greenville, SC

The Biblical View of Self-Esteem, Self-Love, and Self-Image
Dr. Jay Adams
Harvest House Publishers, Eugene Oregon

Who Calls Me Beautiful?
Finding our True Image in the Mirror of God
Regina Franklin
Discovery House Publishers, Grand Rapids MI
Deceptive Diagnosis: When Sin is Called Sickness
Drs. David Tyler and Kurt Grady
Focus Publishing, Bemidji, Minnesota

The Heart of Addiction
Mark Shaw
Focus Publishing, Bemidji, Minnesota

Because He Loves Me
Elyse Fitzpatrick
Crossway, Wheaton, IL

The Cross Centered Life
C.J. Mahaney
Lifechange Books (Multnomah Books)
Colorado Springs, CO

Endnotes

[1] Dick Staub, "Jerry Bridges is Still Pursuing Holiness," Christianity Today Online, April 1, 2004, 48.

[2] Body Mass Index. An approximate calculation of body fat percentage, based on a height/weight ratio.

[3] Spiritual mentoring. In collegiate fellowships and church youth groups, a "discipler" is a more mature believer who is able to model biblical behavior and advise a newer Christian. Often he or she will do one-on-one personal growth assignments and Bible studies with the young believer, serve as an accountability partner, and help answer questions about the faith. In Campus Crusade for Christ, such arrangements have always been completely voluntary and no pressure or manipulation was ever involved.

[4] Naomi Wolf, *The Beauty Myth* (New York: Doubleday, 1991), 205.

[5] Ibid, 208.

[6] Selective serotonin reuptake inhibitors.

[7] Gretchen Smith, "Renovation Biblical Counseling," www.livrite.com (January 2009)

[8] Andrew Murray, as quoted by Stuart Scott, "From Pride to Humility: A Biblical Perspective" (Bemidji: Focus Publishing, Inc., 2000), 2.

[9] Smith, "Renovation Biblical Counseling."

[10] IBID

[11] Dr. Rick Thomas, (Mt. Carmel Ministries). Excerpted from training conference, Heritage Bible Chapel (Princeton, MA), June 10, 2010.

[12] Ed Welch, *Crossroads: A Step-by-Step Guide Away from Addiction* (Greensboro: New Growth Press, 2008), 14.

[13] "Answers from Martha Peace": http://www.marthapeace.com/qa/questions.html © 2001-2005 Martha Peace

[14] Smith, "Renovation Biblical Counseling."

[15] Jay Adams, *Competent to Counsel: Introduction to Nouthetic Counseling* (Grand Rapids: Zondervan Publishing House, 1970), 29-30.

[16] New Life Church ministry webpage: http://www.new-life.net/repentn1.htm (January, 2009).

[17] Marshall, Walter, *The Gospel Mystery of Sanctification*, 1692. Modern version by Bruce McRae. (Eugene: Wipf and Stock Publishers, 2005). Quoted by Martha Peace, "Biblical Counseling and the Doctrine of Sanctification," NANC Annual Conference, October, 2009. "Easy believism" refers to the idea that having a mental belief in Jesus Christ or simply "accepting Jesus into your heart" is the same as obtaining salvation.

[18] Ed Welch, *When People are Big and God is Small: Overcoming Peer Pressure, Codependency, and the Fear of Man* (Phillipsburg: P & R Publishing, 2007), 169-170.

[19] Ibid, 177.

[20] Edward T. Welch, *Addictions: A Banquet in the Grave: Finding Hope in the Power of the Gospel* (Phillipsburg: P&R Publishing, 2001).

[21] John F. Macarthur, *The Freedom and Power of Forgiveness,* (Wheaton: Crossway Books, 1998), 102.

[22] Stuart Scott, *From Pride to Humility* (Bemidji, MN: Focus Publishing, Inc., 2002), 12.

[23] Martha Peace, *Attitudes of a Transformed Heart* (Bemidji, MN: Focus Publishing, 2002), 38-39.

[24] John Calvin, *Romans and Thessalonians, translation Ross Mackenzie* (Grand Rapids, MI: Eerdmans, 1991), 167.

[25] Tony Evans, *Free at Last: Experiencing True Freedom Through Your Identity in Christ* (Chicago: Moody Press, 2001), 54-55.

[26] With the exception of the unforgivable sin, which is blasphemy against the Holy Spirit. Essentially, this is a total rejection of Christ and a complete hardening of the heart.

[27] Regina Franklin, *Who Calls Me Beautiful? Finding Our True Image in the Mirror of God* (Grand Rapids: Discovery House Publishers, 2004), 13.

[28] Jay Adams, *Christian Counselor's Manual*, (Philipsburg, NJ: P&R Publishing Co., 1973), 110.

[29] Table adapted from model used by New Life Community Church, Stafford, VA. Used with permission.

[30] Vernon Grounds, "When and Why the Psychiatrist Can't Help You," Seminary Study Series (Denver: Conservative Baptist Theological Seminary), 3.

[31] Adams, *Competent to Counsel*, 95.

[32] David Tyler and Kurt Grady, *Deceptive Diagnosis: When Sin is Called Sickness* (Bemidji, MN: Focus Publishing, 2006), 41-42.

[33] Rick Thomas, *Counseling Solutions: Connecting the Gospel to Perfectionism,* http://www.competentcounseling.com/2010/06/29/the-gospel-to-perfectionism/ (June 29, 2010).

[34] Mary Fairchild, *Christian Athlete Profile—Laura Wilkinson's Faith,* http://christianity.about.com/od/christiancelebrities/qt/laurawilkinson.htm (July, 2010).

[35] Elyse Fitzpatrick, *Because He Loves Me* (Wheaton: Crossway Books, 2008), 24.

[36] Rick Thomas, *Counseling Solutions.*

[37] Smith, "Renovation Biblical Counseling."

[38] Stanton Peele and Archie Brodsky, *The Truth About Addiction and Recovery* (New York: Fireside, 1991), 23. Quoted by David Tyler and Kurt Grady in Deceptive Diagnosis: When Sin is Called Sickness (Bemidji: Focus Publishing, 2006), 33.

[39] Charles F. Stanley, *When the Enemy Strikes* (Nashville: Thomas Nelson, Inc., 2004), 120-125; 132.

[40] *Heidelberg Catechism, 1563.* From Question 26.

[41] Elyse Fitzpatrick, *Because He Loves Me: How Christ Transforms Our Daily Life* (Wheaton: Crossway, 2008), 153.

[42] Jay Adams, *More than Redemption: A Theology of Christian Counseling* (Philipsburg: P&R Publishing Co., 1979), 165-166.

[43] Adams, *Competent to Counsel.*

[44] Ed Welch, *When People are Big and God is Small: Overcoming Codependency, Peer Pressure, and the Fear of Man* (Phillipsburg: P&R Publishing, 1997), p. 231

[45] For further discussion of the roots of psychology and how it compares to the Bible's view of man, see "Psychobabble: the Failure of Modern Psychology and the Biblical Alternative" by Richard Ganz or "Why Christians Can't Trust Psychology" by Ed Buckley.

[46] Online article "Can Hypnosis End Bulimia?": http://www.hypnosis.org/hypnosis/bulimia.php

[47] Dave Hunt and T.A. McMahon, *The Seduction of Christianity: Spiritual Discernment in the Last Days* (Eugene, OR: Harvest House Publishers, 1985), 140-141.

[48] Counseling should never be done one-on-one with a member of the opposite sex. If pastoral counseling is a woman's only option, a third party should always be present.

[49] "Answers from Martha Peace," http://www.marthapeace.com/qa/questions.html © 2001-2005 Martha Peace

[50] Mahaney, C.J. "Why Small Groups?" Sovereign Grace Ministries. Gaithersburg, MD, 1996, p.5.

[51] Name has been changed to protect privacy.

[52] Adams, *Competent to Counsel*, xv.

[53] Ibid., 181.

[54] Eating disordered women typically attend Overeaters Anonymous (OA), an offshoot of AA. The steps and philosophies of the programs remain essentially the same.

[55] John Lanagan, "C.S. Lewis Warned Against AA Cofounders' Spiritualism," http://www.raptureready.com/index.php (June 2009).

[56] Mark Shaw, *The Heart of Addiction,* (Bemidji, MN: Focus Publishing, 2008), 12-13.

[57] Winston Smith, "Do You Want to Say "No" to Jesus' Touch?" CCEF blog, http://www.ccef.org/node/910 (December 2010)

[58] Matthew Henry, an 18th century Bible commentator wrote: "These are hard lessons to flesh and blood. But if we are thoroughly grounded in the faith of Christ's love, this will make his commands easy to us. Every one that comes to him for washing

in his blood, and knows the greatness of the mercy and the love there is in him, can say, in truth and sincerity, Lord, what wilt thou have me to do? Let us then aim to be merciful, even according to the mercy of our heavenly Father to us." This verse may be understood in a symbolic sense—in ancient Semitic culture, an open-handed slap on the right cheek meant it was rendered by the opponent's left hand, and was more to insult than to do serious bodily injury. It may be from here that we get the expression "left-handed compliment." The implication Jesus seems to be making is that we should bear insults patiently, not repaying in kind. This would align with Proverb 15:1, "A gentle answer turns away wrath, but a harsh word stirs up anger."

[59] Sermon "Forgiveness Made Easy," quoted in John Macarthur's The Freedom and Power of Forgiveness (Wheaton: Crossway Books, 1998), 232.

[60] John Macarthur, op. cit.

[61] Haralan Popov, *Tortured for his Faith,* (Grand Rapids: Zondervan, 1970), 84.

[62] Macarthur, *The Freedom and Power of Forgiveness.*

[63] There are times when reconciliation or "forgetting" the offense is not advisable. A woman may forgive her father for childhood sexual abuse, but leaving her own children alone with him would indicate poor judgment. We need to always do good to those who have wronged us, but this does not negate the need to exercise wisdom.

[64] Jay Adams, *From Forgiven to Forgiving* (Greenville: Calvary Press, 1994), 34.

[65] Macarthur, p. 97.

[66] Courtesy of Casa Palmera Eating Disorder Treatment Center, Del Mar, CA.: http://www.bulimiasideeffects.com/ (June, 2009).

[67] Cited in HealthDay, "News for Healthier Living," http://www. healthday.com/, April 1, 2009.

[68] It should have been known to him, and I was sinning by hiding my bulimic past. See next chapter.

[69] The principle of confessing and asking others for help in over-coming applies equally to any type of disordered eating. However, if you are anorexic, (defined as being at least 15% below normal body weight) or a binge-eater (which frequently leads to obesity), there is a good chance that someone already knows. Bulimia is more easily hidden, and the shame and secrecy attached to the purging usually causes the bulimic to hide her behavior. The thought of confessing her behavior creates an almost irrational fear, therefore, this chapter is primarily aimed at bulimics.

[70] For a more in-depth discussion of the biblical use of the sign gifts, see *Signs and Wonders in the Last Days* by Jay Adams (Time-less Texts) and *Charismatic Chaos* by John Macarthur (Zonder-van).

[71] Quoted by John Macarthur Jr., "And Nothing but the Truth," Grace to You website, http://www.gty.org/Resources/Articles/A116

[72] Quoted from New Life Community Church web page, http://www.new-life.net/ (January 2009)

About the Author

Marie Notcheva is a Christian writer and counselor whose passion is pointing other women towards the Great Physician. A student of Jay Adams' Institute for Nouthetic Studies, she plans to be NANC certified by 2011. Marie's writing has been published in *Christianity Today* and *Baystate Parent*. She and her husband Ivaylo live in Massachusetts and are the parents of four children. She blogs at http://redeemed-fromthepit.blogspot.com/.